Life Beyond

Compelling Evidence for Past Lives and Existence After Death

HANS HOLZER

CB

CONTEMPORARY
BOOKS

CHICAGO

Library of Congress Cataloging-in-Publication Data

Holzer, Hans, 1920–
    Life beyond : compelling evidence for past lives and existence
after death / Hans Holzer.
      p.   cm.
    ISBN 0-8092-3577-3 (pbk.)
    1. Near-death experiences.   2. Reincarnation.   3. Future life.
I. Title.
BF1045.N4H65   1994
133.9′01′3—dc20   94-20617
                                               CIP

Material in this book was published previously in
Life Beyond Life and *Beyond This Life*.

All insert photos © 1994 by Hans Holzer
Cover photo © Westlight
Spine and back cover photos by
Cover design by Todd Petersen

Published by Contemporary Books, Inc.
Two Prudential Plaza, Chicago, Illinois 60601-6790
Manufactured in the United States of America
International Standard Book Number: 0-8092-3577-3
10   9   8   7   6   5   4   3   2   1

Contents

Preface

As you read this book and consider the evidence for an existence beyond physical death, you may well experience a complete about-face in your sense of values and attitudes. I know I did when I first came in contact with hard facts, and the people providing them, many years ago.

It is not a question of belief or disbelief—it is a question of honesty about life and what it really means. I leave the ultimate answer as to who instituted this system, and who appointed the one who did, to the time when I myself come face to face with the ultimate reality.

What I want to convey to you, my dear public, is the need to consider your existence in a new light, the light of total spirituality, where the physical is but one expression of the totality of our existence. Once you have understood and integrated this knowledge into your being, you will have no further doubts about the system or that it works well indeed!

As we are both emotional and rational creatures, we do need a degree of persuasion that this is indeed so. To this end, this work has been assembled. I do not wish to convert the skeptic or materialist or anyone else; but by making the facts available to those who wish to examine them, I hope to contribute to the proliferation of people who regain their inborn (but often neglected) spirituality and thus become parts of a better world for all of us.

Hans Holzer, Ph.D.
December 1993

Part One

Living in Other Worlds

Introduction

When my book *Life After Death: The Challenge and the Evidence* was published in 1969 the question of life after death was debated mainly by two groups of people: the religious establishment, which took the question on a philosophical and perhaps a faith basis, and the metaphysical establishment, ranging all the way from convinced spiritualists to those operating on the fringes of scientific parapsychology, to whom the question of survival of bodily death was one not of *if* but of *how*. Since that time, parapsychology has made great strides. More and more universities have opened their gates to departments in this young and yet very old science, and during the last two years especially, members of the medical fraternity have come to the field of thanatology, the study of death and dying. Some of these medical doctors are no longer searching for the "obvious" explanations to the so-called hallucinations of the dying, or attributing them to final failures of the sensory system. They have at last opened their minds to the *possibility* that life after death is a reality.

Among the pioneers in this work are Dr. Raymond Moody, whose book *Life After Life* was on the bestseller lists for an amazing number of weeks, and the Swiss physician Dr. Elizabeth Kübler-Ross, whose book *On Death and Dying* was a true pioneering effort. Finally there is Dr. Karlis Osis, the research director of the American Society for Psychical Research, whose study of deathbed experiences has been of significant value in this area. Undoubtedly millions of people will have read what these eminent doctors have to say about death and the evidence for survival of human personality. While Dr. Moody defers to his scientific colleagues in the final pages of his book, terming his very scientific work as not necessarily evidence for survival, everything in it points in that direction—although the over-whelming majority of physicians cannot yet accept the reality of human survival. Perhaps the attitude displayed by an increasing number of ordinary people toward the evidence for a life after death was best expressed in the flyer attached to a *Reader's Digest* condensation of Dr. Moody's book. The flyer was titled *Life After Death . . . the Testimony Mounts.*

Between 1969 and the present time much new material has come to my attention pointing in the direction of survival and communication from and with the beyond. In addition I have been the recipient of much mail from people who have read *Life After Death: The Challenge and the Evidence* and found it help-ful in many ways. There were those, first of all, of advanced age to whom the hard evidence of another life beyond this one presented a great deal of comfort. This applied particularly to those who due to their religious background had been brought up to believe in punishment for their misdeeds after death or those, on the other end of the scale, who had always assumed that death was indeed the end. To them, the carefully researched cases in my book presented graphic evidence that their educa-tion in this area had been incomplete or that they had been misinformed about what lay ahead of them.

There was also much mail from young people who were far from the gates of death; to them, evidence for communication with departed ones presented a new and challenging concept, one that they wanted very much to explore on their own terms. If life after death were indeed a reality, then perhaps they could benefit from communication with some of those who had gone before them. An entire generation of young people who have given themselves to the exploration of mysticism and the meta-physical aspects of the occult suddenly found themselves going in the direction of scientific investigation of afterlife evidence.

Instead of the emotional appeal of the cult, they were searching out reliable channels of communication to establish on a purely evidential basis that there was indeed a link with another world beyond this one.

My own investigations into life after death continue and will continue because the subject itself seems to me of paramount importance in the evaluation of any ongoing existence.

Chapter One

Beyond This Life: Testimony of Those Who Have Returned

WHILE THE EVIDENCE FOR COMMUNICATION with the dead will provide the bulk of evidential material for conditions and decrees existing in that other world, we have also a number of testimonies from people who have entered the next world but not stayed in it. The cases involve people who were temporarily separated from their physical reality—without, however, being cut off from it permanently—into the state we call death. These are mainly victims of accidents who recovered, others who had undergone surgery and during the state of anesthesia became separated from their physical bodies and were able to observe from a new vantage point what was happening to them, and, in some instances, people who had traveled to the next world in a kind of dream state and observed conditions there that they remembered upon returning to the full state of wakefulness.

I hesitate to call these cases dreams since, as I have already pointed out in another work on the psychic side of dreams, the dream state covers a multitude of conditions, some of which at least are not actual dreams but states of limited consciousness and receptivity to external inputs. Out-of-body experiences, formerly known as astral projections, are also frequently classed with dreams, while in fact they are a form of projection in which the individual is traveling outside the physical body.

The cases I am about to present for the reality of this phenomenon are, to the best of my knowledge, true experiences by average, ordinary individuals. I have always shied away from accepting material from anyone undergoing psychiatric treatment, not because I necessarily discount such testimony but because some of my readers might.

As Dr. Raymond Moody noted in his work, there is a definite pattern to these near misses, so to speak, the experiences of people who have gone over and then returned. What they relate about conditions on the "other side of life" is frequently similar to what other people have said about these conditions, yet the witnesses have no way of knowing each other's experiences, have never met, have not read a common source from which they could draw such material if they were inclined to deceive the investigator, which they certainly are not. In fact, many of these testimonies are reluctantly given, out of fear of ridicule or perhaps because the individuals themselves are not sure of what to make of it. Far from the fanatical fervor of a religious purveyor, those whose cases have been brought to my attention do not wish to convince anyone of anything but merely want to report what has occurred in their lives. In publishing these reports, I am making the information available to those who might have had similar experiences and wondered about them.

We should keep in mind that the subjects of the experiences would perceive entities and conditions in a three-dimensional way because they themselves are three-dimensional in relation to the experience once they leave their physical bodies. Thus it is entirely possible that a projection of a person would appear to the observer exactly the same way as the person would appear. If we accept the notion that the world beyond this one, in which so-called spirit life continues, is capable of creating by mind actual images of self as desired, even building houses by thought alone, and is able to make them appear as solid and three-dimensional as people and houses are in this world, then the question of seeming contradictions to physical law as we know it is no longer such a puzzling one. Obviously, an entity controlled by thought can pass through solid walls or move at instantaneous speed from one place to another; during the temporary states between physical life and death, individuals partake of this ability and therefore undergo experiences that might otherwise be termed hallucinations.

I cannot emphasize strongly enough that the cases I am reporting in the following pages do not fall into the category of what many doctors like to call hallucinations, mental aberrations, or fantasies. The clarity of the experiences, the full remembrance of them afterward, the many parallels between individual experiences reported by people in widely scattered areas, and finally the physical condition of the percipients at the time of the experience all weigh heavily against the dismissal of such experiences as being of hallucinatory origin.

Mrs. Virginia S., a housewife in one of the western states, had in the past held various responsible jobs in management and business. On March 13, 1960, she underwent surgery for, as she put it, repair to her muscles. During the operation, she lost so much blood she was clinically dead. Nevertheless, the surgeons worked feverishly to bring her back, and she recovered. This is what Mrs. S. experienced during the period when the medical team was unable to detect any sign of life in her.

"I was climbing a rock wall and was standing straight in the air. Nothing else was around it; it seemed flat. At the top of this wall was another stone railing about two feet high. I grabbed for the edge to pull myself over the wall, and my father, who is deceased, appeared and looked down at me. He said, 'You cannot come up yet; go back, you have something left to do.' I looked down and started to go down, and the next thing I heard were the words 'She's coming back.' "

Mrs. J. L. H., a housewife in her middle thirties living in British Columbia, had an amazing experience on her way back from the funeral of her stepfather, George H. She was driving with a friend, Clarence G., and there was a serious accident. Clarence was killed instantly, and Mrs. H. was seriously hurt. "I don't remember anything except seeing car lights coming at me, for I had been sleeping," Mrs. H. explained. "I first remember seeing my stepdad, George, step forward out of a cloudy mist and touch me on my left shoulder. He said, 'Go back, June, it's not time yet.' I woke up with the weight of his hand still on my shoulder."

The curious thing about this case is that two people were in the same accident, yet one of them was evidently marked for death while the other was not. After Mrs. H. had recovered from her injuries and returned home, she woke up one night to see a figure at the end of her bed holding out his hand toward her as if wanting her to come with him. When she turned her light on, the figure disappeared, but it always returned when she turned the lights off again. During subsequent appearances, the entity tried to lift Mrs. H. out of her bed, pulling all the covers off her, thereafter forcing her to sleep with the lights on. It would appear that Clarence could not understand why he was on the other side of life without his friend.

Mrs. Phyllis G., also from Canada, had a most remarkable experience in March 1949. She had just given birth to twin boys at her home, and the confinement seemed normal and natural. By late evening, however, she began to suffer from a very severe headache. By morning she was unconscious and was rushed to the hospital with a cerebral hemorrhage. She was unconcious for three days while the doctors were doing their best to save her life. It was during this time that she had a most remarkable experience.

"My husband's grandmother had died the previous August, but she came to me during my unconscious state, dressed in the whitest white robe, and there was light shining around her. She seemed to me to be in a lovely, quiet meadow. Her arms were held out to me and she called my name. 'Phyllis, come with me.' I told her this was not possible as I had my children to take care of. Again she said, 'Phyllis, come with me, you will love it here.' Once again, I told her it wasn't possible. I said, 'Gran, I can't. I must look after my children.' With this she said, 'I must take someone. I will take Jeffrey.' I didn't object to this, and Gran just faded away." Mrs. G. recovered, and her son Jeffrey, the first twin that was born, wasn't taken either and at twenty-eight years old was doing fine. However, his mother still had a nagging feeling in the back of her mind that perhaps his life may not be as long as it ought to be. During the time when she saw her grandmother, Mrs. G. had been considered clinically dead.

There are many cases on record in which a person begins to become part of another dimension even while there is still hope for recovery, but at a time when the ties between conciousness and body are already beginning to loosen. An interesting case was reported to me by Mrs. J. P. of California. While still a teenager, Mrs. P. had been very ill with influenza but was just begining to recover when she had a most unusual experience.

One morning her father and mother came into her bedroom to see how she was feeling. "After a few minutes I asked them if they could hear the beautiful music. I still remember that my father looked at my mother and said, 'She's delirious.' I vehemently denied that. Soon they left, but as I glanced out my second-floor bedroom window towards the wooded hills I love, I saw a sight that literally took my breath away. There, superimposed on the trees, was a beautiful cathedral-type structure from which that beautiful music was emanating. Then I seemed to be looking down on the people. Everyone was singing, but it was the background music that thrilled my soul. A leader dressed in white was leading the singing. The interior of the church seemed strange to me. It was only in later years, after I had attended services in an Episcopal church and also in a Catholic church that I realized the front of the church I saw was more in their style, with the beautiful altar. The vision faded. Two years later, when I was ill again, the scene and music returned."

On January 5, 1964, Mr. R. J. I. of Pittsburgh, Pennsylvania, was rushed to the hospital with a bleeding ulcer. On admittance he received a shot and became unconscious. Attempts were immediately made to stop the bleeding, and finally he was operated on. During the operation, Mr. I. lost fifteen pints of blood, suffered convulsions, and had a temperature of 106 degrees. He was as close to death as one could come and was given the last rites of his church. However, during the period of his unconsciousness he had a remarkable experience. "On the day my doctor told my wife I had only an hour to live, I saw, while unconscious, a man with black hair and a white robe with a gold belt come from behind the altar, look at me, and shake his head. I was taken to a long hall, and purple robes were laid out for me. There were many candles lit in this hall."

Many cases of this kind occur when the subject is being prepared for surgery or undergoing surgery; sometimes the anesthetic allows dissociation to occur more easily. This is not to say that people necessarily hallucinate under the influence of anesthetic drugs or due to the lack of blood or from any other physical cause. If death is the dissolution of the link between physical body and etheric body, it stands to reason that any loosening of this link is likely to allow the etheric body to move away from its physical shell, although still tied to it either by an invisible silver cord or by some form of invisible tie that we do not as yet fully understand. Otherwise those who have returned from the great beyond would not have done so.

Mrs. J. M., a resident of Canada, was expecting her fourth child in October 1956.

"Something went wrong, and when I had a contraction I went unconscious. My doctor was called, and I remember him telling me he couldn't give any anesthetic as he might have to operate. Then I passed out, but I could still hear him talking and myself talking back to him. Then I couldn't hear him any longer, and I found myself on the banks of a river with green grass and white buildings on the other side. I knew if I could get across I'd never be tired again, but there was no bridge and the water was very rough. I looked back and I saw myself lying there, back in the hospital, with nurses and doctors around me, and Dr. M. had his hand on the back of my neck and he was calling me, and he looked so worried that I knew I had to go back. I had the baby, and then I was back in the room and the doctor explained to my husband what happened. I asked him why he had his hand on my neck, and he replied that it was the only place on my body where he could find a pulse and for over a minute he couldn't even feel one there. Was this the time when I was standing on the riverbank?"

Deborah B. is a young lady living in California with a long record of psychic experiences. At times, when she's intensely involved in an emotional situation, she undergoes what we parapsychologists call a dissociation of personality. For a moment, she is able to look into another dimension, partake of visionary experiences not seen or felt by others in her vicinty. One such incident occurred to Deborah during a theater arts class at school. She looked up from her script and saw "a man standing there in a flowing white robe, staring at me, with golden or blond hair down to his shoulders; a misty fog surrounded him. I couldn't make out his face, but I knew he was staring at me. During this time I had a very peaceful and secure feeling. He then faded away."

Later that year, after an emotional dispute between Deborah and her mother, another visionary experience took place. "I saw a woman dressed in a long, blue flowing robe, with a white shawl or veil over her head, beckoning to a group of three or four women dresed in rose-colored robes and white veils. The lady in blue was on the steps of a church or temple with very large pillars. Then it faded out."

One might argue that Deobrah's imagination was creating visionary scenes within her, if it weren't for the fact that what she describes has been described by others, especially people who have found themselves on the threshold of death and returned. The beckoning figure in the flowing robe has been reported by many, sometimes identified as Jesus, sometimes simply as a master. The identification of the figure depends, of course, on the religious or metaphysical attitude of the subject, but the feeling caused by his appearance seems to be universally the same: a sense of peace and complete contentment.

Mrs. C. B. of Connecticut has had a heart problem for over twenty-five years. The condition is under control so long as she takes the tablets prescribed for her by her physician. Whenever her blood pressure passes the two hundred mark, she reaches for them. When her pulse rate does not respond to the medication, she asks to be taken to the hospital for further treatment. There drugs are injected into her intravenously, a procedure that is unpleasant and that she tries to avoid at all costs. But she has lived with this condition for a long time and knows what she must do to survive. On one occasion she had been reading in bed and was still awake around five o'clock in the morning. Her heart had been acting up again for an hour or so. She even applied pressure to various pressure points she knew about, in the hope that her home remedies would slow down her pulse rate, but to no avail. Since she did not wish to awaken her husband, she was waiting to see whether the condition would abate itself. At that moment Mrs. B. had a most remarkable experience.

"Into my window flew or glided a woman. She was large, beautiful, and clothed in a multicolored garment with either arms or wings close to her sides. She stopped and hovered at the foot of my bed to the right and simply stayed there. I was so shocked, and yet I knew that I was seeing her as a physical being. She turned neither to the right nor to the left but remained absolutely stone-faced and said not a word. Then I seemed to become aware of four cherubs playing around and in front of her. Yet I sensed somehow that these were seen with my mind's eye rather than with the material eyes. I don't know how to explain from any reasonable standpoint what I said or did; I only knew what happened. I thought, 'This is the angel of death. My time has come.' I said audibly, 'If you are from God, I will go with you.' As I reached out my hand to her, she simply vanished in midair. Needless to say, the cherubs vanished too. I was stunned, but my heart beat had returned to normal."

Mrs. L. L. of Michigan dreamed in July 1968 that she and her husband had been killed in an automobile accident. In November of that year, the feeling that death was all around her became stronger. Around the middle of the month, the feeling was so overwhelming she telephoned her husband, who was then on a hunting trip, and informed him of her death fears. She discussed her apprehensions with a neighbor, but nothing helped allay her uneasiness. On December 17, Mrs. L. had still another dream, again about imminent death. In this dream she knew that her husband would die and that she could not save him, no matter what she did. Two days later, Mrs. L. and her husband were indeed in an automobile accident. He was killed, and Mrs. L. nearly died. According to the attending physician, Dr. S., she should have been a dead woman, considering her injuries. But during the stay in the hospital, when she had been given up and was visited by her sister, she spoke freely about a place she was seeing and the dead relatives she was in contact with at the time. Although she was unconscious, she knew that her husband was dead, but she also knew that her time had not come, that she had a purpose to achieve in life and therefore could not stay on the "plane" on which she temporarily was. The sister, who did not understand any of this, asked whether Mrs. L. had seen God and whether she had visted heaven. The unconscious subject replied that she had not seen God nor was she in heaven, but on a certain plane of existence. The sister thought that all this was nonsense and that her dying sister was delirious, and left.

Mrs. L. herself remembers quite clearly how life returned to her after her visit to the other plane. "I felt life coming to my body, from the tip of my toes to the tip of my head. I knew I couldn't die. Something came back into my body; I think it was my soul. I was at complete peace about everything and could not grieve about the death of my husband. I had complete forgiveness for the man who hit us; I felt no bitterness toward him at all."

Do some people get an advance glimpse of their own demise? It would be easy to dismiss some of the precognitive or seemingly precognitive dreams as anxiety-caused, perhaps due to fantasies of their own. However, many of these dreams parallel each other and differ from ordinary anxiety dreams in their intensity and the fact that they are remembered so very clearly upon awakening.

A good case in point is a vivid dream reported to me by Mrs. Peggy C., who lives in a New York suburb. The reason for her contacting me was the fact that she had developed a heart condition recently and was wondering whether a dream she had had twenty years before was an indication that her life was nearing its end. The dream that so unnerved her through the years had her walking past a theater where she met a dead brother-in-law. "I said to him, 'Hi, Charlie, what are you doing here?' He just smiled, and then in my dream it dawned on me that the dead come for the living. I said to him 'Did you come for me?' He said, 'Yes.' I said to him, 'Did I die?' He said, 'Yes.' I said, 'I wasn't sick. Was it my heart?' He nodded, and I said, 'I'm scared.' He said, 'There is nothing to be scared of, just hold onto me.' I put my arms around him, and we sailed through the air of darkness. It was not a frightening feeling but a pleasant sensation. I could see the buildings beneath us. Then we came to a room where a woman was at a desk. In the room were my brother-in-law, an old lady, and a mailman. She called me to her desk. I said, 'Do we have to work here too?' She said, 'We are all assigned to duties. What is your name?' I was christened Bernadine, but my mother never used the name. I was called Peggy. I told her 'Peggy.' She said, 'No, your name is Bernadine.' After taking the details, my brother-in-law took me by the arms and was taking me upstairs, when I awakened. I saw my husband standing over me with his eyes wide open, but I could not move. I was thinking to myself, 'Please shake me, I'm alive,' but I could not move or talk. After a few minutes, my body jerked in bed, and I opened my eyes and began to cry." The question is, did Mrs. C. have a near-death experience and return from it, or was her dream truly precognitive, indicative perhaps of things yet to come?

Doctor Karlis Osis published his findings concerning many deathbed experiences, wherein the dying recognize dead relatives in the room, seemingly come to help them across the threshold into the next world. A lady in South Carolina, Mrs.

M. C., reported one particularly interesting case to me. She herself has a fair degree of mediumship, which is a factor in the present case. "I stood behind my mother as she lay dying at the age of some seventy years. She had suffered a cerebral stroke, and at this particular time of her life she was unable to speak. Her attendants claimed they had had no communication with her for over a week previously. As I let my mind go into her, she spoke clearly and flawlessly, 'If only you could see how beautiful and perfect it all is,' she said, then called out to her dead father, saying 'Papa, Papa.' I then spoke directly to her and asked her, did she see Papa? She answered as if she had come home, so to speak. 'Yes, I see Papa.' She passed over onto the other side shortly, in a matter of days. It was as if her father had indeed come after her, as if she saw him, and she spoke to me clearly with paralyzed mouth and throat muscles."

Sometimes the dead want the living to know how wonderful their newly found world is. Whether this is out of a need to make up for ignorance in one's earth life, when such knowledge was either outside one's ken or ignored, or whether this is in order to acquaint the surviving relative with what lies ahead, cases involving such excursions into the next world tend to confirm the near-death experiences of those who have gone into it on their own, propelled by accidents or unusual states of consciousness. One of the most remarkable reports of this kind came to me through the kindness of two sisters living in England. Mrs. Doreen B., a senior nursing administrator, had witnessed death on numerous occasions. Here is her report.

"In May 1968 my dear mother died. I had nursed her at home, during which time we had become extremely close. My mother was a quiet, shy woman who always wished to remain in the background. Her last weeks were ones of agony; she had terminal cancer with growths in many parts of her body. Towards the end of her life I had to heavily sedate her to alleviate the pain, and after saying good-bye to my daughter on the morning of the seventh of May, she lapsed into semiconsciousness and finally died in a coma, approximately 2:15 A.M. on the eighth of May 1968. A few nights after her death I was gently awakened. I opened my eyes and saw Mother.

"Before I relate what happened, I should like to say that I dream vividly every night, and this fact made me more aware that I was *not* dreaming. I had not taken any drinks or drugs although of course my mind and emotions revolved around my mother. After Mother woke me, I arose from my bed; my hand instinctively reached out for my dressing gown, but I do not remember putting it on. Mother said that she would take me to where she was. I reacted by saying that I would get the car out, but she said that I would not need it. We traveled quickly, I do not know how, but I was aware that we were in the Durking Leatherhead area and entering another dimension.

"The first thing I saw was a large archway. I knew I had seen it before, although it means nothing to me now. Inside the entrance a beautiful sight met my eyes. There was glorious parkland, with shrubbery and flowers of many colors. We traveled across the parkland and came to a low-built white building. It seemed to have the appearance of a convalescent home. There was a veranda, but no windows or doors as we know them. Inside everything was white, and Mother showed me a bed that she said was hers. I was aware of other people, but they were only shadowy white figures. Mother was very worried about some of them and told me that they did not know that they were dead. However, I was aware that one of a group of three was a man.

"Mother had always been very frugal in dress, possibly due to her hardships in earlier years. Therefore her wardrobe was small but neat, and she spent very little on clothing if she could alter and mend. Because of this I was surprised when she said she wished that she had more clothes. In life Mother was the kindest of women, never saying or thinking ill of anyone. Therefore I found it hard to understand her resentment of a woman in a long, flowing robe who appeared on a bridge in the grounds. The bridge looked beautiful, but Mother never took me near it. I now had to return, but to my question, 'Are you happy?' I was extremely distressed to know that she did not want to leave her family. Before Mother left me she said a gentle 'Good-bye dear.' It was said with a quiet finality, and I knew that I would never see her again.

"It was only afterward when I related it to my sister that I realized that Mother had been much more youthful than when she died and that her back, which in life had been rounded, was straight. Also I realized that we had not spoken through our lips but as if by thought, except when she said, 'Good-bye, dear.' It is now three and a half years since this happening, and I have had no further experience. I now realize that I must have seen Mother during her transition period, when she was still earthbound, possibly from the effects of the drugs I administered under medical supervision, and when her tie to her family, particularly her grandchild, was still very strong."

Patricia N., sister to Mrs. B., kindly wrote her own account of the incident, "separately and without consulting each other." As Mrs. N. remembers it, her sister reported the incident to her shortly after it occurred. "My sister told me that she felt herself being gently shaken awake, and when she opened her eyes, my mother was bending over her. She was wearing ordinary dress and looked as she did some twenty-five years earlier." Mrs. N. then goes on to confirm pretty much what her sister had written to me. She adds, "She told my sister she would not be staying where she was but gave no indication as to where she was going. There were no other buildings to be seen in this vast parkland area. It otherwise appeared to be totally deserted and exceptionally beautiful and peaceful. My deepest regret is that my sister and I had never taken an interest in ESP, spiritualism, or mediums up to that time and were therefore totally unprepared for what happened."

Don McI., a professional astrologer living in Richland, Washington, has no particular interest in psychic phenomena, is in his early seventies, and worked most of his life as a security patrolman, his last employment being at an atomic plant in Washington State. After retirement, he took up astrology full-time. Nevertheless, he had a remarkable experience that convinced him of the reality of afterlife existence.

"On November 15, 1971, at about 6:30 A.M., I was beginning to awaken when I clearly saw the face of my cousin beside and near the foot of my bed. He said, 'Don, I have died.' Then his face disappeared, but the voice was definitely his own distinctive voice. As far as I knew at that time, he was alive and well. The thought of telling my wife made me feel uncomfortable, so I did not tell her of the incident. At 11:00 A.M., about four and a half hours after my psychic experience, my mail arrived. In the mail was a letter from my cousin's widow, informing us that he had a heart failure and was pronounced dead upon arrival at the hospital. She stated that his death occurred at 9:30 P.M., November 8, 1971, at Ventura, California. My home, where my psychic experience took place, is at least a thousand miles from Ventura, California. The incident is the only psychic experience I've ever had."

William W. lives and works in Washington, D.C. Because of some remarkable psychic incidents in his life, he began to wonder about survival of human personality. One evening he had a dream in which he saw himself walking up a flight of stairs where he was met by a woman whom he immediately recognized as his elderly great-aunt. She had died in 1936. "However she was dressed in a gray long dress about the turn-of-the-century style, her hair was black, and she looked vibrantly young. I asked her in the dream where the others were, and she referred me to a large room at the top of the stairs. The surroundings were not familiar. I entered the room and was amazed to see about fifteen people in various types of dress, both male and female and all looking like mature adults, some about the age of thirty. I was able to recognize nearly all of these people although most I had seen when they were quite old. All appeared jovial and happy. I awakened from the dream with the feeling that somebody had been trying to tell me something."

There are repeated reports indicating that the dead revert to their best years, which lie around the age of thirty in most cases, because they are able to project a thought-form of themselves as they wish. On the other hand, where apparitions of the dead are intended to prove survival of an individual, they usually appear as they looked prior to death, frequently wearing the clothes they wore at the time of their passing.

Not all temporary separations of the body and etheric self include a visit to the next world. Sometimes the liberated self merely hangs around to observe what is being done with the body. Mrs. Elaine L., of Washinton State, reported an experience that happened to her at the age of sixteen. "I had suffered several days from an infected back tooth, and since my face was badly swollen our dentist refused to remove the tooth until the swelling subsided. When it did, and shortly after the novocaine was administrated, I found myself floating close to an open window. I saw my body in the dental chair and the dentist working feverishly. Our landlady, Mrs. E., who had brought me to the dentist, stood close by, shaking me and looking quite flabbergasted and unbelieving. My feeling at the time was of complete peace and freedom. There was no pain, no anxiety, not even an interest in what was happening close to that chair.

Soon I was back to the pain and remember as I left the office that I felt a little resentful. The dentist phoned frequently during the next few days for assurance that I was alright."

According to one report, a Trappist monk who had suffered a cardiac arrest for a period of ten minutes remembered a visit to a world far different from what his religion had taught him. Brother G. spoke of seeing fluffy white clouds and experiencing a sense of great joy. As a result of his amazing experience, the monk now helps people on the terminal list of a local hospital face death more adequately. He can tell them that there is nothing to fear.

A New Jersey physician, Dr. Joseph G., admitted publicly that he had "died" after a severe attack of pneumonia in 1934 and could actually see himself lying on the deathbed. At the time, worrying how his mother would feel if he died, he heard a voice tell him that it was entirely up to him whether he wanted to stay on the physical plane or go across. Because of his own experience, Dr. G. later paid serious attention to the accounts of several patients who had similar experiences.

The number of cases involving near-death experiences, reports from people who were clinically dead for varying lengths of time and who then recovered and remembered what they experienced while unconcious, is considerable. If we assume that universal law covers all contingencies, there should be no exceptions to it. Why then are some people allowed to glimpse that which lies ahead for them in the next dimension, without actually entering that dimension at the time of the experience? After investigating large numbers of such cases, I can only surmise that there are two reasons. First of all, there must be a degree of self-determination involved, allowing the subject to go forward to the next dimension or return to the body. As a matter of fact, in many cases though not in all, the person is being given that choice and elects to return to earth. Secondly, by the dissemination of these witnesses' reports among those in the physical world, knowledge is put at our disposal, or rather at the disposal of those who wish to listen. It is a little like a congressional leak, short of an official announcement and much more than a mere rumor. In the final analysis, those who are ready to understand the nature of life will derive benefits from this information, and those who are not ready, will not.

Chapter Two

Life and Death: What Are They?

ALTHOUGH HUMANS HAVE WALKED ON THE MOON and will soon reach for the stars, we have yet to learn what we are. After millions of years of existence on this planet, we are still unable to come to grips with the most important question of all: What is man? Why is man? How is man?

❮ To toss the problem of man into the lap of religion by judging it to be the whim of an omnipotent creator is merely to beg the question. Even if we were to accept uncritically the notion of instantaneous creation by a superior force, it would leave unanswered the questions that would immediately arise from such a notion: Who created the creator? ❯

To go to the other end of the scale and ascribe our existence to a slow process of natural evolution in which particles of matter—chemicals—mixed in certain ways to form larger pieces of matter and ultimately reached the stage where life began sounds as if it were a more sensible approach to the puzzle of our existence. But only on the surface, for if we were to accept the theory of evolution—and there is good enough evidence that it is valid—we would still be faced with the very problem religion leaves us: Who arranged things in this way, so that infinitesimal bits of matter would join to create life and follow what is obviously an orderly pattern of development?

Whether we are theistic or atheistic, materialistic or idealistic, the end result, as I see it, seems to lead to the same door. That door, however, is closed. Behind it lies the one big answer man has searched for, consciously or unconsciously, since the dawn of time.

Is man an animal, derived from the primates, as Dr. Desmond Morris asserted in *The Naked Ape*? Is he merely an accidental development whereby at one point in time a large ape became a primitive man? To this day this hypothesis is unacceptable to large segments of the population.

The revulsion against such a hypothesis of man's nature stems largely from strongly entrenched fundamentalist religious feelings rather than from any enlightened understanding that knows better than Darwin. When religion goes against science, even imperfect science, it is bound to lose out.

On the other hand, the less violent but much more effective resistance by scientists, doctors, and intellectuals in general to the hypothesis of man's spontaneous creation by a superior being is so widespread today that it has made heavy inroads in church attendance and forced the religious denominations to think of new approaches to lure large segments of the population back into the fold, or at least to interest them in the nonreligious aspects of church existence. But the professionals and intellectuals are by no means alone in their rejection of traditional views. A large majority of students, on both college and high school levels, are nonbelievers or outright cynics. They don't always cherish that position, but they have not found an alternative. At least they had not until ESP (extrasensory perception) came along to offer them a glimpse at immortality that their scientific training *could* let them accept.

To the average person, then, the problem of what man is remains unsolved and as puzzling as ever. But this is not true of the psychic or esoteric person.

An increasing number of people throughout the world have at one time or another had personal proof of man's immortality. To them, their own experiences are sufficient to assure them that we are part of a greater scheme of things, with some sort of superior law operating for the benefit of all. They do not always agree on what form this superior force takes, and they generally reject the traditional concepts of a personal God, but they acknowledge the existence of an orderly scheme of things and the continuance of life as we know it beyond the barriers of death and time.>

< Many of those who accept in varying degrees spiritual concepts of life after death do so uncritically and believe from a personal, emotional point of view. They merely replace a formal religion with an informal one. They replace a dogma they find outmoded, and not borne out by the facts as they know them, with a flexible, seemingly sensible system to which they can relate enthusiastically. >

It seems to me that somewhere in between these orthodox and heterodox elements lies the answer to the problem. If we are ever to find the human solution and know what man is, why he is, and how he is, we must take into account all elements, strip them of their fallacies, and retain the hard-core facts. In correlating the facts we find, we can then construct an edifice of thought that may solve the problem and give us the ultimate answers we are seeking.

What is life? From birth, life evolves for a human being through successive stages of gradual development that differ in detail with each and every human being. Materialistic science likes to ascribe these unique tendencies to environment and parental heritage alone. Astrology, a very respectable craft when properly used, claims that the radiation from the planets, the sun, and the moon influences the body of the newly born from birth or, according to some astrological schools, even from the moment of conception. One should not reject the astrological theory out of hand. After all, the radiation of man-made atom bombs affected the children of Hiroshima, and the radiation from the cosmos is far greater and of longer duration. We know very little about radiation effects as yet.

That man is essentially a dual creature is no longer denied even by medical science. Psychiatry could not exist were it not for the acknowledgement that man has a mind, though the mind is visible. Esoteric teaching goes even further: man has a soul, and it is inserted into the body of the newborn at the moment of birth. Now if the soul joins the body only at or just before the moment of birth, then a fetus has no personality, according to this view, and abortion is not a "sin." Some orthodox religions do not hold this view and consider even an unborn child a full person. It is pretty difficult to prove objectively either assertion, but it is not impossible to prove scientif- ically and rationally that man *after* birth has a nonphysical component, variously called soul, psyche, psi, or personality.

What is death, then? The ceasing of bodily functions due to illness or malfunction of a vital organ reverses the order of things that occurred at birth. Now the two components of man are separated again and go in different directions. The body, deprived of its operating force, is nothing more than a shell and subject to ordinary laws affecting matter. Under the influence of the atmosphere, it will rapidly decompose and is therefore quickly disposed of in all cultures, to return to the earth in various forms and contribute its basic chemicals to the soil or water.

The soul, on the other hand, continues its journey into what the late Dr. Joseph Rhine of Duke University called "the world of the mind." That is, to those who believe there is a soul, it enters the world of the mind. To those who reject the very notion of a soul factor, the decomposing body represents all the remains of man at death. It is this concept that breeds fear of death, fosters nihilistic attitudes toward life while one lives it, and favors the entire syndrome of expressions such as "death is the end," "fear the cemetery," and "funerals are solemn occa- sions."

Death has different powers in different cultures. To prim- itive man it was a vengeful god who took loved ones away when they were still needed.

To the devout Christian of the Middle Ages, death was the punishment one had to fear all one's life, for after death came the reckoning.

West Africans and their distant cousins, the Haitian, wor- ship death in a strange cult called in Haiti the "Papa Nebo" cult.

Spanish and Irish Catholics celebrate the occasions of death with elaborate festivities, because they wish to help the departed one get a good reception in the afterlife.

Only in the East does death have a benign role. In the spiritually advanced beliefs of the Chinese, the Indians, and the ancient Egyptians, death was the beginning, not the end. Death marked the gate to a higher consciousness, and it is because of this philosophy that the dreary aspects of funerals as we know them in the West are totally absent from eastern rites. They mark their funerals, of course, but not with the sense of finality and sadness that pervades the western concept. Perhaps this benignness has some connection with the strong belief in a hereafter that the people of the East hold, while the western world offers faith in an afterlife but has no real conviction that it exists, except for a minority of fundamentalists to whom the Bible has spelled out everything without further need of clarification.>

There is scarcely a religion that does not accept the continuance of life beyond death in one form or another. There are some forms of "reform" Judaism and some extremely liberal Christian denominations that stress the morality aspects of their religions rather than basic belief in a soul and its survival after death in a vaguely defined heaven or hell. Communism in its pure Marxist form, which is of course *a kind of religion*, goes out of its way to denounce the soul concept.

Not a single religious faith tries to rationalize its tenets of immortality in scientifically valid terms. Orthodox Catholicism rejects the inquiry *itself* as unwanted or at the very least proper only for those inside the professional hierarchy of the church. Some Protestant denominations, especially fundamentalists, find solace in biblical passages that they interpret as speaking out against any traffic with death or inquiry into areas dealing with psychic phenomena. The vast majority of faiths, however, neither encourage nor forbid the search for objective proof that what the church preaches on faith may have a basis in objective fact.

It is clear that one step begets another. If we accept the reality of the soul, we must also ask ourselves, where does the soul go after death? Thus interest concerning the nature of man quite easily extends to a curiosity about the world that the soul inhabits once it leaves its former abode.

Again, religion has given us descriptions galore of the afterlife, many embroidered in human fashion with elements of man-made justice but possessing very little factuality.

Inquiring persons will have to wait until they themselves get to the nonphysical world, or they will have to use one of several channels to find out what the nonphysical world is like. These channels we shall deal with in the next chapter, but inquirers must keep in mind the need, when choosing channels to evaluate the reliability of the channels they use.

When experience is firsthand, one has only one's own status or state of being to consider; waiting for or taking the ultimate step in order to find out about the next world is certainly a direct approach.

Desire to communicate with the dead is as old as humanity itself. As soon as primitive man realized that death could separate him from a loved one and that he could not prevent that person's departure, he thought of the next best thing: once gone, how could he communicate with the dead person? Could he bring him back? Would he join him eventually?

These are the original elements, along with certain observed forces in nature, that have contributed to the structure of early religions.

But primitive man had little or no understanding of nature around him and therefore personified all forces he could not understand or emulate. Death became a person of great and sinister power who ruled in a kingdom of darkness somewhere far away. To communicate with a departed loved one, one would have to have Death's permission or would have to outsmart him. Getting Death's permission to see a loved one was rare (e.g., the story of Orpheus and Eurydice).

Outsmarting Death was even more difficult. Everyman never succeeded, nor did the wealthy Persian merchant who ran away to Samara only to find Death there waiting for him. In these examples Death was of course waiting for the man himself, and it was not a question of getting past him into his kingdom to see the departed one. But it shows how all-knowing the personified Death of primitive and ancient man was.

The West African contact with the dead, which the people of Haiti still practice to this day, has them speaking through the water; again it is a question of either avoiding the voodoo gods or bribing them. Communication with the dead is never easy in primitive society.

In the East, where ancestor worship is part of the religious morality, communication is possible through the established channel of the priest, but the occasion has to warrant it. Here too we have unquestioned adherence to the orders given to the living by their forebears, as a matter of respect. As we dig deeper into the religious concepts of eastern origin, we find such a constant interplay between the living and the dead that one understands why some Orientals are not afraid to die or do not take the kind of precautions western people would take under similar circumstances. Death to them is not a stranger or a punishment or a fearful avenger of sins committed in the flesh.

In modern times, only spiritualism has approached the subject of the dead with a degree of rationalism, although it tends to build its edifice of believability occasionally on very shaky ground. The proof of survival of the human personality is certainly not wanting, yet spiritualism ignores the elements in man that are mortal and yet nonphysical, to give credit to the dead for everything that transcends the five senses. But ESP research has shown that some of these experiences need not be due to the spirit intervention, although they are not explicable in terms of orthodox science. We do have ESP in our incarnate state and rarely use the wonderous faculties of our minds to the fullest.

Nevertheless, the majority of spiritualist beliefs are capable of verification. I have worked with some of the best spiritualist mediums to learn about traffic with the "other world." For the heart of spiritualist belief *is* communication with the dead. If it exists, then obviously spiritualism has a very good claim to be a first-class religion, if not more. If the claim is fraudulent, then spiritualism would be as cruel a fraud as ever existed, deceiving man's deepest emotions.

Assuming that the dead exist and live on in a world beyond our physical world, it would be of the greatest interest to learn the nature of the secondary world and the laws that govern it. It would be important to understand "the art of dying," as the medieval esoterics called it, and come to a better understanding also of the nature of this transition called death.

Having accepted the existence of a nonphysical world populated by the dead that have gone before us, we next should examine the continuing contacts between the two worlds. Here we come to the two-way nature of communications between them: those initiated by the living, and those undertaken by the dead. There is, it would appear, a two-way traffic between the two worlds.

Observation of so-called spontaneous phenomena that have occurred to people will be just as important as induced experiments or attempts at contact. In all this we must keep a weather eye open for deceit, misinterpretation, or self-delusion. So long as there is a faculty of man involved in this inquiry, we must allow for man's weaknesses and limitations. By accepting safe-guards, we do not close our minds against astonishing facts that may be revealed, just because those facts seem contrary to current thinking. But if we proceed with caution, we shall have contributed something that may give beleaguered mankind new hope, new values, and new directions.

Chapter Three

True Communications from the Dead

THE VAST AMOUNT OF MATERIAL I HAVE EXAMINED leads me to believe that there is a certain pattern in the communications between the dead and the living. My research is based solely on first-hand cases that have come to my attention and does not include other researchers' cases, although I have studied most of the authoritative material available. They match many of the already published stories, and that is as it should be, for the law that controls those earlier cases surely must be operating also for the ones I have investigated.

Having disposed of the somewhat tiresome argument of hallucination by vigorously insisting on detailed accounts and properly evaluating my witnesses in terms of reliability and stability, I have accepted the cases I am about to present as genuine because of some very important arguments.

To begin with, I can neither prove objectively nor disprove objectively what human beings experience and register through their senses of sight, hearing, smell, and so on. I must still rely upon their reports unless I am myself the recipient of the unusual experience. Any judgment of people's experiences along these lines must therefore rest on secondary evidence: the person's character, mental and physical health, general behavior patterns, past record, incentive to lie (if any), and a comparison of the descriptive detail of the experiences with information given by other witnesses, whom that person does not know and who do not know him or her. It is scientifically acceptable to consider as true evidence the testimonies given by a number of witnesses in various places and at various times if these witnesses are in no position to influence one another's testimony. The theory of hallucination—that is, imaginary happenings that people believe they are actually experiencing—will simply not cover the majority of cases where contact between the dead and the living has occurred.

It is quite far-fetched to postulate that thousands of people in all sorts of circumstances hallucinate a dead relative under varying conditions, without any common denominator except that a psychic experience results. Far more logical is the assumption that an extraordinary ESP experience does indeed occur to these people, even if it is contrary to orthodox scientific beliefs *at that time.* Parenthetically one should remember that many situations nowadays taken for granted were contrary to scientific beliefs at one time. Television, radio, airplanes, photography, and many other human advances fall under that category. It is not true that science is at the zenith of knowledge today, with little if anything startling yet to come. Far from it. Science, as I define it, is merely a method of learning as much as one can about any given subject. It includes the proviso that one must change one's views and conclusions whenever new findings occur to alter earlier findings. Science is therefore a continually moving force that ought to be flexible and open-minded. It ought to welcome new ideas and investigate them. But it rarely does. Therein lies one of humankind's curious paradoxes: people want to know desperately, but at the same time they fear any knowledge that might upset previously held beliefs.

There are, I find, certain rules that seem to guide communications between the two worlds, and I have presented the material in what I consider the natural subdivisions.

First, there are communications from the dead who are motivated by the desire to let the living know that life continues beyond the veil. This seems to be one of the most common factors with communications, and little wonder, for our upbringing makes a belief in survival after physical death highly unlikely.

❮ True, religion holds out the *promise* of a hereafter to which we go either immediately or at a given point when the trumpets sound. But religion never specifies the nature, the methods, the concept of that transition. Rather does it clothe its promise in pious platitudes and vague promises that the good will be rewarded by being in heaven, and the bad by being relegated to hell. The first place is populated by ethereal beings of great beauty given mainly to uplifting pursuits, while the lower place resembles a low-class Turkish steambath with unfriendly attendants in red underwear. Religion, by and large, has seized upon the very real evidence for the existence of a hereafter as a means to an end: promising heaven or threatening hell keeps the faithful in line.

Unfortunately, people no longer *believe* this. Only a dwindling percentage of religiously oriented people actually accept these hereafter concepts at face value. The majority I have questioned will admit only that they simply don't know if there is such a thing as a hereafter, or they will deny outright that there *could* be. If they practice any religion at all, it is because of moral and social aspects, often even because of economic pressures to belong to an "in" group. But conservative religion on the one hand and extremely liberal religion on the other have both failed to satisfy humanity's eternal hunger for the truth about ourselves. If we are indeed endowed with an immortal soul, we wouldn't know it from our minister, priest, or rabbi.❯

But the searcher just might glimpse a piece of the truth through psychic research. When facts are presented they are subject only to acceptance or rejection. Either does not alter the facts themselves, which are devoid of any personal connotations. When one man shoots another, he may explain his crime in many different ways. The police will explain it in their way, and his defense attorney still another way, and perhaps his mother will have her version of it, too. None of these, however, alters the basic fact that he has shot a man.

So it is, I think, with the material presented here. The facts are recorded for what they are worth; the conclusions drawn are my own views. The views will stimulate people in various ways, no doubt, and that is as it should be. One should arrive at one's philosophy of life by firm conviction based on presented facts. I neither preach nor act as missionary for the cause of a scientifically established hereafter. However, I think the evidence does point toward a life after this one.

❮ Very few people are aware or convinced that death is not the end. Those who think as I do will, I am sure, find the transition far easier to accept than those to whom it comes as a shock. The shock is not so much the fact that one dies but that one is still alive *after* death. The resulting confusion sometimes creates the phenomenon called ghosts, or earthbound spirits.

❮ There are two strong and compelling reasons why dead people want family or friends to know that death is not the end and that they are in fact very much alive in another dimension.

One reason is the continuing ego consciousness of the dead person. He wants to let those closest to him know that he continues to exist as an entity and consequently wishes to be considered a continuing factor in their lives. This is for his own sake.

The second reason is for *their* sake. They too will eventually die. Why not give them the benefit of *his* experience? Why not teach them? Why not help those presumably ignorant of the true situation—that means nine out of ten—and do them the favor of letting them in on the world's greatest and most important secret: that life does not end at the grave? ❯

My own encounter with this type of communication first came in the late fifties, when I happened to drop in at a meeting of the New York branch of the Cayce Foundation. This foundation is also known as the Association for Research and Enlightenment and is dedicated to various forms of psychic and allied research. I sat quietly in the last row of the darkened room, in which there were a hundred or so people listening to a speaker. The lady was just ending her lecture-demonstration. The lights went on, and I was sorry to have come so late, but before I could leave I noticed that the speaker was making her way through the crowd toward me.

"Are you Hans Holzer?" she asked. I nodded, thinking that someone had pointed me out to her. Nobody had, for in those days I was quite unknown. None of my books in this field had yet appeared. Quickly suppressing my ego and realizing that she could not possibly have known my name, I asked what she wanted to tell me.

"I'm Betty Ritter," she explained, "the medium. I have a message for you from an uncle." Well, I thought, bemused, I've got a lot of uncles. She must have felt my skepticism, for she added: "His initials are O. S., he's got a wife named Alice, and she's a blond."

Now I had had an uncle whose name was Otto Stransky; he had died tragically in a streetcar mishap in 1932, and though I had always respected him, I hardly knew him and had not thought of him in many years. His widow's name was Alice. At the time of his passing she was indeed a blond.

There was no further message; this was it. He merely wanted me to know he *existed*. No alternate explanation would make sense. I had not been thinking of him, and if I had I would certainly not have referred to my Aunt Alice as a blond, knowing full well that she had been gray for many years. Only in my uncle's memory would she still be a blond!

Many years later I had the courage to talk of this experience to my aunt, who had moved to Brazil shortly before World War II. She nodded with understanding.

"Shortly before I left Europe," she explained, "I sensed Otto walking next to me. I did not see him with my eyes, but I felt him next to me. There was no mistaking it."

One might rightly ask, why did my uncle choose that particular moment and this medium to communicate with me? I think that two circumstances came together and made this communication possible. He may have waited for such an opportunity for a long time, knowing, with the superior knowledge the dead have in their world free of time and space limitations, that I would be present at this place at a time when a suitable channel would be available. When this became reality, he merely sent his thought message, and it was received and delivered.

Florence Sternfels was a psychic lady of great renown who often worked with law-enforcement authorities such as the FBI and the police in finding criminals or missing persons. Eventually she had her name changed to Florence Psychic, and her little house in Edgewater, New Jersey, became a focal point of activities two afternoons a week, when she gave readings to all comers for a small sum. She was essentially a psychometrist; that is, she touched an object and got impressions from it about the owner or conditions of the person on whose body the object had been. Florence worked not only with me but also with the late Dr. Hereward Carrington, a Los Angeles parapsychologist who died in 1958. We experimented with materializations. I have some interesting photographs taken in darkness with infrared film showing Florence, in trance, creating forms of ectoplasm. But despite her great desire and sincere wish to be a good trance medium, she really was at her best as a psychometrist, working while fully awake.

As her physical health declined, she was not able to get around so much, but she still wanted to volunteer her services and come along on any case I might have that could utilize her talents. Now and again I did call on her, but toward the end of her life I rarely saw her, and her telephone calls became fewer. In the preceding years she would always phone me when something of importance happened in her life. If a magazine writer wanted to interview her, she would first check him out with me. If someone wanted her to "sit" with him, Florence would ask me if that person was all right. I was a kind of friendly consultant to her in her declining years and regret that I did not see her more often than I did.

In early May of 1965 she passed across the threshold into a world she had known all along. For several months before, her heart had been weak, and her death did not come as a surprise. Nevertheless, I was saddened when I heard about it through a friend. That was around the tenth or twelfth of May. Nothing appeared in the newspapers except a small personal notice among the obituary announcements in the Edgewater paper. This was in sharp contrast to the reams of publicity Florence garnered during her active years.

I gave the passing no further thought, feeling that she would be treated like a queen in the world she was now in. I knew that there were relatives and that matters probably were well taken care of, although she had been alone in the house during her last years.

I recall that Florence once said to me how much she liked the heavy oak chair in which she gave her readings. That chair she would have liked to take along into the spirit world, if she could have done so. But other than that, she had no earthly ties or unfinished business. The one great tragedy of her life, the unsolved murder of her son some years before, would also be a matter of little concern since she would now be able to speak to him directly.

On May 19, 1965, I conducted an investigation of a reputedly haunted house at Ringwood, New Jersey, which is not very far from Edgewater. My medium on that occasion was Ethel Johnson Meyers, and we were accompanied by my wife, Catherine, and Haskel Frankel, an editor of the *Saturday Review* at that time and later senior editor on the *Saturday Evening Post*.

We had hardly entered the Ringwood Manor house and seated ourselves at a huge, round dining room table when Ethel fell into a deep trance. Expecting a voice from the past of this historically active mansion, I was startled when a strongly familiar sound came from Ethel Meyers' entranced lips.

"Mr. Holzer . . . hello . . . oh, Mr. Holzer!" The voice spoke out loud. "Hello!"

"Who is it?" I asked.

"Don't you recognize Florence?" the voice reprimanded me. "I'm so glad to talk to you." It was the exact tone of voice, choice of words, and jovial outburst that had always been characteristic of a telephone call from Florence! No mistaking it—this *was* Florence speaking.

"You passed over two weeks ago, Florence," I said gently.

"I just want to say hello."

I repeated my remark. But she brushed it aside and continued with the same excitement in her voice with which she had greeted me.

"I had a visit, I want you to know. I was going to call you and tell you. I can't tell many people, but I can tell *you*, I had a real exceptional . . . visit . . . you know . . . don't tell anybody about it, will you! It's a very deep secret." Florence always had "deep secrets." Every government case brought to her was treated as if she had been entrusted with the key to Fort Knox. But she always confided in me. The phrasing and general tone of voice were truly Florence's own. I doubt that Ethel Meyers, even if she had heard of Florence's passing, could have used such words, words that only passed between Florence and me, words that only made sense between the two of us.

"How did you find me here?" I wondered out loud.

"Well, I've been watching for a long time. . . . I wanted to call you, but I can never get you on the phone. . . . I don't know why, but here you are! Don't tell anybody. You want to know? I've had a very great honor. Great honor."

"What sort of honor?"

"I had a visit from—guess who—the president of—the—United States!" The group around me had fallen silent when this conversation took place. Now they came close to hear.

"He came to see me." Florence whispered, but her whisper always was pretty loud. "Don't tell anybody!"

"I won't," I said, and meant it. I knew this was the voice of the late Florence Sternfels. But how could I be sure the president really went to consult her? In the end, when her illness became fatal, her mind was gone and this might be one of the fantasies such a mind might have concocted out of a mixture of real experiences and unfulfilled wishes. But then again, some pretty important people had found their way to Florence's doorstep over the years in secret. Who was to say that President Kennedy could not have come? She was very famous, and the FBI swore by her.

"When did he come?" I wanted to know.

"It was about—what's the matter with me, I can't think of time—but he came, all in a big, black car—all the people around him."

"What did he want of you?"

"He's afraid—Mr. Holzer, he has fear in his soul—everybody says he is going to die—he wanted to know from me—wasn't that a great honor?"

The expression on Ethel's face was very close to Florence's now. She seemed calmer also, now that she had caught up with me at last!

"Are you all right?" I asked.

"I'm fine," she replied. "Mr. Holzer—what have I got on?" She touched the dress that seemed unfamiliar. Sudden realization that something was different showed on Ethel's entranced face.

"I know you are here. . . . I know I can get to you . . ." the late Florence said. "I want you to know, first from me . . . and I told him, be very careful. . . ."

"Thank you, Florence," I interjected, cognizant of her lifetime tendency to be a bit long-winded.

"I'm so pleased . . ." she said, and a moment later she was gone, and Ethel's control, Albert, was in charge.

"I couldn't stop that," he said by way of explanation. "I'm sorry."

With that we proceeded with the business at hand, which was a fairly routine case involving ghostly manifestations at Ringwood Manor.

But that wasn't the end of Florence by any means. May S., who had been a close friend of the psychic and who had seen her frequently, reported her continuing presence around her from that moment on.

"I feel Florence is trying to tell me something," she confided, "but what?"

Sometimes she even felt a tug at her sleeve.

In May 1967 I met a lady named Margaret S., who brought me further news of Florence. Two of her friends, sisters, who now live in Westchester County, New York, formerly resided in Edgewater, New Jersey, where they had become friendly with Florence. One of the sisters, a Mrs. M., decided to pay Florence another visit. Neither Mrs. M. nor her sister had heard of Florence's passing, so they journeyed back to Edgewater and went up to Florence's house. There they rang the bell and waited. No response. They were about to give up when they heard footsteps inside the house. The steps were coming toward the door, and they immediately recognized them as the characteristic footsteps of Florence, with which they had been familiar.

"She's coming." Mrs. M. nodded to her sister, and they waited for the door to open for them. But when the steps reached the door, the door did not open. The two women thought this peculiar.

"Florence," Mrs. M. finally called impatiently. Suddenly both women felt very strange: it was as if they were being enveloped in an embrace. They felt numb and almost immobile for a moment, then regained their composure and started to leave.

A neighbor had watched their attempts to gain entrance from across the street. When she saw that the two visitors were evidently giving up, she crossed over and spoke to them. "She's been dead quite a while now, you know," she said and looked into two pairs of dumbfounded eyes.

It was Friday morning, July 7, 1967, when Sybil Leek telephoned me in excitement.

"Do you know anyone named Vivian?" she demanded. "I had a curious message from a Vivian last night."

I asked Sybil to be specific, and she explained that a

woman had psychically impressed her to tell *me,* and, on awakening, Sybil Leek did just that. All she could remember was the word *Vivian* and something about "going on a holiday" or a song about a holiday.

I thanked Sybil and took down the information.

Twenty-four hours later, on Saturday, July 8, all newspapers carried the sad news that Vivien Leigh had been found dead in her London apartment. She had died the previous day. Death had come to the famous actress at age fifty-three as a result of a continuing illness. That night, all the London theaters blacked out for a moment of silent tribute. In New York, I excitedly called Sybil and demanded to know if she had ever met Vivien Leigh.

She had indeed, but the thought of connecting the Vivian of her psychic impression with the Vivien Leigh she knew just did not occur to her. Since the message had been to tell Hans, she naturally assumed it was someone I knew or someone who had some link with me.

Now, on looking back, I can see why Vivien Leigh, whom I had never met but who may have known of my work through her private secretary, with whom I was friendly, requested that Sybil give me her message. In publishing the news of her personal survival, she not only continues her influence upon the living—and what actress likes to be forgotten—but she also contributes to the knowledge of that other world into which she had just ascended.

From time to time Vivien Leigh had consulted Sybil as a friend, discussing problems with her in private. In late November of 1966, the actress had made a foursome at dinner at a Manhattan restaurant with her manager, John M., a friend of Sybil's, and Sybil. At that time the British psychic had already had great misgivings about the star's future. She knew that death was near for the actress, but this she did not tell her, of course.

Chapter Four

The Evidence for Survival After Death

FREQUENTLY I AM ASKED BY DOUBTERS, how can one be sure the communication really comes from a dead person and not from the subconscious of the medium? Just as frequently I am asked, in cases in which there is no intermediary involved and the contact is directly between a supposedly dead individual and someone in the physical world, how can one know that the living person is not hallucinating or imagining the whole thing? Finally, how does one know these communications aren't just coincidences?

Some people like to dismiss the facts by blandly claiming that "the majority of ESP experiences can be chalked up to coincidence." It is an all too human tendency to resort to pat statements whenever one does not *want* to examine evidence for fear that one's preconceived notions may have to be changed.

When the content of a message is such that it fits only the dead person as originator and when that communication is with a person who has no possible knowledge of the content beforehand, then we are certainly dealing with a psychic phenomenon. It is psychic because the information has been obtained through other means than the ordinary five senses. Has the receiver used his or her own ESP to obtain the information without requiring the presence of a dead communicator on the other end of the line of communication? Has this psychic person somehow drawn from his or her own unconscious or subconscious (pick your term) the very specific message that concerns another person known to be dead? Occasionally this may be possible, though it is by no means likely. But on numerous occasions it simply is impossible. Messages from the dead to the living speak of specific events that have not yet become objective reality to *anyone*.

Later these events occur, and in retrospect the receiver of the message realizes that a dead individual has foreseen them. Or the receiver does not know the personal circumstances of the dead communicator and therefore does not have in his own unconscious storehouse the detailed knowledge to draw upon if the message were to originate within himself. Time and again, receivers are taken by surprise and do not expect the contact from the beyond. There is nothing in their thoughts to link them with the dead person. And yet communications of this kind occur with considerable frequency.

Imagining information, if that were possible, will again have to be judged on the truth of the information. If it turns out to be correct and unknown to the receiver at the time of the contact, then it is pretty much a moot question whether the receiver "imagined" it psychically or had a genuine communication from the psychic world. Either way it is what we call *paranormal*.

Finally, the word *hallucinating* has been bandied about indiscriminately by would-be parapsychologists explaining phenomena they have not themselves witnessed or investigated. Their aim is to explain these occurrences in terms of orthodox science; they forget that science is a *changing* concept.

When a person hallucinates an image or sound, that person is the originator of it and is presumed to have an abnormality of mind or emotional constitution that permits these phenomena to occur. But no one has ever proved that a person manufactures such hallucinations when we are dealing with supposedly "normal," well-adjusted people who do not have a medical history of mental disease or have not partaken of hallucinogenic drugs. *Healthy* people do not hallucinate. In addition, there is a sharp distinction between the phantasms created in the sick mind and those experienced by the healthy as spontaneous experiences. The true hallucinations of mentally sick individuals or of people under the influence of certain drugs are illogical, often monstrous images and symbols far removed from possible reality.

Psychic phenomena, on the other hand, have the ring of truth in them. They seem perfectly logical and well ordered in their sequence of events, and they differ from ordinary life experiences only in that they have not yet occurred or that they are unknown to the recipient at the time they occur.

Coincidence, another term thrown around with abandon by some would-be scientists, is a word requiring further definition. Strictly speaking, it means that events happen in objective reality that are totally unconnected by the common laws of cause and effect but that somehow *seem* to be connected, while in fact they are not.

Coincidence was a strong argument of the materialistically inclined to deal with the strange links between people that only psychic research can explain in some manner, those weird patterns of fate that defy the laws of cause and effect. Then Carl Jung wrote a fundamental book called *The Law of Meaningful Coincidence or Acausal Synchronicity*, in which he painstakingly documented the existence of a second set of laws beyond the common laws of cause and effect. This second set of laws, which he called "the laws of meaningful coincidence," do, in his view, connect events and people that are apparently not at all connected in terms of logic. Carl Jung has taken a great deal of the wind out of the sails of those who still accept the possibility of "coincidence" in our universe.

I am not one of them. I do not envision any coincidence at all in what appears to be a marvelously well-arranged world where nothing is left to chance. There are connections beyond our understanding, at least our present very limited understanding, but there is nothing in our universe that does not obey *some* set of laws. When the elements of each authenticated case are carefully examined, one realizes that coincidence as a possible explanation is completely out of the question. What we are left with in those cases is the realization that there is no better or alternate explanation than the one that sounds most logical: true contact between the two worlds.

I met Mrs. Claude T. in the winter of 1967 through a mutual friend in the music business, Robert L., who had known her late bandleader-composer husband. Mrs. T., a well-read person with a broad educational background, played an important role in international society. A native of the state of Washington, Ruth T. had her first encounter with the psychic when she was twelve, but it failed to get her particularly interested in the subject, and she took her later experiences in stride, neither rejecting them nor unduly dwelling on them.

Her parents had purchased an old house near Olympia, Washington, and as her uncle and aunt had a house next door to the one the family had just bought, Ruth and a girlfriend were given permission to go up there and have a look at the empty place as long as they stayed with her relatives. But the two girls decided to rough it and sleep at the other house, which had stood empty for many years.

Ruth and Marjory set up two army cots in an upstairs bedroom. There was an enclosed staircase leading to the upper floor, and a door at the bottom of it. The first night in the old house, the two girls, feeling adventurous, cooked a meal on a stove they had brought with them. They were tired and went to bed fairly early.

Falling asleep almost immediately, Ruth was awakened by the sound of someone walking up the stairs. Marjory, who also heard it, sat up straight in bed and listened. It was a bright, moonlit night, and they could clearly see each other across the room. The footsteps sounded like the steps of a heavy man. When they had reached the top of the stairs where there was a landing, the girls waited for the intruder to show himself, terrified, of course, as twelve-year-olds would be.

But nobody came into their room, and nobody went down the stairs again. They jumped out of bed, lit whatever lamps they had, and finally opened the door. They found no one in the house except themselves, although they searched.

Ruth's cousin Harold M., a student at Oberlin, in his early twenties, was staying with Ruth's uncle at the time. The next day the two girls asked him to sleep in the house with them. He agreed, and set up a cot in the front bedroom. Needless to say, it made the two girls very happy to have a man in the house, and they outdid each other in preparing a good dinner. Afterward, they retired to their respective rooms, the girls upstairs and Harold directly under them.

In the middle of the night, when everyone was asleep, the

footsteps started up again. Harold heard them too, for he opened his door and called up: "Ruth, are you walking around up there?"

The girls rushed downstairs and finally told him *why* he had been invited to share the house with them. Harold did not believe in the psychic and examined the house very carefully. But he decided to stick around with them in the old house until he could find a logical explanation for the footsteps. For ten days, the three young people became ghost hunters. Every night the steps returned, and every morning the three were dumbfounded.

Finally Ruth's parents arrived with the furniture for the house, accompanied by her brother and a little dog named Trixie. Ruth's mother entered the house first, followed by Trixie. But when the dog crossed the threshold, he stopped dead in his tracks. His hair bristling, he whimpered and cried as if begging them not to go into that house! Nothing could make him go into the house, and he shot out from under them into the open yard. Ruth's mother then proceeded into the house alone. She had been psychic on occasion, and this was one of those occasions.

"There is something here!" she declared.

Ruth's father, Roy M., an engineer by profession, scoffed at the idea. The dog's behavior, however, upset him.

"We've made a mistake," Mrs. M. said, but they had bought the house and would have to make the best of it. The men were unloading the furniture now, and Mrs. M. went inside to direct them. The rest of the family stayed outside while she entered the house ahead of the moving men, addressing herself to the unseen guest from another age. Here and there she stopped and said a prayer for his peace of mind.

When the furniture was all in place, Mrs. M. came out and told her family to come on in. Everything would be all right now. Even the dog no longer bolted.

They never were able to trace the previous owners, and as the house had been empty for more than thirty years, there might have been some trespassers in addition to the legal tenants. But whatever or whoever it was who walked up those stairs, walked no more.

Premonitions, true dreams, and hunches filled the years as Ruth grew up. Despite several such experiences, she never involved herself in the study of the phenomena except where they concerned her personally.

Many years after her initial experience in the state of Washington, Ruth lived at Cannes on the French Riviera, married to Paul L. A friend of hers by the name of Count Antoine S. had a small villa at Cap d'Antibes called the Villa Lilliput. He suffered from heart trouble, and as Ruth's husband owned a hotel at the spa of Royat, famed for its salubrious cures, she suggested the count go there and spend some time as their guest at the hotel.

He agreed to go there with his valet, but he had invited them for dinner that night, and would go the day after. Another friend of the count's, Princess Ghika, and two others were also present at the count's dinner party that evening. It was a gay evening, and the count even got Ruth's promise to visit him at Royat and play cards with him during his cure. The party broke up, and Ruth was happy in the thought that her friend would be on his way to Royat the next morning for his much-needed cure.

The following night she awoke from sleep because of a vivid nightmare. The vision was so strong she could not shake it. She had seen a walled garden with a driveway coming out of it, and there was a hole in that wall. Outside the driveway, she had seen a car. Two men came out carrying a man, and when they came closer she saw it was her friend the count. He seemed very white, and Ruth had the distinct impression that he was very ill and needed help.

"Do something for him," she heard herself say. Neither the garden nor the men seemed at all familiar.

But one of them said to her: "We've done all we can. I'm his doctor."

She was crying now and replied: "Don't put him in a car, put him in a bed!"

"That's what we're doing," the man said. "We're taking him back to Villa Lilliput to put him to bed."

"But he looks as if he's dead," she heard herself say.

"He is," the man replied gravely, "but we're taking him back."

Now another person entered the dream vision, the then still-living author Somerset Maugham, whom Ruth knew very well. She turned to him now and asked that he intercede and not allow the count's body to be driven back like that. Maugham, in the dream, replied not to worry about it and said that the count was "a scoundrel." That of course struck Ruth as very odd. Somerset Maugham and the count had been very good friends, and she had met the count through the author.

With that, Ruth awakened, and her husband also woke up. She discussed her nightmare with him, and her husband calmed her, or tried to, pointing out that by now the count was already at Royat or nearby. It was 4 A.M., and he urged her to go back to sleep. But her sleep was interrupted again, this time by the ringing of the telephone. It was the manager of their hotel in Cannes. He had received a call from Princess Ghika that Count S. had died the previous night! Apparently he had gone to have dinner at her home and had taken sick after dinner. The princess's house was on the outskirts of Cannes.

When Ruth later described the dream to her, the princess pointed out that the walled garden was at her home, although Ruth could not have known this, never having been there.

"What did the doctor in your dream look like?" she asked Ruth.

"He looked like the man who is just coming in the door there," Ruth pointed out. They were at the bar of the hotel.

"But that *is* the doctor," the princess said.

"The only thing strange in my dream is that you took him back to his house in the car," Ruth continued.

Meanwhile the doctor had come up and heard her remark.

"But that's exactly what we did," he confirmed. "How did you know?"

Everything happened in her dream as it had simultaneously happened miles away, except for the presence of Somerset Maugham. She could not puzzle out why he had entered her psychic vision, until a few days later she received a letter from Mr. Maugham. It was an invitation to join him for lunch.

Because she knew of the close friendship between the late count and Maugham, Ruth tried to console him over the count's death.

"Oh, don't worry about it," Maugham said with a twinkle in his eyes. *"He was a scoundrel."*

Suddenly Ruth realized why Maugham had appeared in her psychic dream. A strange mixture of the dead reaching out to the living to let them know of their passing, and the ability of the dead to foresee the future, is at the heart of this experience.

Mrs. T. has had other encounters with the unknown. To her, at least, the unknown is a lot less mysterious than to the person to whom nothing of this kind ever happens.

The incident with the count happened in May 1946. Some time afterward Ruth married Claude T., the bandleader and composer. T. died in 1965, and the following year his widow moved into an apartment in one of New York's smart East Side hotels while at the same time retaining her ownership of the house she and T. had bought for their weekends in nearby New Jersey.

Her husband had never had any heart trouble. But one night in July 1965, he suddenly complained of chest pains as he was resting quietly in bed prior to going to sleep. By the time the doctor arrived, however, he felt better. Nevertheless, he was given an injection. A few moments later he complained of feeling very odd. A moment later he was gone.

The doctor worked over him in vain. As she picked him up to put some pillows behind him, Ruth noticed a shimmering light around his head. His hair seemed full of electricity. It was just for an instant, but when it ceased she knew he was gone for good.

Mrs. T. made no immediate attempt of her own to make contact with her husband. But three days after his death, a first link was made for her from "the other side," so to speak. She felt an impulse to call Bonnie L., a lady she scarcely knew, who had casually met her late husband only twice during his long career. Miss L. was a writer and actress. Soon after Mrs. T. obtained her address and called her, Miss L. came to see her.

That night they tried automatic writing, a talent Miss L. had. There was another friend present, a lady from Texas named Cathy N. who was somewhat psychic too. Suddenly Bonnie L. started to write. The first words purported to come from Mrs. T.'s mother. They were in her style and used a favorite phrase of hers, "Now you listen to Mary." Even the handwriting seemed like Mrs. T.'s mother's. Bonnie L. could not have known these details, as she had not met Mrs. T. until that evening.

Next the automatist wrote four bars of music. There followed a message from Ruth's late husband. The other lady, who knew Claude T.'s handwriting, immediately identified it, corroborating her.

"He wants you to ask questions," the medium said.

"Are you all right?" Mrs. T. asked.

Immediately the pencil in Bonnie L.'s hand began to move across the paper again.

"I'm fine and on my way, *Peedee*."

Mrs. T. was visibly moved. "Peedee" was the nickname her husband called her in private. No one but she and her husband knew the spelling of this unusual name.

One night not long after, she was alone at home in the house in New Jersey. She was expecting the local minister to call and whiled away the time at the piano. She played one of her husband's compositions, "Memory of an Island." She felt she was playing it very well and felt rather proud of herself. "He should hear this," she thought.

As if in answer to her silent thought, she heard a voice speak to her: "Yes, but watch your fingering!"

The voice originated at the other end of the piano, and it sounded exactly like her husband's voice in life. Shocked, she looked down at her fingers and discovered that her fingering *was* wrong. This was two months after his death, and suddenly his presence with her was very strong again. The bell rang. It was the minister she had been expecting, and the spell was broken.

Mrs. T. kept herself busy around the house after her husband's untimely passing. On a busy summer day that same year, she was stripping wallpaper from the living room walls. She was standing on a ladder, something her husband had always forbidden her to do. A young girl from the neighborhood was with her that afternoon, helping around the house. The piano was in the living room at that time. The young girl, Kay C., excused herself and went into the kitchen. Mrs. T. saw her pass the piano and disappear into the kitchen. That moment she heard the piano playing *by itself*. It started softly at first, as if the music came from far away; then it began to build, and her first thought was that Kay must be at the piano. The piano was playing the "Paganini Variations of Brahms," one of the pieces her late husband frequently practiced on this very piano. It was a good piece to strengthen his technique.

Ruth T. came down from the ladder to look and walked to

the entrance of the dining room; at the same time Kay walked in from the kitchen with a blank look on her face.

"Were you playing the piano?" the girl asked. That instant the playing stopped.

Both women had heard the music. It was the piece he had practiced on his last day. Kay had been in the house that day on a visit. She remembered it well.

After his death, Ruth T. had lent the car to the band, which continued to work under a different leader. Somehow the car papers were mislaid, and when she wanted to sell the car, she could not find them. No matter how much she searched, the papers remained lost, and she finally asked her attorney to get her a duplicate set of ownership papers.

One day she was alone in the house. It was around four in the afternoon on a fall day. It had been a tiresome day filled with problems, some of them unsolved, and she stood by the window and looked out into the sunset. Suddenly she had an impulse to go over to where she had left a Ouija board the night before. The board was considered more a toy than a serious instrument of communication, but she had one in the house and used it now and again.

"Nonsense," she thought, and tried to ignore the impulse. But the urge was stronger, and finally she reached the board and placed her hands ever so lightly upon the indicator. Instantly there was contact!

"Go to my music" was the message spelled out. "You're tired, but before you go to sleep tonight, work on my music."

Now, she had been over his arrangements thousands of times. The music was all over the place—in the basement, in the garage—and it would be quite a task to look at all of it. But the message had been very insistent, and there was nothing more.

She had dinner and decided she just could not do any more work that night, message or no message. She went upstairs to bed but could not fall asleep.

"It's no use," she said to herself. She got dressed again and went down into the basement of the house, standing in the middle of the piles of music around her. She had no idea where to start. Finally she decided the only thing she could do that night would be to look through the music that had been used the time she lent the car to the band, when she had last had the documents. It seemed like a small job, just about all she might manage that night.

She picked up the piano book from the arrangements case and took it up to the dining room. She opened it, and on the third page, there were the car papers!

"I try not to call him," Mrs. T. explained to me. "I feel he has a great deal of work to do. He told me he is happy, and I know we will see each other again. It would be selfish of me to harp on him."

Mrs. T.'s "open channel" did not operate only for her late husband. There were others who wished to let her know that their existence continued or who took an interest in what she was doing here on the physical side of life.

Shortly after she moved into her town apartment in the winter of 1966, she went to Europe. Returning in time for the Christmas holiday, she was expecting her brother Don M. to come to California to spend Christmas with her. Christmas dinner was shared with Kay and the man she had married. Mrs. T. felt extremely tired and rather detached that evening. She describes her condition as "floaty," and that is exactly the word for the start of mediumistic conditions. Her mind was not on the conversation that evening.

When Ruth went to bed, she fell asleep almost instantly. She was awakened by raps on the wall separating the room she slept in from the one her brother was using. Her first thought on awakening was to blame the neighbors for making the noise. She saw that it was 1 A.M. when she turned on the light. She then realized it was not a party next door but something uncanny that was disturbing her.

"If you're trying to communicate with me," she thought, "will you rap twice?"

There came two distinct raps, followed by a flurry of signals that she tried to dismiss. Underneath she knew very well that someone was trying to reach her. She got up and went into the pantry to put on some tea. She waited a few minutes for the tea to be strong enough.

When she left the pantry and looked across the room toward the hallway leading into the bedroom, she noticed a man standing there. Her eyesight was not very good, and she thought it was her brother Don. The figure was of his height, so she was not at all afraid but waited for him to say something and explain his presence. Instead the figure started to dissolve *from the top down*. There was a small mirror in back of where the man stood, and gradually the mirror became visible through his body, until the body completely disappeared.

She walked over to the spot and found herself quite alone. Moreover, the door to her brother's room was tightly closed. Inside, her brother was fast asleep; the light was out, and it was obvious that he had not stirred. There was no light whatsoever in the passage, nothing that could have created the illusion of a figure.

Ruth was not sure who the caller had been—not because it was a spectral figure but because of her poor eyesight. She could not have identified even a flesh-and-blood figure under the light conditions and at the distance across the apartment from which she had been standing. She went back to bed, puzzled. Who might the person have been? From the height of the figure, she was sure that it had not been her husband. But who was it?

The man, whose facial features she had not been able to distinguish, had dark hair and wore a dark suit of some kind. That much she had seen. Back in bed, she had trouble falling asleep again, so she read for an hour and a half. Suddenly her brother rushed into her room in great excitement.

"Were you calling me?" Ruth assured him she wasn't. What had awakened him from deep sleep was the sound of a voice saying, "Don, Ruth needs you!" and at the same time he saw a figure standing beside his bed and felt someone shake him as if to arouse him. He felt the touch at the same time that he heard the voice calling. The voice had been very much like their mother's voice. Had she thought that the previous experience had so unnerved Ruth that she needed her brother's help to calm down?

Quickly she filled him in on what had happened during the two hours just past. As she spoke of the raps, the raps returned in force. Her brother had been a complete skeptic until that night, but he too heard the raps. Eventually he returned to his room, but neither of them found any more sleep that night.

It was 7 A.M. when he came back into her room. He had just listened to a television news broadcast. "Are you awake?" he asked, and when she nodded, he added: "Well, *I know who it was.*"

"Who was it?"

"The morning news just announced that Nick Dandolas has died." The news brought an immediate reaction from Ruth. "Nick the Greek" had been a dear and close friend of hers for many years. In retrospect she realized that the dark figure indeed looked like him. The famed gambler had been psychic himself in his time, and they had often discussed their various experiences in this field.

But there was an unseen presence that kept intruding itself on her after her husband's death. This presence at times wanted to take her over, and she fought it; she did not feel that it was a welcome presence, and it frightened her despite her knowledge of the unseen world. She felt it in the house in New Jersey and in her apartment in Manhattan, but she also knew this was neither her husband nor her mother. This was someone else.

Under the circumstances I thought it wisest to send Ruth to see Betty Ritter and to examine whatever material Betty might get about any "hangers-on." Mrs. T. phoned Mrs. Ritter without telling her who she was and after some difficulty Mrs. Ritter agreed to see her on November 8, 1967, at her apartment on the East Side. Mrs. T. found Betty charming, and the two women got along well. I had asked her to keep an exact transcript of whatever was said during her sitting.

Before she went to see Betty Ritter, Ruth T. had again tried her hand at the Ouija board. Her partner was the local minister, of all people, and the message purported to come from her late husband. Although she discounted much of it simply because it could very well have emanated from her own unconscious, there was nevertheless an urgent request contained in it that concerned Claude T.'s musical estate. The late composer wanted her to contact Robert L. the publisher, whom he had known for many years, and subsequently Ruth did. Now when she arrived at Betty Ritter's apartment and had scarcely sat down, Betty insisted she had just gotten a name of some importance to her, and she wrote down *Robert L.*

"A man is standing behind you: he leans down and kisses you and says: 'This is my girl!' I see a name; it is dim—I'm sure of the CL."

Betty had no idea who Mrs. T. was, nor did she know that Claude T. had passed on.

The communicator continued through Betty: "What can I do? It was God's will. I love you."

Betty continued her sitting, very much relaxed now, by

describing some other members of Ruth's family. Then she spoke of a man who had committed suicide . . . a very large and insistent S. She added: "I see someone who hung himself . . . M."

Later Mrs. T. explained that a long time before, she had had a suitor, a Russian gentleman initialed S. who was possessed of a large ego. When he received no encouragement from her, he eventually shot himself. This man had indeed been "insistent." But there was also another friend first-named Michael who had committed suicide by hanging when he felt himself grown old.

Was either of the two behind the insistent presence at her New York apartment and in the country house? Ruth wondered. Anyone saying "coincidence" here would be stretching a point beyond belief: two suicides, and the exact initials named, under circumstances that exclude any foreknowledge by the medium of any circumstances surrounding her caller.

"A lovely mother stands behind you," Betty continued. "Mary . . . Marie? No, Mary."

Betty then told her that she was being annoyed at night in her bedroom by "someone" pulling her covers off. Ruth nodded. It was perfectly true, and she wished she knew *who* was doing it.

Betty then described a dead person, a man who was furious at something concerning a watch. He is in a temper at something that happened to him, Betty explained, and she quoted him as complaining that someone had "knocked him down."

But to Ruth this expression made immediate sense, even though the incident had happened in the 1950s and had hardly been on her mind. The gentleman friend initialed S. whom Betty had sensed as one of two suicides trying to communicate with her had indeed been involved in an incident with a watch. The watch was Ruth's, and she had asked him to have it repaired when it stopped. When she got it back, he had taken it upon himself to have his name engraved on the back of it. This made her very angry, and she broke off their friendship because of it. Someone had "knocked him down," meaning "put him down." "Put him down" would have been the expression this Russian gentleman would have used!

As Betty continued her messages, she brought Ruth assurance that her husband would watch over her and protect her. "He has just handed you a large rose—he says it's his love!"

Although many people express their love with flowers, the rose had been a constant and special symbol in the T.s' life. Ruth considered this symbol very characteristic of Claude.

Although I was not present at this reading, I was mentioned. Betty, of course, did not know my connection with Mrs. T., but she mentioned that she "saw" something going into a book and that a writer was involved—and here I am now.

Betty Ritter then described the house she had never visited, complete even to the stacks of manuscripts lying around. During all this, Mrs. T. kept her mouth shut and her mind as much a blank as she could manage.

Suddenly she said: "Ruth . . . what does Ruth mean? It must be you, because the voice said, 'Do this, Ruth!' "

Mrs. Ritter thought he meant that certain business arrangements should be made concerning the "papers."

I had asked Mrs. T. to let me have the transcript of her next sitting with Betty Ritter, especially those portions that seemed to prove communication with the dead.

On November 26 Ruth returned for a second visit with Betty, without, however, having disclosed anything to her concerning herself or the results of the first sitting. Immediately upon Ruth's arrival, Betty described the presence of Mrs. T's family "in spirit": "A mother . . . Marie . . . Charles . . . William . . . John, and two others . . . they are a family."

Mrs. T.'s mother, Mary or Marie, did have seven brothers, among them John, William, and Charles.

"A man standing behind you places his hands on your shoulder, smiles, and says, 'This is my wife,' " Betty continued, and added that Ruth's late husband showed Betty that Ruth was writing her *memoirs*—Betty had trouble with that word—and also spoke of a Dr. R., with the first initial A. The interesting thing about this message was that Dr. A. R. was a dear friend of both Ruth and Claude T.; the latter had once saved his life. The doctor's wife had been urging Ruth to write her memoirs, and she was about to do so!

"Your husband is kissing you. He is so sorry and seems to repent about something. He shows me the words *exchange* and *stock market*, things dwindling down. . . . I see him on his knees beside you."

Apparently Mr. T. had bought some stocks against his wife's advice and had refused to sell them when she suggested that he do so. They were now quite worthless. As there were not many of them, the matter was not very important to Ruth, but her husband would have taken precisely the attitude Betty described—exaggerating where his wife's welfare was concerned.

To further prove his identity—not that Ruth doubted it by now—Betty Ritter described Ruth's husband bringing in a woman now whom he called Louise. The interesting fact is that Mr. T. had always carried a small card with Aunt Louise's name on it, a card that Louise's husband, Ruth's uncle, had given him after her death. Mr. T. was quite sentimental about it and about her.

But the door to the other side allowed others to pass through to greet her, too. Evidently her own psychic potential had been added in some way to Betty's for an overall topnotch reading.

"I see the spirit of a man with mustache, hard of hearing in his left ear. He had to do with chemicals. Peter . . . and he said, show you the anchor of a ship."

Such a detailed and specific message would certainly be capable of verification, I thought, when Mrs. T. showed me the transcript. Needless to say, Betty still knew nothing whatever about Ruth or her friends.

Well, some years ago Mrs. T. had befriended a gentleman named Peter. He had a mustache, was hard of hearing in one ear, and was an executive with Shell Oil, in charge of some tankers. It had been many years since she saw him, and a check in the London telephone directory showed only his wife—or widow—listed.

Not every person is as fortunate as Ruth T. in making contact with the beyond both personally and through an intermediary. Perhaps she is a better channel than most, and, having served others as psychic spokeswoman, she was rewarded by meeting the right people to allow her an evidential contact through a medium such as Betty Ritter.

The material Ruth obtained in her two sessions with Betty, reinforced by her own primary experiences with the surviving personalities of her husband and several others whom she knew, gave her the conviction that life does indeed continue and we need not fear death or consider a separation caused by the dissolution of the physical body as final.

In telling her personal story, I hope I'm reaching out to the many who have wondered about such things and who may have had similar proof themselves but have not been sure.

Chapter Five

The Channels of Communication

THE DESIRE TO COMMUNICATE WITH THE DEAD goes back to the beginning of human existence. It is usually the result of personal anxiety of one kind or another. The bereaved want to know that their loved ones live on. The weak hope for sage counsel from a departed one who is thought to know more than mortals. The nagging doubt whether there is a hereafter also drives many people to seek communication with the dead. A small fraction of those seeking this link are motivated by scientific interest rather than personal curiosity.

Even among those making serious scientific inquiries into channels of communication between our two worlds, there are different points of view. Conservative parapsychologists will not accept the *a priori* view that the hereafter exists. They will exhaust every other possibility before admitting that the communication is genuinely a link between the living and the dead. I find some researchers going to extremes at times to disprove any form of survival hypothesis.

I am not a *conservative* parapsychologist, and so, happily, I have no preconceived notions as to what the channels of communication are and represent. My view is that a hereafter exists because of the weight of evidence already on hand; pri-

54

marily spontaneous cases in large numbers suggest it. But I too would like to know more about the laws that govern the non-physical side of life and communication with it. In this I shall probably have to reject as unsatisfactory a great deal of material that the spiritualist inquirer would accept without hesitation. This does not mean that this material is false but that the rigid standards concerning alternative explanations have not been met in such cases. Nothing is so damning to a new view of the world as an incomplete or doubtful argument. I would rather have ten strong cases for survival of human personality than ten thousand mixed ones where alternate explanations have not been rigorously excluded. 〉

As previously noted, there are two big areas of communications, as different as day and night in the way we relate to them. First, there are communications initiated by the dead. These are dramatic, often sudden, often surprising, and occasionally frightening linkups between the two worlds. There are a number of reasons why I think the dead want to communicate with the living, and I shall presently detail these reasons along with actual cases.

The advantage, from the scientific observer's point of view, in spontaneous phenomena of this kind is the state of mind of the recipient of the communication. Since the recipient has not actively sought it, the elements of wish fulfillment are mostly absent. The unconscious does not play so large a part in this type of contact as it may play with induced communications, and the genuine emotional conditions that are usually behind such spontaneous contacts to begin with are present to their full extent. This is the sort of psychic phenomenon one cannot possibly reproduce in the laboratory because it involves unique, personal, and deeply emotional experiences at both ends of the channel.

The "sender" in the nonphysical world is motivated by some need or urge to communicate with the living person for whom the communication is meant. The receiver, impressed emotionally by the content and form of the communication and the further implications of it, is doubly involved in each and every communication from the other side. To create similar conditions *artificially* in a laboratory, with routine technicians or even with talented ESP subjects, is impossible. We are dealing here with far more complex situations than the mere reading of thoughts or the influencing of the fall of dice via psycho-kinesis. Dr. Joseph Rhine's experiments were great beginnings for a science that needed a first step in the right direction. Here the conservative parapsychologist and of course the hostile scientist are totally off the track: this phenomenon is not even capable of confinement within a laboratory, much less capable of being artificially created or recreated.

But there isn't any need for a laboratory. Many important events of nature are not susceptible to laboratory tests. The actual eruption of a volcano, or an underwater quake, or a major holocaust cannot be staged at will in the research center, yet the actual event may be observed on the spot by competent witnesses. Even the study of disease often simulates its subject rather than actually recreating it, for obvious moral reasons. And simulation is not duplication.

We do not as yet know all the laws that govern this kind of communication. It may well be that what is required is the uniqueness and genuineness of the emotional situation. Unless there is real need for the communication to take place, the link is not established. If there were not some kind of restraining rule, I think we would have conversations between the dead and the living all day long, and the phenomenon would cease to be unusual. But such conversations are unusual; while the bulk of evidence is very heavy, they are by no means an everyday occur-rence, nor is the establishing of channels an easy task. That, however, need not militate against scientific acceptance of spon-taneous communications. Many things in the universe are un-usual or rare and still are part of the orderly scheme of things. For instance, a black hole—created when a star implodes, or burns itself out and then falls into itself—occurs far fewer times than the creation of a new star or a comet or passing asteroid. Nevertheless, black holes are susceptible to proper observation and evaluation. Albinism occurs among people and animals with some degree of regularity but is still considered unusual. Just the same, albinos are part of nature, and by no stretch of the imagination can they be termed unscientific or unreal phenomena. Large numbers of examples do not necessarily make an occurrence scientifically valid, nor do few examples make it less so.

If we were able to control the spontaneous communication channels from the nonphysical world, we would indeed have a major key in our hands. Perhaps the "board of directors" that runs all this does not want us to hold that key. On the other hand, nothing stops us from searching for our own channels, starting on our end. 〉

Communications initiated by the living compose the second large group of communications. They too fall into many categories, depending on the nature of the channel used and on the approach by the individual making the contact, or attempting to make it.

The intermediary between a living person and the inhabitants of the nonphysical world is called the *instrument.*

Putting aside here the belief that priests and ministers are intermediaries between human beings and the divine—which they may or may not be—and reducing the attempt to communicate to its individual, personal level, we still have to have at least three elements or three persons: one who desires the contact, the instrument who makes the contact possible, and one who receives the communication. Once the initial contact is established, the receiver also turns sender, and the initiator of the contact becomes a receiver. But the instrument remains the same—an intermediary whose sole function is to make contact possible as clearly and as untouched by the instrument's own personality as possible. This is not so easy as it may sound. The instrument's own personality cannot be set aside without proper training and discipline, and even then there is always an element of that personality present in almost all communications between the two worlds.

The instrument can be a professional or an amateur "medium," a person with a gift of *dissociation of personality,* in the case of trance, clairvoyance, clairaudience, or clairsentience; if a so-called mental medium, the instrument does not lose consciousness during a séance. The séance does not denote a mysterious ceremony in a darkened room when spirits descend upon the mortals to amaze them. *Séance* means to "sit down" with someone. Most communications are very simply held in a room, in normal light, with two or more people sitting quietly and trying to establish contact with the nonphysical world. Only in Hollywood movies does mumbo jumbo enter the picture.

When a sitting utilizes the services of a trance medium, the departed will use the vocal chords of the medium to speak and may even rearrange facial expressions to approximate his or her own face. There may be physical movements by which the departed might wish to prove identity; specific phrases, words, nicknames, and personal bits of information are given as a means of identification so that the one seeking the contact can be sure it has been established with the right person.

There aren't many good trance mediums in the world. I am always looking for new people to train in this profession. By far the majority of instruments are mental mediums who act as go-betweens and relay messages and phrases from the alleged dead to the living. Depending on the ability of the individual medium, these messages will be straight or garbled, and whenever symbolic messages or images are involved, interpretation by the medium of the image impressed on his or her mind can also play a large role in the success of the undertaking. There are no hard and fast rules as to what a medium should produce or do or not do. Each case is an individual attempt in a largely uncharted land and must be evaluated on that basis. As yet we cannot computerize the results of mediumship, and I hope to God we never shall!

Among the mental mediums there are many who are called psychometrists. They are able to touch an object that was once the property of the departed and induce certain visions and impressions from it. Quite naturally, in using psychometric methods in attempting communication with the dead, one should be careful to disallow anything about the departed that might have been obtained by the medium from the touching of the object handed him or her.

But it is equally wrong to assume that *all* the information that may follow is obtained merely in this manner. I have witnessed a number of sittings where the touching of the object served as an opening door for the discarnate (dead individual or individuals) to enter and continue the sitting. Once the alleged dead is "present," the sitter will have to evaluate the messages received on their own merits. Although objects do carry a certain amount of information about their former owners, to my knowledge they do not contain complete biographies and detailed histories of that person. The only exceptions are cases where people died violently or other forms of emotional trauma were present when the object was in the possession of the discarnate owner. Then the entire scene might very well have been imprinted on the object and could be read by the psychic person.

Mediums are not easily found when a person lives in a rural area or small community outside the big cities. Still, the desire for communication is not confined to the "convenient" areas of the world. People who cannot obtain the services of psychics and who desire to initiate contact with departed ones have found alternative ways to do so.

There is, first of all, that most satisfying route of the direct communication. By training and by the sheer good fortune of having innate psychic talents, a person can establish a direct link with the world of the departed by developing mediumship. Depending again on the particular "phase" of that ability and the degree with which it is practiced, we find a number of do-it-yourself mediums enjoying contact with the other world. The most common form of this contact is again through clairvoyance, clairaudience, or clairsentience—but of the induced kind. Usually this is done through periods of withdrawal or regular meditation. Another form is automatic writing, wherein a dead person allegedly controls the hand of the medium and communicates through writing. I have examined many such cases and found that a fair number of the automatists are indeed controlled by dead correspondents. The proof will be found in the nature and contents of the writings, the appearance of the handwriting and whether it is similar to the deceased person's own hand, and the absence of detailed knowledge of the dead person's life and habits on the part of the automatic writer. All these are criteria I take into consideration when judging the genuineness of automatic scripts. There is a large amount of this material that is either a product of the writer's own unconscious mind, giving vent to suppressed ideas and wishes, or not conclusive enough to say with certainty that it is dictated by a discarnate person. Standards of acceptance of this form of communication have to be high, higher perhaps than warranted by facts. But I feel that discarnate persons capable of extensive memories and full personality traits should also be able to remember their style and handwriting.

Certainly, when a stranger communicates through automatic writing, the believability of the phenomenon is much greater. The late *New York Daily News* columnist Danton

Walker once received many pages of material allegedly from a Russian officer killed in the Sino-Japanese War of 1895. The whole matter seemed preposterous to Danton, who was an enlightened skeptic although fully aware of his own mediumship. But he checked the name and data given by the person and found that an officer of that name and description had indeed served and died in the Sino-Japanese War.

Last, and perhaps least, there are the man-made instruments by which many seek communication with the world beyond. Whether it is called a planchette or a Ouija board, a plain piece of wood inscribed with the letters of the alphabet and some figures serves as probably the best-known apparatus of attempted communication. Today this apparatus is manufactured by the millions and has captured the fancy of youngsters and grown-ups alike. There isn't a day when I don't receive an inquiry about it. Rarely do I lecture at a college when someone doesn't bring it up. Ouija boards were created after World War I when a wave of spiritualism swept England and the United States. The board was a way, it was thought, to contact the loved ones, and depending upon where the indicator—or a water glass, if one preferred—would point, the answer was either yes (*oui, ja*) or no.

The board has no supernormal faculties whatever. If any genuine communications result from its use by two or more people, then one must examine first of all whatever knowledge those present might have had of the subject.

Only when a person is found to communicate via the board who is totally unknown to all present and is afterward found to have existed as a person, and in the way the communicator claims, do we have a reputable communication. For Ouija boards, along with crystal balls, tea leaves, and coffee grinds, merely serve as concentration points for the reader's own unconscious. It is the psychic ability of the ones using the board that makes the communication, if one occurs, possible.

On occasion genuine contacts with the dead do come about in this manner, but they are not common. I recall one particular case involving medium Ethel Johnson Meyers in New York. A soldier announced himself by making our indicator run to certain letters of the alphabet. He gave a name, serial number, and the name and address of his parents, saying that he had been killed in the Philippines during World War II and that he had served in a paratroop outfit. I managed to contact his relatives and establish that there was indeed such a person.

There is also a certain risk involved in the indiscriminate use of the board. A person capable of deep trance mediumship and not aware of this potential ability might conceivably play with the board and "pick up" an undesired and undesirable discarnate person. Once an initial contact has been made, it is often difficult to get rid of the tie, and unless the involuntary medium has professional guidance, all sorts of difficulties could result. For that reason I hold a dim view of parlor games called ESP and the light touch given to what is essentially a very serious and important human faculty. People who have had trance experience or who know that they are true mediums should be very careful before using a Ouija board alone or without the assistance of a trained psychic researcher who might help break an unwanted trance state, should this be required.

Chapter Six

When the Dead Reach Out to the Living

THE ANNALS OF PSYCHIC RESEARCH ARE FULL of verified cases in which the dead come to bid the living a last good-bye. But the thought of separation is often overshadowed by the desire to announce the continuance of life. This, of course, is implied in the very fact of an appearance after death: only a person who survives can come to say good-bye. Orthodox psychiatry has labored hard and long to explain most of these appearances as "hallucinations," but the fact is that the majority of cases show total ignorance on the part of the recipient that the person who communicates after death is no longer alive. You cannot hallucinate something you don't know.

This type of communication occurs frequently with professional psychics. Eileen Garrett once reported to me that she was riding in a taxi down New York's Fifth Avenue when a long-dead friend spoke to her clairvoyantly and advised her that Marie H., whom both knew, had just passed on and was over there with him. Mrs. Garrett looked at her watch and registered the time. Shortly after, when she reached her offices, she put in a call to California, where Miss H. lived. The message was correct, and when she compared the time of passing as recorded in California with the time she had received her message, she found that, allowing for the time differential, it had been given her a moment after Miss H.'s death! But laypeople, that is, people not at all concerned with the psychic or even interested in it, who are often skeptics and firm nonbelievers in an afterlife—are frequently the recipients of such messages and experience communications from the dead.

Once, when I was lecturing at Waynesburg College in Waynesburg, Pennsylvania, I was approached by a young lady who had had a most interesting experience along such lines in April 1963.

Sandra R. lived with her family in a house in a small town south of Pittsburgh. Her brother Neal R., then aged twenty-two, had been working as a bank teller for the past three years. Young Neal had often expressed a dislike of going into the army; he had a feeling he would be killed. As a consequence, his mother and sister, to whom the young man was quite close, persuaded him to join the National Guard for a six-month tour of duty. Since he would be drafted anyway, he might thus shorten the period of his service.

Neal finally agreed that this was the best thing to do under the circumstances, and he joined the National Guard. He resigned his position at the bank and seemed reconciled to making the best of the situation.

In April he got his orders and tickets and was to report for basic training a week from the following Monday. Several times during those final days at home, he mentioned the fact that he was to leave at 5 A.M. Sunday, as if this were indeed something important and final. On the Monday preceding his departure, he visited friends to say good-bye. Leaving home as usual with a kiss on the cheek for his mother, he gaily said, "I'll see you," and went out.

He never returned. The following morning the family was notified that he had been found dead in his car parked along a lonely country road about two miles from his home. He had committed suicide by inhaling carbon monoxide.

The news created a state of shock in his family. At first they would not believe the news, for they were sure he would have left some sort of note for his family. But nothing was ever found, even though the family searched the house from top to bottom. He had put all his things in order, leaving no debts or commitments, but there was no message of any kind for anyone.

He was buried in his hometown, and the family tried to adjust to their great loss. Sandra, his sister, was three years his junior, but the two had been close enough to have many telepathic experiences in which they would read each other's thoughts. She could not understand why her brother had not confided in her before taking this drastic step.

In the house, both Sandra's room and Neal's had been upstairs. After the boy's death, Sandra could not bear the thought of sleeping so near to her late brother's room, so she slept on a rollout divan placed in the living room downstairs. The day of the funeral was a Friday, and it seemed to Sandra that it would never pass. Finally, after a restless, almost sleepless night, Saturday dawned. All day long she felt uneasy, and there was an atmosphere of tension in the air that she found almost unbearable. When night came, Sandra asked that her mother share the couch with her. Neither woman had taken any tranquilizers or sleeping pills. They discussed the suicide again from all angles but failed to arrive at any clues. Finally they fell asleep from exhaustion.

Suddenly Sandra was awakened from deep slumber by a clicking sound. It sounded exactly as if someone had snapped his fingers just above her head. As Sandra became fully awake, she heard her mother stir next to her.

"Did you hear that?" her mother asked. She too had heard the strange snapping sound. Both women were now fully awake.

They felt a tingling sensation pervading them from head to toe, as if they were plugged into an electric socket! Some sort of current was running through them, and they were quite unable to move a limb.

The living room is situated in the front part of the house. The blinds were all closed, and no light whatever shone through them. The only light coming into the room came from a doorway behind them, a doorway that led into the hall. All of a sudden, they noticed a bright light to their left, moving toward them. It had the brightness of an electric bulb when they first saw it approach. It appeared about two feet from the couch on the mother's side and was getting brighter and brighter. "What is it, what is it?" they cried to each other, and then Sandra noticed that the light had a form. There was a head and shoulders encased in light!

Frightened, her heart pounding, Sandra heard herself cry out: "It's Neal!" At the moment she called out her late brother's name, the light blew up to its brightest glare. With that, a feeling of great peace and relief came over the two women.

Mrs. R., still unable to move her body, asked: "What do you want? Why did you do it?"

With that, she started to cry. At that moment waves of light in the form of fingers appeared inside the bright light *as if someone were waving good-bye.* Then the light gradually dimmed until it vanished completely.

At that instant a rush of cold air moved across the room. A moment later they clearly heard someone walking up the stairs. They were alone in the house, so they knew it could not be a flesh-and-blood person. Now the steps approached Neal's room upstairs. When they reached the top step, the step squeaked as it had always done when Sandra's brother had walked up the stairs. Over the years, Sandra had heard this particular noise time and again. Neal's room was directly over their heads, and there wasn't a sound in the house. Except those footsteps overhead. The two women were lying quite still on the couch, unable to move even if they had wanted to. The steps continued through the hallway and then went into Neal's room. Next they heard the sound of someone sitting down on his bed, and they clearly heard the bed springs give from the weight of a person! Since the bed stood almost directly over their heads down in the living room, there was no mistaking these sounds. At this moment, their bodies suddenly returned to normal. The tension was broken, and Sandra jumped up, turned on the lights, and looked at the clock next to the couch. The time was five o'clock Sunday morning—the exact moment Neal had been scheduled to leave, had he not committed suicide!

With this, all was quiet again in the house. But Sandra and her mother no longer grieved for Neal. They accepted the inevitable and began to realize that life did continue in another dimension. The bond between their Neal and themselves was reestablished, and they felt a certain relief to know he was all right wherever he now was.

At different times after that initial good-bye visit, they experienced the strong smell of Neal's favorite after-shave lotion in the house. At the time of his death, he had a bottle of it in the glove compartment of his car. As no one else in the house was using any after-shave lotion, an alternative explanation would be hard to come by.

Neither Mrs. R. nor her daughter is given to hysterics. They accepted these events as perfectly natural, always carefully making sure no ordinary explanation would fit. But when all was said and done, they knew that their Neal had not let them down, after all. The bond was still unbroken.

Mrs. G. B., a housewife living in a Pittsburgh suburb, and her brother, Frank G., had been close in their childhood, which may be of some importance in the event I am about to relate. Whenever there exists an emotional bond between people, the communication between the world of the dead and that of the living seems to be easier. But this is by no means always the case, as even strangers have communicated in this way with each other.

Frank G. and forty-one others were aboard a navy transport flying over the ocean. On the nights of October 26, 27, and 28, 1954, Mrs. B. had a vivid dream in which she felt someone was drowning. This recurrent dream puzzled her, but she did not connect it with her brother as she had no idea where he was or what he was doing at the time. On October 30, 1954, she was awakened from sleep by the feeling of a presence in her room. This was not at her own home but at the house of her in-laws. Her husband was sleeping in an adjoining room. As she looked up, fully awake now, she saw at the foot of her bed a figure all in white. A feeling of great sorrow came over her at this moment. Frightened, she jumped out of bed and ran to her husband.

The following evening, the telephone rang. Her brother, Frank, crewman on an ill-fated air transport, had been lost at sea.

Mrs. William F. of Salem, Massachusetts, no witch but rather a well-adjusted housewife, had what she calls a "spiritual experience," which was enough to assure her that life did indeed exist beyond the grave.

In 1957, her aged grandmother had passed on, leaving the care of her grandfather to her parents. The old man was lost without his companion of so many years, and eventually he deteriorated to the point where he had to be placed in a hospital. He died in 1961, and the family went jointly to the local funeral parlor for a last good-bye.

Mrs. F. and her older sister were sitting in the room where the body lay, when suddenly both of them—as they later realized—had the same strange feeling of a presence with them. The feeling became so strong that Mrs. F. eventually lifted her head, which had been lowered in mourning. It may be mentioned that she did not like funeral parlors and had never been inside one before.

As she looked up beyond the coffin, she saw her grandfather and her grandmother with smiles on their faces. Although their lips did not move, the girl got the impression her "Nana" was saying to her: "It's all right now. I am taking care of him now. Don't be sad. We're together again."

The parents did not see this vision, but the older sister did.

The apparitions of the dead wish to be recognized as the people they were and are. Thus the majority of them appear looking as they did in physical life—that is, wearing the clothes they had on when they died or clothes they liked to wear ordinarily. But there are also cases where the dead have appeared dressed in a simple white robe instead of their customary clothing. I myself saw my mother several years after her passing, wearing what I then called "a long nightshirt." The moment was brief but long enough for me to realize I was fully awake and that she cast a shadow on the opposite wall.

I think that this white robe is perhaps the "ordinary" dress over there, with the earth-type clothing optional when and if needed. No doubt the white robe is behind many legends of white-robed angels appearing to mortals and the generally accepted description of ghosts being "white." It is also true that ectoplasm, the material of which materializations of the dead are created, is white. It is an albumen substance that has been analyzed in laboratories and that is drawn from the living during physical séances.

The white color has some bearing on the need for darkness whenever such manifestations are induced in the séance room. Evidently strong white light destroys the material, perhaps because light and psychic energies are traveling on collision courses and might cancel each other out. But the ectoplastic substance is tangible and real and is by no means a figment of the imagination.

Mrs. C. M. R., a widow living in eastern New England, was married more than forty years to her husband, John, who passed away in 1966. John R. had worked as a machinist for a leather factory. When he complained of pain in his chest, his ailment was diagnosed as pleurisy, and he was told to stay in bed. There was no indication of imminent death on that March day in 1966. The doctor left after a routine inspection, and John

R. went back to bed.

Between 2 and 3 A.M., he suddenly complained of pain. He was sitting on the bed when his wife rushed to his side. She made him comfortable, and he went back to sleep—never to wake up again. Because of the complaint, Mrs. R. kept a vigil close to the bed. Suddenly she saw a white-robed figure rise up from the bed and sit on it for a moment, as if to get its bearings. There was a rustling sound of sheets moving. Since the figure's back was turned toward her, Mrs. R. could not make out its features. But it was a large person, and so was her husband. At the same time, she had a peculiar sensation inside her head. Suddenly, as if a balloon inside her had burst, the sensation stopped and all was silent. The white-robed figure had disappeared. She stepped to the bed and realized that her husband was gone.

Mrs. R.'s brother, Robert C., was a lieutenant in the army during the Second World War and later worked for the C.N.R. railroad in Canada. Mrs. R. had not been in constant touch with him, since she lived a thousand miles away. But on April 11, 1948, she and her daughter were in their bedroom when both women saw the figure of Robert C., dressed in black, looking into the room, his hand on the doorknob. He smiled at them and Mrs. R. spoke to her brother, but he vanished into thin air. That was between midnight and 1 A.M. Hospital records at the Halifax Victoria General Hospital show that Lieutenant C. passed away officially at 7 A.M., April 12, 1948. Evidently he had already been out of the body and on his last journey several hours before. Stopping in at his sister's house on the way, he had come to say good-bye.

Diane S., a high school graduate and as level-headed as you would want to meet, did not show the slightest interest in psychic matters until age seventeen. She lived with her parents in a medium-sized town in Michigan. Her friend Kerm was the apple of her eye, and vice versa. No doubt, if things had preceded normally, they would have married.

But one night, after he had driven her home, Kerm was killed in a car accident on the way to his own place. The shock hit Diane very strongly, and she missed him. She wondered whether there was anything in the belief that man survived death.

One week after the funeral of her friend, she smelled the scent of funeral flowers on arising. For five days this phenomenon took place. There were no such flowers in the house at that time. Then other things followed. Diane was on her way home from a girlfriend's house. It was around midnight. As she drove home, she gradually felt another presence with her in the car. She laughed it off as being due to an overactive imagination, but the sensation persisted. She looked around for a moment, but the back seat was empty. Again she focused her eyes on the road. Suddenly she felt something touch first her left hand, then her right. There was no mistaking it; the touch was very real.

At another time she awoke in the middle of a sound sleep. She felt the presence of something or someone in the room with her. Finally, she opened her eyes and looked in all directions. She saw nothing unusual, but she was sure there was another person sitting on the second bed, watching her. The feeling became so intense that she broke out in a cold sweat. But she did not dare get up, and finally she managed to get back to sleep. The next morning, when she awoke, her first act was to have a look at the other bed. There, at the foot of the bed, was an imprint on the bedspread, as if someone had been sitting on it!

After that there was a period of quiet, and Diane thought with great relief that the psychic manifestations had finally come to an end.

But in late July of 1965, something happened that caused her to reconsider that opinion. A young man named Jerry had been a steady companion of hers since the unfortunate accident in which Kerm had been killed. There was a party at Diane's house one evening. After the company left, Jerry stayed on.

Together they sat and talked for several hours. It grew late, and dawn began to show itself. The two young people were sitting on the couch downstairs when suddenly Jerry looked up and asked if her mother was standing at the top of the stairs! Diane knew that her mother would be asleep in her room, yet she followed Jerry's eyes to the top landing of the stairs.

There was a figure standing there, rather vaguely outlined and seemingly composed of a white filmy substance. At its base there was a luminous sparkle. As the two young people stared at the figure, without daring to move, it gradually faded away.

Jerry then left for home, and Diane went to bed. As he drove down the road, he was about to pass the spot where Kerm had been killed a couple of months before. He stopped for a moment and got out to stretch his legs. When he walked back to his car, he noticed that it was enveloped by a thick fog. He got into the car, which felt strangely cold and clammy. He glanced to his right, and to his horror he saw a white, cloudlike object cross the road toward the car. As it approached the car, Jerry could make it out clearly enough: it was a blurred image of a human body, but the face was as plain as day. It was Kerm. He got into the front seat with Jerry, who shook with terror. Jerry's eyes were watering, and he dared not move.

"Take care of Di," a strangely broken voice said next to him. It sounded as though it were coming from far away, like an echo.

Then a hand reached out for his, and Jerry passed out. When he came to, he found himself parked in front of the local cemetery. How he had got there he did not know. It is some distance from the spot of Kerms accident to the cemetery. But there he was, barely able to start his car and drive home.

When he told his story to his parents, they thought he had dreamed it. Jerry was sure he had not. The events that followed bore him out. It would seem that Kerm wanted to make sure Jerry took good care of his former girlfriend. At various times, Jerry would feel a hand at his shoulder.

At this point Diane got in touch with me. As I could not then rush out to Michigan, I sent her explicit instructions about what to do. On the next occasion when the restless form was in evidence, she was to address him calmly and ask that he cease worrying over her. Jerry would indeed look out for her, and they would rather not have him, Kerm, around also. Three does make a crowd, even if one is a ghost.

Apparently Kerm took the hint and left for good. But to Diane it was an indication that there is another world where we all may meet again.

Although many visits of departing loved ones take place while the recipients of the message are fully awake or as they are being awakened to receive the news, there are many more such incidents on record where the events seemingly occur in the dream state. I devoted an entire chapter to the many-sided nature of dreams in my book *ESP and You*. Many dreams are physically caused or are psychoanalytical material. But there are such things as true dreams and psychic dreams, in which precise messages are received that later come true.

Mrs. Madeline M. lives in a large Eastern city. She is a "true dreamer" and has accepted her ESP abilities calmly and without fears.

"True dreams I can't forget on awakening, even if I try," she explained to me, "while the ordinary kind fade away quickly and I couldn't recall them no matter how hard I try to."

When Madeline was fourteen, her mother was taken to the hospital with a fatal illness. The girl was not aware of its seriousness, however, and only later found out that her mother knew she would soon die and was worried about leaving her daughter at so tender an age.

At the time, Madeline had accepted the invitation of a friend and former neighbor to stay overnight with her. That night she had a vivid dream. She saw her mother standing at the foot of the bed, stroking her feet and smiling at her with a sweet yet sad smile. What puzzled Madeline, however, was the way her mother looked in the vision. To begin with, she wore a strange dress with tiny buttons. Her hair was done in a way she had never worn it before. Both dress and strange hairdo impressed themselves upon the young girl, along with a feeling of emptiness at the sight of her mother.

"I have to leave now, Madeline," the mother said in the dream.

"But where are you going?" Madeline heard herself ask in the dream.

"Never mind, Madeline, it's just that I *must* go!"

And with that remark, her mother eased herself toward the door, gently closing it behind her and looking back once more, saying: "Good-bye, Madeline."

With that, the door was shut.

The next thing Madeline knew, she found herself sitting on the bed, sobbing hysterically, "Mother, don't go, please don't go!" Her hostess was next to her trying to get her out of the state she was in.

"It's only a dream," the friend explained, "and look, it's late—*five minutes past two*! We must both get some sleep now!"

With that, Madeline and her friend went back to sleep, but not until after Madeline had reported her vision to her friend in every detail.

She was roused from deep sleep by her friend early the next morning.

"Your brother is here to have breakfast with us," her friend explained. Hurriedly Madeline got dressed to meet her brother.

"Tell him about your dream," the friend nudged her.

There was a pause, then the brother remarked: "I'm

jealous, Madeline; why didn't she come to *me*?"

He then informed the girl that their mother had passed away at *five minutes past two* the previous night.

Too stunned to cry, Madeline realized that her mother had come to say good-bye. In the dream state the connection can be made a lot easier, because there is no conscious thought wall to penetrate and that interferes with the flow of communication.

They went to the viewing of the body. When Madeline caught sight of her mother's body, she grabbed her brother's hand and dug her nails deeply into it.

"What is it?" he asked with surprise. She could only point to her mother's appearance: the dress with the tiny buttons she had never worn before and the strange hairdo—exactly as Madeline had seen it in her "dream."

Evidently Madeline M. was and is a good recipient of messages from the departing and departed. Many years later, in 1957, she had another true dream. This time she saw herself walk into a house, go straight to the back of the house, and stop in a doorway that opened into a large dining room. As she stood in this doorway, in the dream, she noticed her dead father seated at the head of the table. Her dead mother walked in just as Madeline arrived at her observation point. Her mother now stood next to her father, whose face was aglow with joy. Both father and mother appeared very much younger than they were at the time of their deaths, and both seemed very excited. But it was not the dreamer's presence that caused all this commotion; in fact they paid no attention to her at all. In her dream Madeline felt left out and wondered why she had not been asked to sit down at the dinner table, since there was an extra place set at the table.

"Isn't it wonderful that we are all here together again?" she heard herself ask. "Where is my brother?"

Finally her mother spoke up, pointing to the empty chair. "Oh, he will be here; we're expecting him—in fact, he is on his way now!"

The next morning Mrs. M. recalled her dream vision only too clearly. But it was not until nine months later that the events alluded to in the dream became reality. Her brother had the same fatal illness that had taken her mother, and after a brief hospital stay he too passed into the world of the spirit, where a place had already been set for him at Thanksgiving the year before.

There are instances when the dead wish to let someone living know that they are across the veil and not merely somewhere on earth and out of touch. Especially in the United States, where the movement of people is unchecked by police registration, people can easily drop out of one another's sight and may be hard to trace or track down. One case involved a young lady who had moved in with a married sister in coastal Virginia.

Mrs. Doris S., the married sister, has a husband in the army, and consequently they move around a lot. But at that time she had a house, and her sister was welcome in it. The sister was engaged to a young man with whom she had kept company for several years. Her weakness was cigarettes, and even her young man frowned on her excessive smoking.

"I'll be back in one month to take you with me," he had promised before he left, "and if you've cut down on cigarettes to ten a day, I'll marry you!"

Soon after he had left, strange occurrences began to puzzle the two women. The sister's clothes would be moved around in her closet without any reason. Cigarette butts would be found all over the house like markers, although neither sister had put them there. One of the dresses disappeared completely, only to show up a week later, neatly folded, in another drawer. There was walking upstairs at times when there was no human being in that part of the house. Then one day a shoe of the sister's walked down the steps by itself—as if someone were moving it!

Mrs. S.'s husband was impressed with the unaccountable events she wrote him about, and it was decided that they would look for another house. Then, when he had some leave coming to him, the family decided to go home to Pennsylvania. There they found out something they had not known before: the sister's friend had been killed in a car accident several weeks earlier. As he didn't have any family, nobody had let them know of his death.

"It must have been he," Mrs. S. remarked, "trying to keep his word. After all, he did promise to get sister in a month."

After that there were no unusual happenings in the house.

Mrs. Darlene V., a housewife in suburban New York City, has had numerous premonitory experiences. But the incident that convinced her that she had a special gift happened when she was sixteen years old and a junior in high school in Beaver Dam, Wisconsin. Mrs. V., a Catholic, attended a religious study course at the time. It was held at the local church, and the group consisted of youngsters of both sexes. During her study sessions she noticed a certain young man who sat all by himself on the side; his sad and lonely expression attracted her interest. She inquired about him and learned that his name was Roger but that his friends called him Rocky. He had been studying for the priesthood but had had to stop recently because of illness. He was then in his early twenties. A bond of friendship grew between Darlene and this unhappy young man, although her mother did not approve of it.

Around the end of October, he failed to show up at the study evenings, and it wasn't until the week before Christmas that Darlene found out why. Her parish priest informed her that Rocky was very ill and in the hospital. She asked her mother for permission to visit her sick friend, but her mother refused. The following day she had the strongest feeling that Rocky needed her, so she went anyway, after school. The young man was overjoyed and confirmed that he had indeed wanted to see her very much.

During the next two months, she went to visit him as often as she could. In February she had an accident in her gym class that forced her to remain in bed for two weeks. But she continued her interest in Rocky through telephone calls to his mother, whom she had never met. The young man had cancer and had been operated upon, and the mother gave Darlene daily reports of his progress.

On a Friday in February she was able to return to school, and it was her intention to visit her friend Rocky at the hospital that Friday afternoon. But before she could do so, her brother showed her the morning paper: Rocky had died the night before. The shock sent Darlene back to bed.

Very late that night she awoke from deep sleep with the feeling that she was not alone. She sat up in bed and looked around. There, at the foot of her bed, stood her friend Rocky. His features were plain, and he was surrounded by a soft glow. As soon as he noticed that she saw him, he held out his hands toward her and said: "Please help my mother; she wants and needs you." Then he was gone.

Darlene called the boy's mother the next morning. Before she could relay her message, the mother broke into tears, saying that she had been trying to locate Darlene, whose family name she did not know.

Darlene was at Rocky's mother's side from then until after

the funeral. It was only then that she finally told the boy's mother what had happened the night after Rocky's passing. It was a great comfort to the mother, but the parish priest, whom Darlene also told of her experience, tried to convince her that it was all "a young girl's emotional imagination."

Visual phenomena are not the only way by which the dead seemingly assert themselves to the living. Sometimes the phenomena are only auditory but no less evidential. It is somewhat like playing an instrument: some people gravitate toward the piano, others to the violin—but both make music. So it is with psychic communication, which, more than any ordinary communication, depends on the makeup of both individuals, the receiver as well as the sender.

Mrs. William S. is a housewife in Pennsylvania. A friend of her husband's by the name of Paul F., who was employed by a large mail-order house, died in his early fifties of a heart attack. A few weeks after his death Mrs. S. was in her bedroom making the bed when she suddenly heard him call out to her. There was no mistaking his voice, for she knew it well. He had called her by name, as if he wanted her attention. The voice sounded as if it came from the adjoining room, so she entered that room and responded by calling Paul's name. There was no answer. A religious person, Mrs. S. then knelt on the floor and prayed for the man. She has not heard his voice since.

For many years, Elizabeth S. had been friendly with a young woman named Dorothy B. This was in Pittsburgh, and they were almost next-door neighbors. Dorothy had a sister named Leona, who was a housewife also. She passed away suddenly, only twenty-eight years of age. The shock was very great for Dorothy, who could not reconcile herself to this passing. Despite attempts by Mrs. S. and others to bring her out of this state of grief, Dorothy refused to listen and even cried in her sleep at night.

One night Dorothy was awakened by something or someone shaking her bed. She got up and looked but found no explanation for this. Everybody in her house was fast asleep. As she stood in front of her bed, puzzled about the strange occurrence, she clearly heard footsteps on the stairs. Frightened, she woke her husband, and together they searched the whole house. They found no one who could have caused the steps. The following night, the same phenomena occurred. Again there was no natural explanation.

But during that second night, a strange thing also happened to Mrs. S., five doors away. She was in bed, reading a book, when all of a sudden the printed page seemed to disappear in front of her eyes, and different words appeared instead. Mrs. S. shook her head, assuming her eyes were tired, but it happened again. At this point she closed her eyes and lay back in bed, when she heard a voice beside her pillow calling her name, "Betty!" It was a very sharp voice, full of despair. Although Mrs. S. had never met Dorothy's sister Leona in life, she knew it was she, calling out for recognition.

The two women got together the next day and compared experiences. It was then that they decided Leona wanted them to know that she continued to enjoy a kind of life in another world, and to stop grieving for her. It was the push that Dorothy had needed to get out of her grief, and the two women became like sisters after this common experience. Leona never called on either of them again.

I have often doubted the reliability of Ouija boards as a means of communication between the two worlds, but once in a while something genuine can come through them. The proof must rest with the individuals operating the board, of course, and depends upon the presence or absence of the information in their unconscious minds. But Mrs. S. had an experience that to me rings true.

At the time, she was nineteen, as yet unmarried, and lived with her parents. She did not really believe there was anything supernatural in a Ouija board. More to amuse themselves than for any serious reason, she and a neighbor sat down to try their luck with a board. Hardly had they started to operate the indicator when it moved with great rapidity to spell out a name. That name was Parker. It surprised Elizabeth, for she had not thought of this person in a long time. Now one might argue that his name would always be present in her subconscious mind, but so would many other names of people who had gone on before.

"Do you want anything?" Elizabeth cried out.

The board spelled "yes," and at the very same moment she clearly felt a kiss on her right cheek. It was not her imagination. The sensation was quite physical.

Parker S. was a young man she had dated two years before, and the two young people had been very much in love. At the time he worked at a service station. One day, on his way to see her, he was killed in a car accident. Mrs. S. feels he had finally delivered his good-bye kiss to her, albeit a little late.

Lastly, there are phenomena of letting the living know that death has taken a loved one. The thought going out from the dying person at the moment of separation is not strong enough or not organized sufficiently to send a full image to a loved one remaining behind. But there is enough psychic or psychokinetic energy to move an object or cause some other telltale sign so that the loved ones may look up and wonder. The Germans call these phenomena *gaenger*, or goers, and they are quite common.

A typical case is the experience Mrs. Maria P. of California shared with her husband a few days before Christmas 1955. The couple were in bed asleep in their Toronto home, when suddenly they were awakened by the noise of a knickknack falling off a bookshelf. The object could not possibly have fallen off accidently or by itself. At the same moment, the woman was impressed with the idea that her father had just died. A few days later she learned that her father had indeed passed on at that identical moment in his native Germany, across the ocean.

This was not the first time Maria had experienced anything along these lines. When she was only five years old and her mother left for the hospital, the little girl said, "You will not come back, Mother." It was nine days later that the entire family heard a loud, snapping noise in the main bedroom. All the clocks in the house stopped at that instant. The time was 1:10 P.M. A few hours later, word came that her mother had died at that hour.

There are other cases involving the falling of paintings, or the moving of shutters at windows, or the closing of doors in a gust of wind when no wind was blowing. All of these supernormal phenomena are, in my estimation, different ways of saying the same thing: I am going, folks, but I'm not finished.

Sometimes the message needs no words: the very presence of the "deceased" is enough to bring home the facts of afterlife. Once, my friend Gail B., public relations director for many leading hotels, called me to ask my help for a friend who was extremely upset because of a visit from the beyond. Would I please go and talk to her? I would and I did.

Carina L., a onetime professional singer who later went into business in New York City was originally from Romania and a firm "nonbeliever" in anything she could not touch, smell, see, hear, or count. Thus it was with considerable apprehension that she reported two seemingly impossible experiences.

When she was a young girl in the old country, Carina had a favorite grandmother by the name of Minta M. Grandmother M. lived to be a hale and healthy eighty-six; then she left this vale of tears as the result of a heart attack. To be sure, the old lady was no longer so spry as she had been in her youth. One could see her around the neighborhood in her faded brown coat and her little bonnet and special shoes made for her swollen feet, as she suffered from foot trouble.

She had a shuffling walk, not too fast, not too slow; her gait was well known in her neighborhood in Bucharest. When Grandmother M. had called it a day on earth, her daughters inherited her various belongings. The famed brown coat went to Carina's Aunt Rosa, who promptly cut it apart in order to remodel it for herself.

Grandmother was gone, and the three daughters—Carina's mother and her two aunts, Rosa and Ita—lived together at the house. Two months after Grandmother's death, Ita and her little son went to the grocer's for some shopping. On their way they had to pass a neighbor's house and stopped for a chat. As they were standing there with the neighbor, who should come around the corner but Grandmother, the way she had done so often in life. Ita saw her first and stared, mouth wide open. Then the little boy noticed Grandmother and said so.

Meanwhile the figure came closer, shuffling on her bad feet as she had always done. But she didn't pay any attention to the little group staring at her. As she came within an arm's length, she merely kept going, looking straight ahead. She wore the same faded brown coat that had been her favorite in life. Ita was dumbfounded. By the time she came to her senses, the figure had simply disappeared.

"Did you see Mrs. M.?" the neighbor asked in awe. Ita could only nod. What was there to say? It was something she never forgot. On getting home she rushed to her sister's room. There, cut apart as it had been for several weeks, lay the brown coat!

Many things changed over the years, and finally Carina found herself living in New York City. Her Aunt Ita, now living in Toronto, decided to pay her a visit and stayed with Carina at her apartment. About two weeks after the aunt's arrival, she accompanied her niece on a routine shopping errand in the neighborhood. It was a breezy March afternoon as the two ladies went along Broadway, looking at the windows. Between West

Eighty-first and Eighty-second Streets, they suddenly saw a familiar figure. There, coming toward them, was Grandmother M. again, dressed exactly as she had been twenty-five years before, with her faded brown coat, the little bonnet, and the peculiar shoes.

The two ladies were flabbergasted. What does one do under such conditions? They decided to wait and see. And see they did, for they stopped and let Grandmother M. pass them by. When she was only inches away from them, they could clearly see her face. She was as solid as anyone in the street, but she did not look at them. Instead, she kept staring ahead as if she were not aware of them or anyone else around. As she passed them, they could clearly hear the sound of her shuffling feet. There was no mistaking it: this was Grandmother M. dead twenty-five years but looking as good as new.

When the figure reached the next corner and disappeared around it, Carina sprang to life again. Within a few seconds she was at the corner. Before her, the side street was almost empty. No Grandmother. Again she had disappeared into thin air. What had the old lady wanted? Why did she appear to them? I could only guess that it was her way of saying, "Don't you forget your Granny. I'm still going strong!"

Chapter Seven
Unfinished Business

THE SECOND CATEGORY OF "SPIRIT RETURNS," as the spiritualists like to call it, is unfinished business. While the first thought of a newly dead person might be to let the grieving family know there is no reason to cry and that life does continue, the second thought might well be how to attend to whatever was left unfinished on earth and should be taken care of.

The evidence pointing to a continuance of personality after dissolution of the body shows that mundane worries and desires go right along with the newly liberated soul. Just because one is now in another, finer dimension does not mean one can entirely neglect one's obligations in the physical world. This will vary according to the individual and his or her attitudes toward responsibilities in general while in the body. A coward does not become a hero after death, and a slob does not turn into a paragon of orderliness. There is, it appears, really nothing ennobling in dying per se. It would seem that there is an opportunity to grasp the overall scheme of the universe a lot better from over there, but this comprehension is by no means compulsory, nor is the newly arrived soul brainwashed in any way. Freedom to advance or stand still exists on both sides of the veil.

However, if a person dies suddenly and manages to move

on without staying in the earth's atmosphere and becoming a so-called ghost, then that person may also take along all unresolved problems. These problems may range from such major matters as insurance and sustenance for the family, guidance for the young, lack of a legal will, unfinished works of one kind or another, incomplete manuscripts or compositions, disorderly states of affairs leaving the heirs in a quandary as to where "everything" is, to such minor matters as leaving the desk in disorder, not having answered a couple of letters, or having spoken rashly to a loved one. To various individuals such frustrations may mean either a little or a lot, depending again on the makeup of the person's personality. There are no objective standards as to what constitutes a major problem and what is minor. What appears to one person a major problem may seem quite unimportant when viewed through another individual's eyes.

Generally speaking, the need to communicate with living people arises from a compulsion to set matters right. Once the contact has been made and the problem understood by the living, the deceased's need to reappear is no longer present, unless the living *fail* to act on the deceased communicator's request. Then that person will return again and again until he gets his way.

All communications are by no means as crystal clear as a Western Union message. Some come in symbolic language or can only be understood if one knows the communicator's habit patterns. But the grasping of the request is generally enough to relieve the very real anxieties of the deceased. There are cases where the request cannot possibly be granted, because conditions have changed or much time has gone on. Some of these communications stem from very old grievances.

A communicator appearing in what was once her home in the 1880s insisted that the papers confirming her ownership of the house be found and the property be turned back to her from the current owners. To her the ancient wrong was a current problem, of course, but we could not very well oblige her eighty-five years later and throw out an owner who had bought the property in good faith many years after her passing. We finally persuaded the restless personality that we would *try* to do what she wanted, at the same time assuring her that things had changed. It calmed her anxiety, and because we had at least listened to her with a sympathetic ear, she did not insist on actual performance of the promise.

An extreme case of this kind concerns a Mrs. Sally V. of Chicago. This lady was married to a plasterer who gave her ten children, but in 1943 she nevertheless divorced her active spouse. She then married a distant relative of her husband's, also called V. But divorce did not stop the plasterer from molesting her. He allegedly threatened her over the years until she could stand it no longer. It was then that the woman, in her despair, decided to get rid of her ex-husband in a most dramatic and, she thought, final way by murdering him.

The opportunity came when a nineteen-year-old cousin of hers stopped in on leave from his outfit, which was stationed at Fort Benning, Georgia.

"Would you kill my ex-husband for me? I'd give a month's pay for it."

"You've got yourself a deal," the cousin is quoted as saying obligingly, according to the United Press, and when she offered him $90 for the job, he thought $50 was quite enough. To a soldier conditioned to war, human life is sometimes cheap.

Soon afterward Mr. Charles V. was found dead in his basement apartment, his head bashed in by a hammer.

The story might have remained a secret between the willing widow and her obliging cousin had it not been for the unwilling spirit of the late Mr. V.

The murder took place on a Tuesday night, right after she made the deal. On Wednesday morning, August 5, 1953, Mrs. V. was startled to see her late husband standing before her in a menacing attitude. She was terrified and called the police. The detectives took a dim view of her ghost story, but in the questioning her own guilt was brought out and the soldier was arrested. One certainly cannot blame the late Mr. V. for wanting the unfinished business of his murder cleared up.

The psychic experience of Clarence T. of California is particularly interesting, because Mr. T. has been blind all his life. In 1946 he was married in San Francisco to a lady who is still his wife. They went to New York shortly afterward, and he did not know any of his wife's friends or family at the time.

Mr. T. remembers the day of his arrival in New York: it was the day famed baseball player Babe Ruth was to be buried. Mr. T. and his wife were to stay with his new mother-in-law on the lower East Side.

The mother-in-law worked as a janitor and usually came home around 1 A.M. The apartment itself was on the ground floor, the last apartment on the floor, about seventy feet from the front door of the house. It was a warm night, and the newly married couple decided to sit up and await the mother's return. The radio was playing a rebroadcast of the solemn mass given at Babe Ruth's funeral, and the time was just eleven o'clock.

At the moment when the music started, both Mr. and Mrs. T. heard the front door open and someone walk down the hall toward them. With Mr. T.'s extrasensitive hearing—many blind people have this—he could distinguish the fact that the person coming toward them wore no shoes. Then this person came through the door, and Mr. T. felt a hand go over his eyes. He thought it was the mother-in-law and said, "Mother?"

Mrs. T. assured him he was mistaken; there was no one to be seen, although she, too, had heard footsteps. Now the invisible person walked past T. and turned around, facing him. All at once both T. and his wife noticed the strong smell of garlic, and each asked the other if he or she was cleaning garlic! But even stranger, T., who is totally blind, could suddenly *see* a woman standing before him—a short woman with long hair, wearing a loose dress and no shoes. Over the dress she wore an apron, and she had one hand in the apron pocket. There was a noise coming from the pocket as if paper were being crumpled. Her eyes were droopy almost to the point of being shut. T. stared at the apparition for what seemed like a long time to him. Finally the woman spoke: "Tell Julia to throw away those stones!"

She repeated it twice. When the religious music on the radio had ended, she turned and walked from the room, although neither of them could hear any footsteps this time. But T. *saw* her walk away. All the time the visitor had been with them, they had felt very strange, as if they were paralyzed. They could not move and just sat there in a daze. The moment the figure disappeared, the spell was broken, and they discovered to their surprise that it had lasted a full hour.

Since Mrs. T. had not seen the figure, T. told her what the woman had said. Mrs. T.'s first name is Julia, but the message made no sense to her. While they were trying to figure out what had happened to them, the mother-in-law returned, and they reported the incident to her.

"My God," the mother-in-law exclaimed, "what does she

want?" There was *another* Julia whom she knew, and the message might apply to her. It seemed that this Julia had been in the apartment the night before and was due to return the next morning for another visit. Why not question her about the apparition? Next morning, the Ts. met the other Julia and described their experience to her in every detail. The young woman nodded with understanding.

"That was my mother," she cried. "She's been dead for two years."

Then she explained that her late mother had been in the habit of carrying garlic on her person, in her apron pocket to be exact. She had collected small stones wherever she went and would put them into small containers to keep. These containers with the stones her mother had collected were still cluttering up her home. Under the circumstances, the young woman decided to take the stones and scatter them over her mother's grave. The apparition has not returned since.

The Ns. lived in a large brick house on Delaware Avenue, Buffalo, in one of the better residential districts. They shared the house with the actual owner, Mr. N.'s uncle by marriage. After Mr. N's aunt died, strange knockings began to disturb the inhabitants of the house. There never was any rational explanation for these raps. Then, several months later, Mr. N. happened to be cleaning out a closet in what had been the aunt's storeroom. There she had put away personal souvenirs and other belongings. In the cleanup, he came across a wrapped package in a drawer. He picked it up, and as he did so he distinctly heard a voice—a human voice—talking to him, although he knew he was quite alone in the room. It was not clear enough for him to make out the words. It was late at night; no one else was stirring in the house, and there was no radio or TV playing.

Mr. N. took the package with him and walked down a long hall to the bedroom where his wife was reading in bed. For a distance of seventy-five feet, all along the way, the voice kept talking to him!

As he entered the bedroom, Mrs. N. looked up from her book and said: "Who was that talking to you?"

Mr. N. became very agitated and somehow found himself taking the strange package to the basement. As if he had been led there he then opened the furnace and threw the package into it. He had the strong feeling that his aunt did not wish to have that package opened or found. As soon as the flames had destroyed the contents of the package, Mr. N.'s mood returned to normal. There were no further psychic occurrences in the house after that. Evidently the aunt did not wish to have her private correspondence or other papers made public, and once that possibility was obviated, her need to communicate ended.

Sometimes the "unfinished business" is monkey business. A person who dies but is unable to accept the change in status, unable to let go of earthly appetites, will be drawn back to the people he or she was close to, and sometimes this return may express itself rather physically. Wild as it sounds, it is entirely possible for a dead man to express love to a living woman, and vice versa. It is not proper, of course, not because of moral reasons but simply because it is very impractical and truly "out of its element." But it does happen.

Mrs. Audrey L. of Baltimore, Maryland, has been a widow for four years. As soon as her husband died, her troubles started. She would hear him "still around." He would call her by name. He would move around in his usual manner in what used to be his house. Mrs. L. did not see this, but she heard it clearly. At night she would hear him snore. Finally she decided to sell their house and move to an apartment.

For a while Mr. L. was not in evidence. But not for long. The nocturnal disturbances began again. This time the phenomena were also visual. Her husband's figure appeared next to her bed, grabbed her by the wrists, and tried to pull her out of bed. She looked at him closely, despite her terror, and noticed that the familiar figure was somewhat transparent. Nevertheless, he was real, and the touch of his hands was the touch of two strong hands.

There is no easy solution for this type of "unfinished business." Exorcism will yield results only if the other part is willing to accept it. But if the dead husband's moral level is not attuned to that approach, the service will not work. Only the woman herself can reject him, if she is strong enough in her determination to close this psychic door. For it is true that there may be a deep-seated desire present in the unconscious that permits the transgression to take place.

Sometimes the business the departing person wishes to complete cannot be finished until many years later. Yet there are cases where the dead communicator somehow knows this beforehand, indicating that the threshold of death removes also the limitations of time.

An interesting case in point concerns a prominent mid-western physician's wife, herself an educator. A number of years ago Mrs. B. was married to a professional gentleman. They had two children. Their marriage was happy, there were no financial or professional problems, and yet the husband was given to unaccountable depressions. One evening the husband went out, never to return. Hours went by. Mrs. B. anxiously awaited his return, although she had no suspicion that anything drastic had happened. Her husband had been in excellent spirits when he left. Finally she became too tired to sit up and wait for his return. She went to bed, assuming her husband would be coming in very late.

Her sleep was interrupted in the middle of the night by the feeling of a presence in the room. As she opened her eyes and looked, she discerned at the foot of her bed the form of her husband, and all at once she realized that he had gone across to the hereafter.

"You are not to worry," the husband spoke; "everything will be all right. Wally will take care of you and the children." The apparition vanished.

Early the next morning she was notified that he had fatally shot himself, evidently overcome by a fit of depression. In her great grief she tried to pass the visitation off as a dream, although she knew in her heart that she had been quite awake at the time she saw her husband standing at the foot of her bed.

Two years passed, and the matter sank into the deepest recesses of her subconscious mind. At the time of the message, she had not been able to make much of it. Wally was a dear friend of her late husband and herself but nothing more. Out of a clear blue sky the telephone rang one day, and before she picked up the receiver Mrs. B. *knew* it was Wally! The friendship was resumed and ultimately led to marriage, and Wally has indeed taken care of her and the children ever since!

Bernhard M., sixty-four, happily married, and a largely self-taught scholar, makes his home in Southern California. His literary criticism and philosophical essays have appeared largely in such scholarly publications as *Books Abroad*. A disability pension augments his income from writing. His mother,

Frances M., was a gifted musician who has always shown an interest in psychic research. When Mr. M. Senior, who had been with the San Francisco Symphony Orchestra, had passed on, the family went through difficult times, and young Bernhard had to work hard to keep the family in groceries. At the age of forty-two, Mrs. M. died of a stroke at her place of work, the Conservatory of Music and Drama in Point Loma, California.

A few days after her passing, Bernhard attended the funeral. At the time, he was told that the ashes would be placed in a niche in Greenwood Cemetery. With that reassurance, he left town. Returning to Point Loma from his business trip a month later, he had a strange dream. His late mother appeared to him in what seemed to be a small room, quite dark, and she seemed in great distress.

"Everything went wrong," she complained. "Even my ashes are mislaid!"

Her son remonstrated with her in his dream, assuring her that this could not be the case. But in reply she showed him a little table on which there was a wire basket containing a small copper box.

When he awoke the next morning, Bernhard M. rejected what he thought was an absurd dream brought on, no doubt, by his grief and recent upset over the death of his beloved brother. But it so happened he had planned on going into town to see if his mother's name had been properly inscribed on the door to the niche at the cemetery.

On the way he ran into a friend, May L., a singer, who informed him that she had just been to the cemetery to pay her respects to Mrs. M.—and his mother's ashes were not there!

On hearing this, Mr. M. asked Mrs. L. to return to the cemetery with him to make inquiry. Sure enough, his father's ashes were there, but his mother's were not. He questioned the caretaker, who checked the entries in his books.

"No record of a Mrs. M.," the caretaker informed him.

With mounting agony and anger, Bernhard M. went to the funeral parlor.

After some embarrassing investigations, it developed that the box of ashes had never left the building. Bernhard then took them personally out to the cemetery, to make sure everything would be as it should. By a strange quirk of fate, he traveled the identical route he had often taken with his mother when they had gone together to Point Loma.

When Mr. M. related this experience to me, he suddenly felt his mother's presence again, as if she were pleased at his having told me, so that others might know that the dead *can* return.

Florine McC.'s solid stone house, built on one of San Francisco's many hills in the year 1895, has withstood earthquakes and the big fire and is likely to withstand the next catastrophe, if one comes. Mrs. McC.'s brush with the uncanny started in 1929, when she was a newlywed living in Tampa, Florida. To everyone's surprise—including her own—she suffered an unexpected heart attack. A doctor was summoned to the home and, after examining her, pronounced her dead. A towel was then placed over her face and the doctor started to console the young husband.

"I'll have to pass the undertaker on the way, and I'll leave the death certificate there," the doctor said to her husband.

"But she's so young," the husband sighed, for Mrs. McC. was only nineteen at the time.

The strange part of it was that Mrs. McC. could hear the conversation, although she could not move. Despite the fact that her eyes were covered, she could *see* the entire scene. Moreover, she had the strangest sensation that she was about two inches high!

Then, it seemed to her, through her mouth came a replica of her own body, very small and without clothing. She went up to the corner of the ceiling and stayed there, looking down. She had left her body down below. The landlady had joined the mourners now, and young Mrs. McC. thought what fun it would be to wiggle her hands and frighten the woman. The thought of seeing the landlady scurry from the room in haste amused her. But then she became serious and suddenly dived down and reentered her own body through the nostrils, or so it seemed. Her physical body then became warm again, and she broke into an uncontrollable burst of laughter. Immediately the doctor proceeded to give her an injection to revive her. As soon as she was conscious she explained what had happened to her.

The doctor shook his head. But he listened with widening eyes when Mrs. McC. repeated every word that had been said during the time she had been "legally dead."

She had noticed, during her temporary stay at the ceiling, that the doctor had squeezed her arms, perhaps to bring her back to life, and she wondered if she would feel sore when she returned into her body. But the arms did not feel painful. A curious thought, though, kept intruding: "He forgot something. . . . Whoever was in charge forgot some duty I had to do, . . . but I don't understand it."

Perhaps that was why she was still alive. Someone forgot to pull a switch?

Throughout the years, Florine McC. displayed extrasensory abilities. These ranged from such simple things as foreknowledge of events or places where she had not been, to the more disturbing forebodings of trouble affecting her loved ones, and her subsequent ability to come to the aid of her troubled family.

Her father, Olaus S., born in Norway and brought to the United States at age two, was in the hotel business until his retirement many years later. He passed away in 1946 at age seventy-nine, after a full and satisfactory life.

About a month after his death, Mrs. McC. was in bed in her room on the fourth floor of the house on Grove Street, which had been her father's. She had not been asleep long when she was awakened by a knock at the door. She woke up, and to her amazement she saw her late father stick his head into the opened door, calling out in a cheery voice: "Hi there, Florence!"

Mrs. McC.'s baptismal name is Florence, but she has never liked it, preferring the form "Florine" instead. However, her father liked to tease her about it, and on such occasions he would call her Florence.

It was about two o'clock in the morning. Mr. S. entered the room of his daughter and stood near the bed, looking at her.

"You can't find it," he said.

Mrs. McC., fully awake now, observed her father's apparition. She noticed that he wore a tweed overcoat, his customary shirt and tie, and his hat. He removed the hat and put his hands into his pockets. The strange thing was that she could see *through* him, and he was surrounded by the most beautiful blue rays, lighting up the entire room.

"Dad, come over and sit down," she said, and pointed to the chaise longue. There was no fear, even though she was aware that he was dead. It seemed somehow perfectly natural to her now. Although she had heard of psychic matters, she had been raised in a house where such matters were neither discussed or believed.

The apparition walked over and sat on the chaise longue, putting his feet on a stool, as he had often done in life. This was his chair.

"You're looking for a paper, Florine," her father said.

"Yes, Dad," she nodded, "and I can't find it."

"You go down to my bedroom and take the top drawer out," her father instructed her, "and underneath the drawer you will find it pasted on. Also, honey, you will find a letter!" The voice sounded as normal and steady as her father's voice had always sounded.

"Dad, I'm going to cover you up," the daughter said, and she took a robe to place over his feet, as she had often done in his life.

The moment the robe touched her father's legs, the apparition disappeared—gone like a puff of smoke!

"Did I dream it?" she asked herself, wondering if it had really happened. She felt awake, but she was still not sure whether she was in the midst of a dream. She decided then and there, with the curious logic of dreamers who see themselves within the dream, not to touch anything and to go straight back to bed. This she did and quickly went off to sleep.

In the morning, she arose and inspected the room. The door, which she had closed firmly on retiring, was still ajar. Her robe was lying on the chaise longue. She looked closer and discovered that the material was still folded in a way that indicated that it had been supported by a pair of legs! She then knew she had not dreamed the visitation.

She ran downstairs and looked for the drawer her father had indicated. There, underneath, were the papers that had been missing. These papers proved her father's birth and nationality and were of great importance in the settling of the estate. There was also the letter he had mentioned, and it was a beautiful farewell letter from a father to his daughter. Throughout his long life, Olaus S. had never scoffed at the possibility of personal survival. The family took a dim view of Florine's experience, but the close communion father and daughter had always enjoyed during his lifetime was the reason she had been singled out for the visit—plus the fact that there was a real need, unfinished business, that only a visit from the deceased could bring to a close.

Chapter Eight

When the Dead Help the Living

WE HAVE SEEN HOW THE DEPARTED MANIFEST to the living to let them know that their lives continue in another world or because they have some unfinished business in the mundane sphere that needs completing. Having thus manifested, they will not communicate again unless a crisis comes up in the lives of their loved ones or friends and their services are perhaps "required." This is another category of communication, and it is one that also occurs frequently.

In many recorded instances, people who have died will nevertheless retain an interest in the affairs of those they have left behind. It is moot what drives them to do this. Is there a law over there that rewards them for shepherding or watching over their people? Are they doing it because virtue has its own rewards? Are they compelled to continue the bond from a motivation of ego importance? Do they want not to be left out of the continuing lives of their families? Or is it because the living so strongly need their help that they are drawn back to intercede by the very need for their intercession? I am rather inclined to think that there are set rules as to when there may be this kind of communication and how far they may go in warning the living of impending dangers or other future developments.

What this law is in detail is not easy to fathom, and even more difficult is the question of who originated the law and who created the originator. Suffice it to establish rationally and methodically that the law exists and that there are bona fide instances of an interest taken in the affairs of the living by their dead.

This interest can take many forms, but the common denominator is always the fact that the communication results in some benefit to the living from the knowledge obtained through the communication. This may be a warning of disaster or a foretelling of events to come that cannot be changed, but if one knows what is in store ahead of time, the blow is softened for him.

The interest in the living may be less striking and merely gently supervisory, a part of seeing how things are going or of encouraging a depressed person. It is not at all like a Big Brother feeling, with the invisibles watching you, but it gives a warm, comfortable impression that one is not alone and that forces greater than oneself *care*.

Thus this interest is an expression of love, and as such it is certainly a positive force, far from frightening or dangerous.

The living who are fortunate enough to have a deceased relative take an interest in their lives should accept this as natural and live with it. They should not defer decisions to the spiritual watchdog, of course, but make their own mundane decisions as they feel best. Nevertheless, sometimes the greater knowledge of the ones beyond the veil can help the living understand their own problems better and thus provide them with ammunition for a better judgment.

Mrs. Harry C. lives near a large city in Pennsylvania. Of Irish-English ancestry, she was born in North Carolina and came from an old family that was given a land grant there by George III. The psychic gift was not unknown in her family, mainly on her mother's side. After a year in college, Mrs. C. became a trained practical nurse. She married a soldier from Pennsylvania in 1945 and over the years bore five sons.

Although she had had clairvoyant experiences from time to time, it was not until she was eleven years old that she received a visit from the beyond. At that time an aunt was living with her family to look after the children while their mother worked. Thus it happened that in her childhood Mrs. C. spent many hours with her aunt; they read and sewed together, and there was a strong bond between them. Until the aunt died, Mrs. C. had shared a room with her mother, but after the death of the aunt she was given her aunt's bedroom. A few weeks after the funeral, Mrs. C., then eleven, was sitting on the porch of the house when she heard her name being called. She glanced up and saw her late aunt standing in the door, holding it ajar.

"Gretchen, will you please come in here for a moment. I have something to tell you," the aunt said in the same tone of voice Mrs. C. had heard her use while alive. Obediently and not at all frightened, the eleven-year-old girl put down her sewing and followed her beckoning aunt into the house. But as she started to go in, the apparition slowly faded away! What did the aunt want to tell her little companion? That life continued and that she still cared how the family was?

A few weeks after this incident, a girlfriend of Gretchen's by the name of Maxine F. stopped in so that they might attend a movie together. Just as the two girls were about to leave, Mrs. C. heard her name being called. All set to go to the movie, she decided to ignore this. But the voice called again: "Gretchen! Gretchen!"

"Your mother's calling you," Maxine said, and waited.

So the two children went back to the kitchen, where Gretchen's mother was washing dishes. The mother had not called her. Other than the three of them, the house was empty at the time. But Gretchen knew her late aunt was calling her.

As the days went on, the aunt continued to make her presence felt in the house. She was not about to be abandoned at the cemetery but insisted on continuing with her duties—and rights—in the household. At night, Gretchen would hear someone drumming fingernails on the table. This was a lifelong habit of her aunt's. Often she would awaken to see the aunt standing at the foot of her bed, looking at her. Gretchen was by no means alone in observing these phenomena. A friend of her mother's by the name of Mary L. once occupied the same room. She too heard the drumming of the invisible fingernails.

It also fell to Gretchen to go through her late aunt's effects. This was a very difficult task. On certain days she felt her aunt's overpowering presence hovering over her, taking a keen interest in what she was doing. When the pressure became too great, Gretchen threw her aunt's old letters down and ran out of the house for a breath of fresh air. Somehow she knew her aunt would not follow her there.

Many years later, when Gretchen had become Mrs. Harry C., she and her husband occupied a house in Pennsylvania. At first Mrs. C. thought they had acquired a "resident ghost," something left over from the past of one of the earlier owners of the house. The house itself had been built in 1904 as part of a "company town" for the Westinghouse Corporation. The houses then were occupied by workers of that corporation, but in the 1920s the company decided to get out of the real estate business, and the houses reverted to individual ownership. A number of tenants then occupied the house in succession. Several ladies had died on the third floor of the house, center of the psychic manifestations during the time Mr. and Mrs. C. occupied the dwelling. But none of these people had died violently or were part of a tragic situation of the kind that may sometimes create a ghostly phenomenon. Of course, the early history of the house when it was a company property could not be checked out as there were no records kept of the tenants during that time. Mrs. C. thought that perhaps one of the early owners of the house had been the victim of a tragedy and that it was the restless shade of that person that was staying on. Her belief was reinforced by the fact that since her childhood and the encounters with her late aunt, she had not experienced anything so strong in the other houses they had lived in. But her clairvoyance had been active elsewhere, and she has never been entirely without some form of ESP experience.

The phenomena were mainly footsteps on the third floor of the house and someone walking down the stairs when the occupants knew no one was up there. In 1961 Mrs. C. learned that their unseen guest was a woman. One of her boys was in delicate health and had major surgery when only seven weeks old. One night Mrs. C. woke up to hear the baby crying. At the same time, however, she became aware of another voice, someone singing softly as if to quiet the baby. Wondering who it might be, Mrs. C. rose and went into the baby's room.

There, near the crib, stood a lady. She was a small woman with a lovely face, dressed in what seemed World War I clothes and hairstyle. The dress was pale lavender trimmed with black braid and filigree buttons. It had a lace bodice and jabot and a hobble skirt in the manner of the turn-of-the-century clothes.

Far from being terrified by the stranger, Mrs. C. stepped closer. When she approached the crib, the lady smiled and stepped to one side to let her pass so that she might tend the baby. When she looked up again, the lady was gone. The visitor's presence was no longer required; the mother had come to look after her own.

After that first time, she saw the lady several times—sometimes in the baby's room, sometimes going up and down the third-floor stairs. Later Mrs C. had another baby, and the stranger also occupied herself with the new arrival, as if tending babies were something very natural and dear to her. But who could she possibly be?

When Mrs. C.'s five-year-old son was sick in the fall of 1967, he once asked his mother who the strange lady was who had come and sung to him, and he proceeded to describe her. Mrs. C. had never discussed her own experiences with the boy, but she knew at once that he too had seen the lady upstairs.

By this time it began to dawn on her that perhaps this lady was not a "resident ghost" but a deceased relative continuing an interest in her family. But she could not be sure one way or the other, and there the matter stood when her oldest son Lonnie and his wife Sally came to spend their Christmas weekend with her in 1967. Sally is a registered nurse by profession and scientifically minded. For that reason Mrs. C. had not seen fit to discuss psychic experiences with her or to tell her of the unusual goings-on on the third floor of the house.

It so happened that the young couple were put into the third-floor bedroom for the weekend. Because they were both tired from the trip, Mrs. C. thought it best to put them up there, as far removed from street noises as possible. The room is rather large, with one bed on each side and a dormer window between the two beds. The daughter-in-law took one bed, the son the other. They were soon fast asleep.

On Saturday morning Lonnie, the son, came down first for breakfast. He and his mother were having coffee in the kitchen when Sally arrived. She looked rather pale and haggard. After Mrs. C. had poured her a cup of coffee, Sally looked at her mother-in-law.

"Mom, did you come up to the room for any reason during the night?"

"Of course not," Mrs. C. replied.

"Did *you* get up during the night, Lonnie?" Sally turned to her husband. He assured her that he had not budged all night.

"Well," the girl said, swallowing hard, "then I have something strange to tell you."

She had been awakened in the middle of the night by a voice calling her name. Fully awake, she saw a lady standing beside her bed. She was not sure how the apparition disappeared, but eventually she went back to sleep, being very tired. Nothing further happened. What she had seen, she was sure of. That it was not a dream—that, too, she knew for a fact. But who was the stranger? The two young people left a couple of days later, and nothing further was said about the incident.

About three weeks after Christmas, Mrs. C. went to North Carolina to spend a week at her mother's home. During a conversation, Mrs. C.'s mother mentioned that she had recently been going through some things in an old trunk in the attic. Among many other items, she had found a small photograph of her grandmother that she did not know she had. If Mrs. C. wanted it she would be happy to give it to her, especially as Grandmother L. had always shown a special interest in her family.

Mrs. C. thanked her mother and took the little photograph home with her to Pennsylvania. In her own home she propped it up on the dresser in her room, until she could find a proper frame for it. But after it had stood there for a couple of days, Mrs. C. thought that the old photograph might become soiled and decided to put it away in the top dresser drawer.

That night Mrs. C. was almost asleep when she became aware of a humming sound in the room. She opened her eyes and noticed that the air in her room was as thick as fog and she could scarcely see the opposite side of the room. In a moment, her grandmother walked in from the hall and stood beside her bed. Mrs. C., now fully awake, raised herself up on one elbow so that the apparition would know she was awake and observing her. Immediately the figure turned and put one hand on Mrs. C.'s dresser, on exactly the spot where the picture had been until two days ago. Then she turned her head and looked directly at Mrs. C. Somehow Mrs. C. understood what her grandmother wanted. She got out of bed and took the picture from the drawer and put it back on top of the dresser again. With that the apparition smiled and walked out of the room. The air cleared, and the humming stopped.

Mrs. C. had been "aware" of her grandmother's presence in the house for some time but never in so definite a way. She knew that Grandmother L. still considered herself one of the family and took a keen interest in the living. That is why she had appeared to Mrs. C.'s daughter-in-law Sally, not to frighten her or even to ask for anything or because of any unfinished business, but merely to let her know she *cared*.

As a member of the household, Grandmother L. had naturally felt a bit hemmed in when her picture was relegated to a stuffy drawer. Especially as she had probably instigated its rediscovery to begin with! Until the picture turned up, Mrs. C. could not have been sure who the lady was. But now that she realized she had her own grandmother to protect her family, Mrs. C. did not mind at all. With help being scarce these days, and expensive and unreliable, it was rather comforting to know that an unpaid relative was around to look out for the well-being of the family.

But the lady did not show up after the incident with the photograph. Could it be that, like Lohengrin, once she was recognized her usefulness to the Cs. had come to an end?

Mrs. Betty S., a California housewife, has not the slightest interest in the psychic. When her father passed away in 1957 she mourned him, but since he left his wife well provided for, she did not worry unduly about her mother, even though they lived in different cities. Shortly after, she had a vision of her late father so real that she felt it could not have been a dream. Dream or vision, there stood her father wearing a white shirt and blue pants. He looked radiant and alive.

"Is mother all right?" he asked.

Mrs. S. assured her father everything was just fine. The apparition went away. But a few days later Mrs. S.'s mother was on the telephone. She was in great distress. Someone had been in her bank deposit box, and two valuable deeds had disappeared without a trace! In addition, money and bonds had also been taken, making her position anything but financially secure.

All at once Mrs. S. realized why her late father had been concerned. Evidently he knew or sensed something she had not yet become aware of.

Her father never reappeared to her. But the missing two deeds mysteriously returned to the deposit box about three months later. To this day this is a puzzle Mrs. S. has not been able to solve. But it was comforting to know that her late father had continued to care for her mother.

It is well known that often grandparents get very attached to the offspring of their children. When death separates a grandparent from the third generation, a desire to look in on them can be very strong. Consider the case of Mrs. Carol S. of Massachusetts.

In 1963 her first son was born. On one of the first nights after her return from the hospital, she awoke in the night to see a misty light near the ceiling of her room. It hovered between the baby's bassinet and the foot of the bed. A moment later the light took the form of her late grandfather's face and continued to glow. At the same time, Mrs. S. had the impression her grandfather had come to see his first great-grandchild.

She herself had been a first grandchild, and her mother had been the grandfather's firstborn; the interest would have been understandable. For a moment the face remained, then it drifted into a fog and soon disappeared altogether.

In 1969, Mrs. S.'s other grandfather—on her father's side of the family—also passed away. A little later her grandmother gave his bed to Mrs. S. The first night her six-year-old son slept in it, he reported a strange "dream."

His great-grandfather had come to him and told him he lived in heaven and was happy and could look down and see him. This "dream" was strange because the boy had no knowledge that the bed he slept in had any connection with the great-grandfather.

Mrs. Joseph B., a housewife living in a medium-sized eastern city, a member of the Girl Scout council, a Sunday school teacher, and a busy, average person with a good, healthy mind, has no time for fantasies or daydreaming. Of Pennsylvania Dutch background, she is married to a steelworker of Italian antecedents. Her hobbies are bowling and reading, not psychic research.

She and her husband and son shared a house, while her mother lived across town by herself. But every ten days or so her mother would visit them. The mother was familiar with the house and would always let herself in by the front door. These visits became a normal routine, and the years went by peacefully until the mother died. She was not forgotten, but neither did the B. family go into deep mourning. Her death was simply accepted as a natural occurrence, and life went on.

One year after her passing, Mr. and Mrs. B. were getting ready for bed upstairs in their house. Their son was fast asleep in his room. The time was 1 A.M. Mr. B. was in the bathroom, and Mrs. B. had just gotten into bed, looking forward to a good night's sleep. Tomorrow was Saturday, and they could sleep longer.

At this moment she heard the downstairs front door of the house open. Her husband, who had evidently heard it also, came to the bathroom door and said: "I thought I heard someone come in."

"So did I," replied Mrs. B., and she called downstairs: "Who's down there?"

Her mother's voice came back. "It's only me; don't come down—I'm not staying!" Then they heard her familiar steps resounding through the house as she walked about and finally left by the back door.

As if it were the most ordinary thing in the world for her mother to visit them at 1 A.M., the husband returned to the bathroom, and Mrs. B. went back to bed. The power of the routine they had grown accustomed to over the years had left them immune to Mother's visits as being anything but routine. They were both tired and fell asleep soon afterward. In the morning, Mr. B. looked at the doors, both the front and the rear doors. They were locked *from the inside*, just as he had left them the previous night before retiring! As Mrs. B came down for breakfast he silently pointed at the door. It was then that it hit them with sudden impact that the mother had been dead for just a year.

They talked it over. Both agreed that the voice they had heard had been the mother's voice and that it had sounded the same as it used to. Evidently this was Mother's way of saying she was still visiting them. Nothing more was heard from her for a long time. Perhaps she had other things to do or found her new world more intriguing.

But on January 9, 1967, Mrs. B.'s older sister woke up to hear her mother calling her urgently. She immediately got out of bed to answer her mother, completely forgetting for the moment that her mother had been dead for all those years. Three times the voice called, and the tone was one of great distress. Was she trying to tell her something, and if so, what?

The following night, Mrs. B.'s sister found out. Her husband died quite suddenly. Perhaps her mother had tried to soften the blow by forewarning her.

Not every communication from the dead is welcomed by the living. A certain percentage of superstitious people might even consider such contacts evil or devil-inspired or dangerous. Otherwise rational people refuse the proffered hand from beyond the grave. They don't doubt that their loved ones continue to exist in another world. They just don't want those loved ones around in *theirs*.

A Mrs. Marge C. in New Jersey has had trouble with her grandfather for years. It all started when he was dying in the local hospital and asked to see her. Although she had not been really close to him, it was his dying wish; yet her mother did not grant it. Soon after, she felt a strange chill. Later she realized that it had occurred at the very moment of his passing, but she did not know it at the time.

Still a little girl, Marge was present when her uncle and aunt brought their new baby home with them. She happened to look up, and there at the back door stood her grandfather, watching. As he noticed her look, he reached out to her. But instead of compassion for the old man, she only felt terror at the thought.

A little later, one evening as she was getting ready for bed she heard someone calling her. This was peculiar because she was home *alone*. But she went downstairs to the kitchen. There was her grandfather, gazing at her. She yelled in fright, and he vanished.

The next time the unwelcome visitor made an appearance she was sixteen. This time she was at a girlfriend's house and happened to glance out the window at a quiet moment. There was Grandfather again, looking at her from outside. She still did not want any part of the manifestations.

Just before she met her husband in 1965 she saw her grandfather again. He reached for her and tried to speak, but she yelled and fainted. Perhaps the grandfather got the message that appearing in all his celestial glory was frightening to his granddaughter; at any rate he did not come back again. But the problem was by no means solved. Frequently Marge could sense him around and hear him call out to her. Even her husband heard the voice and of course could understand it. Finally, Marge took her problem to her mother to find out why her grandfather was so insistent. Her mother had been his favorite child, it seems, and Marge, ever since she was born, had grown into the image of her mother. Was that the reason her grandfather wanted to communicate with her?

I explained the possible reasons to Mrs. C. and asked her to be understanding toward her grandfather. I never heard anything further from her, so perhaps Grandfather has given up.

Dr. Lucia B., a medical doctor specializing in cancer research and a graduate of a leading European university, has had a distinguished medical career as a chest specialist. A vivacious lady, she speaks several languages. Her parents moved from her native Vienna to Prague, where her father was editor and publisher of a group of magazines. Later her father lived in Berlin, where he ran a successful publishing house.

Dr. B. is married to a retired Italian army general and lives in an apartment on New York's West Side. She has lived in the United States on and off since 1932. Prior to that, she was a physician with the Health Department of Puerto Rico. Her major contribution to medicine, she feels, was the discovery of the enzyme that inhibits the cancer cells of the respiratory system. Unfortunately the New York climate did not agree with her, and when I met her she was ready to pull up stakes again and return to Italy.

Dr. B. came to my study in New York to talk about some unusual psychic experiences she wanted explained. As a medical doctor, she had a certain reluctance to accept these events at face value, and yet, as an observant and brilliantly logical individual, she knew that what had happened to her was perfectly real and not the result of an overactive hallucinatory imagination.

In 1940, when the first of these astounding events took place, Lucia B. lived at the famous Villa Horace in Tivoli, Italy. World War II was on, and her husband was on active duty as a major in the Italian army. They had just been transferred to Tivoli and lived at the villa, which was then the property of an Englishwoman whom the Fascists did not touch because she had lived among the Italians for a very long time. Dr. B. was and is a U.S. citizen, and there was some concern felt for her status. But for the moment no overt move had been made against her, and as the wife of an Italian officer she seemed safe for the time being, especially since the United States had not yet entered the war.

In May of that year, the Englishwoman left for two days to visit friends. Major B. had gone off to Civitavecchia to get some briefings at the military academy, leaving Dr. B. all alone for a day. She decided to make good use of her "freedom" to go to nearby Rome the next morning for a full day's visit. It was a beautiful, warm evening, and there was one of those marvelous early summer sunsets Italy is famous for. Dr. B. stood by her windows and looked out into the landscape, unusually happy despite the heavy clouds of war all around her.

They had a pet turkey, which she went to visit in the downstairs portion of the villa. The house, built upon the original Roman foundations and incorporating much of the ancient house, is one of the great historical attractions of the area and is listed in most guidebooks. After a brief visit with the bird, she returned to her quarters and went to bed in a serene frame of mind.

She had left word to be awakened at 7 A.M. This was to be the duty of Gino, her husband's young aide-de-camp. But she was aroused from deep sleep at 6 A.M. not by Gino but by Oscar, Gino's orderly.

"Wake up—it's six o'clock," he said, and shook her.

Dr. Barrett was upset at this unusual treatment. "But it's supposed to be at seven," she countered, "and not you, but Gino's supposed to wake me. What are you doing in here? Get out!"

With that, the orderly fled, and Dr. B. tried to go back to sleep. But she could not. She got up and opened the shutters that let in the light of the already bright day. Then she opened the door that led to a long, spacious room called the mensa that was used as a mess hall. There was a chapel within the walls of the villa, and a row of benches formerly in the chapel had been placed along the walls of this long room so that people might sit there and pray, or just rest. Dr. B. stepped into the mess hall. On one of the first bench seats she saw a man sitting. It was her father, and then she realized why the orderly had awakened her out of turn: to let her know that her father had arrived.

"So you're not dead after all," she said, and went over to greet him.

Her father had left New York in October 1938 and gone back to Prague. In February of the following year she received a telegram from her father's mistress advising her briefly that her father had died and had been buried. There were some suspicious circumstances surrounding his death, Dr. B. learned later when she went to Prague to investigate. It was not a natural death, and there were witnesses who said he was afraid that he was being poisoned. But there was nothing she could do. Prague was already German-occupied, and it was difficult to open old wounds. She could not locate the ashes, but she did find the man who had signed her late father's death certificate. He freely admitted that he had not examined the body, but the death had occurred on the day the Nazis took over Czechoslovakia, so he took it for granted that it was suicide as he had "been told." Dr. B. has always suspected her father was "done in" through a plot involving a mistress, but she cannot prove it. She left Prague again, sure only that her father was indeed no longer alive.

But there he was, exactly as he used to look in the happy days when they went hiking into the mountains together. He was dressed in a brown tweed suit, a suit her mother had loathed because it was so old. His head was bent down, and at first she did not see his face. He wore a wide-brimmed hat.

"You're here," Dr. B. exclaimed. "I knew you weren't dead!"

For the moment she had forgotten all about her trip to Prague and the certainty of his demise. But she was otherwise awake and alert, and the day was already very bright.

She knelt down to look into his face and noticed how worn his suit was. He was as solid a man as ever, nothing transparent or vague about him. She started to talk to him in a voice filled with joy. He lifted his head somewhat, and the hat moved back up on his head a little. Now she could see his forehead and face more clearly, and she noticed that his skin was *greenish*.

"You must have been ill," she said, puzzled by this strange color. "Or have you been a prisoner?"

He answered her in a voice that came from his lips with great difficulty. "Yes," he said, "they let me sit in the sun so you would not get so scared."

(A materialization in full daylight requires a great deal of power and preparation, I thought, and is not at all common. But evidently the people arranging this strange encounter had seen a way to bring it off successfully.)

Dr. B. did not grasp the meaning of his remark. "You've been sick," she repeated. "Who brought you?"

Her father pointed to the rear of the huge room. Dr. B. looked in that direction. There were six other benches behind the one her father sat on, and then there was a buffet where the soldiers quartered in the house would eat, and beyond that, next to a wide open door, she saw standing Dr. K., a friend of both her father and herself. At the time she saw this man, he was living in New York, but as it dawned upon her that her father was a visitor from the other side, she asked him whether Dr. K. was also dead.

His reply came in a faltering voice, the way an invalid might speak. "No. *They* brought me."

Dr. B. looked again and saw behind the erect figure of Dr. K. five yellow-skinned people of small stature, apparently East Indians. They stood at a short distance from the doctor in a respectful position and were dressed in dark clothes.

"Who are these men?" she asked.

"They are from Java," her father replied. "They brought me here."

This did not make any sense whatever. She took her father's hand into her own now. It felt like ice. Now she realized that her intuitive feeling a moment before had been right.

"You are ——— ?"

He nodded.

"Why did you come? There must be a reason for it."

"Yes, there is."

"Am I in danger?"

"Yes," he replied, "you are. You must join the mountaineers."

"I must *what*?"

"Go over the mountains," her father admonished. "You must get guides."

This made very little sense, but before she could question her dead father further, he added: "When you're on the ship, these Javanese will look after you."

"But I don't need to be looked after."

"They'll watch you during the sea voyage," he repeated in a tired, faraway tone of voice.

At this moment, Gino the aide-de-camp who was supposed to wake her at 7 A.M., burst through the door. Seeing her already up and about, he became agitated.

"Who are all these people?" he demanded. Evidently he too could see them! "Who opened the gates for them?"

As Gino thundered into the mess hall, Dr. B.'s attention was momentarily distracted by him. When she looked back to her father, he had vanished! She glanced toward the other end of the room and found the Javanese and Dr. K. had also disappeared.

She explained that Oscar had awakened her an hour earlier. Gino swore he would punish the orderly for doing this and left immediately. Fifteen minutes later Gino returned rather sheepishly. It seemed that Oscar was supposed to get up at 5 A.M. but did not. No matter how the soldiers tried to rouse him, he would not wake up but seemed to be in a strange stupor. He was still asleep when Gino saw him, and there was no question that he had never set foot into the mensa room that morning!

Evidently Oscar was a physical medium, and it was his "substance" those in charge of "arrangements" had borrowed to make the materialization of Dr. B.'s father possible.

An additional proof that it was not the real Oscar but only a projection or simulation of the orderly that had awakened her at 6 A.M. could be seen in the fact that the keys to the outer gates were still in Gino's possession. No one else had a set of keys, and yet the doors were open when Gino arrived! They could not be opened from the inside; only with a key put into the lock from outside the gates could they be opened.

A long succession of soldiers testified that Oscar had never left his bed. At 7:10 A.M. he was still unconscious, and awoke only much later in the day.

When questioned by his superiors and Dr. B., Oscar was as mystified as they were. He recalled absolutely nothing and had never had a similar experience before.

"I should have known something was odd when he touched me and shook me violently to awaken me," Dr. B. said as an afterthought. "In Italy that sort of thing just isn't done—you don't touch the *Signora*."

The real Oscar, of course, would never have dared to, but apparently the astrally projected Oscar, perhaps under the control of another will, *had* to awaken her in order for her to receive the message her father had brought. It seemed to me like a wonderfully well-organized psychic plot.

With all the commotion, Dr. B. had completely forgotten she had to catch the eight o'clock train to Rome. Getting hold of her emotions, she made the train just in time. When her husband returned two days later, she did not tell him about the incident. It wasn't the sort of thing an Italian officer would accept, she felt, and she thought it best to put it aside. Time would tell if there was something to all this.

Two months later her husband left for the war in earnest. This left her alone at the villa, and as the Germans took over more and more in Italy she was advised by the U.S. consul to leave the country. But just as she was ready to leave for Switzerland, the Italian government confiscated her passport. Marriages between Italian officers and foreigners were dissolved, leaving her in even greater difficulties.

All this time her husband was fighting somewhere in Greece, and she had very little news of him. There was a hint she might wind up in a detention camp. She decided to leave while she could.

"Go over the mountains," a friend suggested, and suddenly it hit her what her father had meant.

Twice she was unsuccessful. The third time she succeeded and wound up in a French prison for two months. As she was a good skier, she had crossed the Little St. Bernard pass on skis. However, in order not to get caught and sent back again she had taken a guide. Just as her dead father had predicted she would!

Her mother in New York arranged for her to come back and got her to Lisbon, where she was to take a boat. Through a highly placed acquaintance in Washington her mother arranged for passage aboard a tiny vessel never meant for the Atlantic passage. The boat belonged to a Portuguese industrialist, and there were just twelve cabins aboard.

The yacht was named the *Cavalho Arrujo*, or Red Horse, and it took twenty-one days to cross the ocean. When the ship reached the Azores, a Dutch radioman and five Javanese crewmen from a torpedoed Dutch ship were taken aboard. Evidently they had been torpedoed by the Germans and taken blindfolded to the Azores, then neutral. In a rare gesture of humanitarianism the Germans left them there to be rescued and sent home.

From the very first, the five Javanese attached themselves to Dr. B., watching over her just as her father had told her they would. They looked exactly as they had appeared to her in the glimpse into the future her father had given at the villa in Tivoli!

After she landed in New York and joined her mother, she never saw the Javanese crewmen again. They vanished as quickly and quietly as they had entered her life.

Just as soon as she could, she looked up Dr. K. She was sure he would not believe her, but she was determined to tell him what she had seen.

To her amazement Dr. K., a celebrated biochemist, did not scoff. They compared the time differential to determine where he had been at the time she had seen him in Tivoli. He had been at work in his New York lab and had felt nothing special at the time.

Since there was no close connection between Dr. B. and Dr. K., she was puzzled as to why her father had "shown" him to her at the time of his visit. But Dr. K. represented New York to her father, and perhaps this was his way of saying: "You'll get to New York."

Since Dr. K. did not project his image to Italy, I can only assume that what Dr. B. saw was a simulation—that is, a materialization created by the same powers that arranged for her father's temporary return. Ectoplasm can be molded in many ways, and as Dr. B. did not actually speak to the Javanese and to the Dr. K. she saw in Tivoli, they might also have been merely projections or visions. Whatever the technique of their amazing appearances, the purpose was clear: to give her a glimpse into the future.

Her father never contacted her again after her safe return to the United States.

Dr. B.'s encounters with the supernormal have been rare and far between, but whatever experiences she has had were unusually vivid. Shortly after her marriage she was spending some time alone in a summer resort not far from Venice, where she and her husband were living at the time. Two days before she was to rejoin her husband in the city, she was dressing for dinner. It was the last Sunday, and she was putting on her fanciest evening gown for the occasion. It was a warm June evening. She was sitting in front of the dresser, and as she bent forward to put on her lipstick, she suddenly saw in the mirror that *two candles* were burning behind her. She turned around, but there were no candles in back of her. She looked back into the mirror, and there were the two candles again! Back and forth her head went, and the candles were still there—but only in the mirror.

"It must be some kind of reflection," she said to herself aloud and rose to look for the original candles. She examined first the windows, then the doors and walls, but there was no possible way in which two burning candles could appear in her mirror. Disquieted, she sat down again and looked. Perhaps it was only her imagination. But the two candles were back again! Only this time one of the candles flickered, and the flame moved a little.

It was seven o'clock. She was hungry and thought: "I've got to go down. I don't care, candles or no candles."

No sooner had she thought this than she heard a voice behind her—a woman's voice, speaking in Italian.

"Promise me never to abandon him!"

"Of course not," she replied, without thinking how a disembodied voice could suddenly sound in her room. She turned around. There was no one there!

She wondered: Who was she never to abandon? It could only be her husband, Alberto.

She decided she had had enough unusual experiences for one day and left the room. Coming down the stairs, she was met on the second floor by her husband, racing up to meet her. He seemed upset.

"What is it?" she asked.

"Mother died. I've just come from her funeral." Tears streamed down his face. He had not wished to alarm her or to allow his grief to interfere with their vacation. His mother had been buried the day before, and he thought it best to come and tell her personally rather than to telephone.

The voice Dr. B. had heard had been her mother-in-law's.

Years later the request made strange sense to her. Between 1941 and 1945, when she was in New York, her husband was a prisoner of the Germans. She had no contact with him and knew nothing about his fate. The Red Cross told her that he had died, so legally she could remarry after five years. But the voice of a mother from beyond the grave stuck in her mind, and she realized what the voice had meant; she never abandoned her husband, and eventually she was reunited with him.

Loved ones or known members of one's family are not the only ones who communicate with the living. Sometimes a total stranger may do so.

Before the war, Dr. B. spent some time vacationing in Arosa, Switzerland. She stayed at a modest pension at the time, as it was toward the end of her vacation and she was beginning to run low on funds. Her room was on one of the upper floors.

She had just rung for her breakfast, which the maid would very shortly bring her. But before this happened, the door was flung open, and a woman burst into her room. She wore a kind of negligee, and her black hair was flying behind her in disorder. Out of breath, the woman demanded: "You must tell him. It is very important! Please tell him!"

Her hands moved with great agitation. Dr. B. was annoyed by the intrusion. She eyed the woman coolly and asked her to leave the room, assuming the woman had stepped into her room in error. The woman had spoken German.

"*Raus!*" Dr. B. said, and the girl tried once again to implore her to "tell him." Then she *backed out* of the room by sliding backward.

The next moment the maid came into the room carrying the breakfast tray. "Who was that crazy woman who just came in?" Dr. B. demanded.

"What woman? There is no one else on this floor."

"But she was just here this minute."

"Impossible. You're the only one on this floor. There is no one left. After all, this is the end of the season." The maid shook her head and left, wondering about the good doctor.

It was late, so Dr. B. did not bother to make inquiries at the desk downstairs about the strange visitor. She took her skis and went out to the slope. She had a favorite spot on the mountain where she could enjoy a marvelous view of the surrounding countryside. She could not get up there fast enough this morning. As she approached the spot, she suddenly saw a man coming toward her from behind some trees.

"May I join you?" he said. He looked like a nice young man and she was not afraid, but she told the young man as gracefully as she could that she was a married woman.

"No, no, it's nothing like that," he assured her. "I just want to talk to you for moment."

He was a physician from Zurich whose first practice had been here in Arosa. At that time he had treated a young woman for advanced tuberculosis. When he first saw the patient, she was a great beauty. They were almost instantly in love, but to his horror he realized that she had only a short time to live. The girl was only eighteen at the time, and he was a young doctor just starting out. But he would not accept this verdict and decided he could somehow change her fate.

"I'm going to die," the girl said. But the young doctor asked for her hand in marriage and, despite her parents' objection, insisted on marrying her. Since both the doctor's family and the girl's people were well off financially, he gladly signed the waiver as to her fortune and promised in addition to take care of her, no matter what.

Dr. B. listened to the story with keen interest. He asked her to accompany him a bit farther and showed her a small chalet where he and his bride had spent their honeymoon. Everything had been brand-new. He had bought the chalet for her, and it looked for a while as though the dire predictions about her death would not come true. Months went by, and her condition, far from worsening, gradually improved.

The doctor spent every moment of his time with her, completely putting aside his career and never leaving her. But when she seemed to be improving so much, he decided he should see a few of his patients again. He thought it safe and did not think she would die now.

One day there was an emergency in the village. An accident occurred, and he was called. While he was gone, something strange must have happened to the girl. Suddenly she left the chalet and came running down the winding road to the village in sheer terror. Whether it was a sudden realization that her protector was not by her side for a few hours or because of some inexplicable worsening of her condition, no one knew. She came running down the hill after him. When she got to the little pension, her physical strength gave out. Her disease-ridden lungs could not stand the great strain of running. Collapsing in the pension, she was carried to one of the rooms upstairs, where she died without ever seeing her husband again.

"One of the rooms?" Dr. B. asked. "On the third floor?"

The young man nodded.

She then described her experience of that morning to him.

"That's she, all right," the young man acknowledged sadly. "Wasn't she beautiful?"

Every year the young physician would come to Arosa on the anniversary of her death, always hoping to find out why she had run out of their chalet.

Today was that day.

After a moment of reflection, Dr. B. told the young man that she too was a physician. It pleased him to know this, and he asked her whether she had read anything in the wraith's face that might have indicated the nature of her fears. Had she seen death approaching, and did she not want to go without her husband by her side? Or was it something else, something they might never know, that drove her to undertake her fatal dash?

Dr. B. conjectured that perhaps the girl discovered she was pregnant and wanted her husband to know right away. But there was a telephone in the chalet, and the doctor had told his wife where he was going. She could have reached him at the scene of the accident, or she might have waited for his return.

Two days later, Dr. B. left Arosa and never returned to the little pension. But the young man probably continues to come back on the anniversary of the day when his loved one was taken from him. And on the third floor of the pension a tragedy will be enacted once a year, a tragedy involving a beautiful girl with flying black hair, until the two lovers meet for good in the land beyond the veil.

Chapter Nine

How to Make Contact
with the Dead

THE DESIRE TO CALL UP UNCLE JOE IN the great beyond is as old as humanity. All the weaknesses inherent in such a daring proposition must be traced to the eagerness to make a contact *from this end* rather than waiting for contact to happen, naturally and of necessity, from the other end of the "line."

Of course, not everybody considers it proper to make contact with deceased relatives; some people hold peculiar views about the propriety of such attempts. This is partly due to religious pressures and ingrained prejudices and partly due to fear of the unknown. However, there is a substantial segment of the population that considers such contacts not only proper but even desirable. Their motives vary from greed to genuine spiritual curiosity. There isn't a day when my mail does not bring a request for an introduction to a good medium. The purpose is always personal; the goal is always some sort of contact with a loved one. People want to know about their future, and the loved ones are asked advice on the doubtful premise that a dead person might know more than a living one.

This does not follow. Passage into the nonphysical world creates no sages. It does not make angels out of sinners or saints out of good people merely because they happen to be dead.

Death does not purify, but it does allow willing souls to learn something new, something the soul probably did not know until then: namely, that life continues and that a person's consciousness can be expanded over there precisely as it can over here, if the person is interested. *Some* individuals attain a higher degree of knowledge after their death, and this includes foreknowledge of future events. This happens because in the nonphysical world the time and space barrier preventing everyday precognition on earth does not exist. Events shape up independently, and a clear-eyed person can look ahead into time and possibly speak to a living relative about it. But it does not follow that *all* dead can do this or that being dead helps them to do this if the personal desire to learn is not present.

Among simple people there has grown up an almost mystical belief in the supernatural powers of the dead, as if they were an army of soldiers ready to interfere in the lives of the flesh-and-blood world. Nothing could be further from the truth. The only difference between the living and the dead is the degree of density of their bodies and, consequently, the greater maneuverability of the spiritual body in comparison with the clumsy physical "encasement."

To seek contact with the dead, therefore, is a matter for only well-adjusted individuals to undertake. It is particularly ill suited for the neurotic or newly bereaved, at least without proper instruction by a psychic researcher. The dangers are twofold. To begin with, people unable to accept the loss of a loved one may place too much emphasis on the life beyond and abandon themselves to a concept for which they are not prepared. The physical body must have its due, and the dead cannot ever take the place of the living in human relations. A bereaved person might substitute a strong bond with the dead for the continuing search for relationships among the living, which nature has intended.

The concept of bereavement is a false notion that death is a disaster and a final, destructive event beyond which lies nothing but despair. Some religions encourage this view in order to keep a firmer hold upon the living while they are able to contribute spiritually—and materially—to the welfare of the church.

The religious do this even though some clergymen—of various denominations—have expressed doubt that man possesses an immortal soul or that the tenets of the religion they preach concerning immortality, resurrection, paradise, and heaven and hell are anything other than symbolic fables of moral significance and not to be taken literally or seriously.

When bereaved people find little or no personal solace in the church of their choice but instead are sent away with vague promises of a distant reunion with loved ones, they may quite naturally seek their own channels. Some of these channels are genuine, and some are not. Most people under emotional stress are quite incapable of distinguishing the true from the false. Moreover, the desire to communicate and the hope that one will succeed are powerful inducements to make a person overlook fraud or self-deception.

Spontaneous phenomena—that is, communications induced by the dead—are by their very nature devoid of the elements described above. The living person is not involved until the actual contact has been made and the message forwarded, so that elements of the receiver's own knowledge cannot be taken into account if the message contains specific information unknown to the medium or if communication was direct to the recipient.

A person who has not thought of Uncle Joe for ten years and who suddenly hears Uncle's voice giving a specific message for his widow cannot be accused of "hallucinating" it, especially if it is acknowledged to be a valid message. Hallucination is an even less tenable explanation when a stranger communicates through a psychic person and the recipient has to be sought out in order to deliver the message.

There are legitimate reasons for a living person to wish communication with someone known to be dead. Some unfinished business that only the dead person can clear up, or a desire to assure oneself of the loved one's well-being and continued existence, or a nonspecific interest in learning more about life beyond—these are certainly good reasons for establishing a channel. Less desirable but certainly understandable are requests for information regarding one's own fortunes, love life, and prospects. I feel that such interests belong more properly to the province of clairvoyants who specialize in predictions. But when a person wants to know what horse to bet on in a certain race I draw the line. Let the Gypsy fortune-teller break *that* bad habit.

A borderline question concerns the material obtained from clairvoyants covering one's future: Are they obtaining it through their ESP, or are they listening to the advice of deceased relatives supplying information beneficial to the one asking the questions? Either way, the results are paranormal, of course.

Let us assume you are a person interested in making contact with a dead relative for one reason or another. How do you go about it?

The simplest form of communication would be a kind of telephone directly from you to him. As the phone company has not yet invented such a gadget—they may in time—a good substitute might be a Ouija board. I have already discussed Ouija boards and planchettes—pieces of thin wood inscribed with *yes, no,* and the letters of the alphabet.

A small, wooden indicator glides across the board and stops at the desired letter or word. Your hand and one or two other hands rest lightly upon the indicator. A turned-down water glass will serve just as well. Ouija boards have no mystic powers whatever, and when anything of a paranormal nature comes through them, you or your guests are the originators. That is to say, the information may be totally unknown to you or anyone with you at the time, but it may rest deeply buried in your unconscious minds. Since the Ouija board can be used to draw out your unconscious, material thus obtained would not be proof of actually speaking to a discarnate or dead person. Once in a while, however, genuinely unknown material is obtained in this manner, and what appear to be the dead communicate with the living. The proof of this can be found only in the strictest application of sensible controls: make sure that the alleged communicator gives you proof of identity of the kind you could not have known yourself but that is capable of being verified *afterward* by your questioning someone not present in the room at the time.

A disturbing element I find is communications through the board obtained from seemingly genuine personalities of whom no one has ever heard or who cannot be checked out despite the fact that they give convincing details of their lives. Some even go so far as to give birth data, army records, precise information about their families and other data with the ring of truthfulness to them. Nevertheless, after careful search none of these things can be verified. Perhaps these are figments of the recipients imagination, split-off personality imposters created as attention-getters? Or is the search for verification merely incomplete?

I cannot conceive of spiritual imposters—that is, deceased individuals pretending to be someone other than themselves. I do not for a moment take seriously the theory of demons or other fabled creatures that have sprung from the fertile and sometimes demented minds of the religious practitioners in the past.

There are other forms of communicating with the dead without involving another person. Even the Ouija board does involve at least one other person, although as an assistant rather than a channel.

Those who prefer their contacts to be direct and private need to possess paranormal powers themselves. If they have some incipient ESP, they can develop such powers through taking certain steps.

Paramount among such steps is the practice of various forms of meditation, or withdrawal from the world of objective reality. In these withdrawn states the ordinary bonds between the conscious or logical mind and the unconscious are relaxed, permitting communication to take place from mind to mind. More often than not, communications are initiated from the other side when an individual thus prepares for it by withdrawal. Usually this happens long before the person is capable of initiating the contact. Thus there are few cases where communication is genuinely started on the initiative and under the control of a living person, but it does sometimes occur and is a valid method of reaching out to the nonphysical world and its inhabitants.

The least complex method would involve thought images being created in the mind and directed outward toward a loved one. In a way, this is like prayer except that the goal is not divine intercession but human response. In times of great need or duress, such communications are apt to be more successful, proving again how closely all psychic phenomena are tied in with the emotions and the actual emotional and spiritual needs of the individual.

The majority of people are not successful in getting through by themselves in this fashion, simply because they lack the training, patience, or other attributes of the professional medium. Those who are successful merely prove to be mediums of professional quality who have not used their powers until then, or have not cared to.

What remains for the average person to do, who wishes to contact a dead relative or friend, is to search for a reputable channel—a medium capable of making this contact possible. With the proper safeguards, visiting a medium is neither dangerous, sacrilegious, nor unnerving. It may well be a waste of time, if the results are nil or unsatisfactory.

But is it not the same with a visit to a doctor or lawyer? Good results are never guaranteed in advance. People are good, bad, or indifferent. Lawyers and doctors can be anything from excellent to fraudulent. So can mediums.

Judging by the large number of letters requesting the names of professional mediums for personal reasons, I can only assume that a lot of people would like to communicate with the dead.

Some mediums work clairvoyantly. That is, they are fully awake; they simply relay the messages from the dead, who presumably are standing next to them, though unseen by the outsider, answering questions from the medium or volunteering information.

To be sure the material obtained through the medium is genuine and not colored by something said, the sitter—that is, the person asking for the communication—must never *volunteer* any information. A "good" sitter never says anything other than yes or no, for it is useful to either confirm or deny statements by the medium. The confirmatory yes helps steady the contact, and the damning no makes the medium work harder! Other than that, it is unwise to elaborate on anything unless one is finished with both sitting and medium—that is, one does not intend to return for another reading.

Honest mediums do not *want* to know anything about sitter or communicator. They are merely the channel. They pass on information for which they are not responsible, nor are they interested in its content. The late Betty Ritter of New York, for example, insisted that her sitters not talk about themselves at all.

A lady named Freda Z. was desolate when her husband passed away on March 23, 1966. A friend had heard of Betty Ritter, and Mrs. Ritter consented to see the bereaved lady, a complete stranger.

A month after her husband's death, Freda Z. went to Betty's apartment. As soon as Mrs. Z. had closed the door behind her and without anything more than a hello having been exchanged, Betty Ritter looked at Mrs. Z. and exclaimed: "Your husband just passed away. . . . He is here and keeps asking me to tell you that he is here."

Betty then explained that the husband was kissing Mrs. Z. on the cheek and was asking her not to cry.

"Your name is Freda," Betty continued, and then Mrs. Z. spent a moving hour speaking to her late husband through Betty. In a statement voluntarily signed by her, Mrs. Z. said: "It was truly my husband speaking to me through her." So much of the material thus received was genuine that Mrs. Z. felt sure it was her late husband who was communicating. Some of the things he told her, through the medium, were in the future and unknown to her at the time of the sitting. But they occurred just as she had been told.

I myself have had many proofs that Betty Ritter did indeed speak to the dead, and the dead to her.

On August 20, 1966, I had just returned home from Europe, as my father had unexpectedly passed away on July 25, 1966, while I was abroad. As soon as Betty had taken a seat across from my wife Catherine and me, she explained that my father was present and that he had passed over. Now I am not altogether sure that she did not know he had died, but I certainly did not bring it to her attention. But if she knew of his passing, she could not know when, where, or how. Yet she immediately launched into a specific description of his last weeks on earth. She described his room and added: "Leo . . . Anna throws you kisses . . . Father says, Dr. K. did the best he could."

I am sure Betty Ritter did not know my father's first name, Leo, nor that our old cook who had been with us for thirty years and was like one of the family was named Anna. Anna passed on in 1964. The remark about Dr. K. I found particularly revealing. One of my father's best friends was Dr. Bruno Kisch, the noted heart specialist. In his last years, however, my father had trouble remembering people's full names and always referred to the doctor as "Dr. K." Although my father held dim views of the other medical men who treated him when necessary, he had only the highest regard for Dr. K.

I telephoned Dr. K.'s house in Brooklyn, New York, immediately to tell him of this unusual remark. But it was the doctor's *widow* who answered me. Doctor K. had also passed away unexpectedly while abroad. My father died July 25, Dr. K. passed on August 12, and Betty Ritter "brought in" my father through her mediumship on August 20. Thus, when my father remarked that Dr. K. had done all he could, Dr. K. must have been standing right next to him!

During his lifetime my father never believed in survival after death, and though he became less hostile to the idea as time wore on, he never really interested himself in the subject.

"God bless you," he said to me then, through Betty Ritter. "I didn't believe it, but you indoctrinated me—it helped when I went over—it's true!"

He added that some money that had been laid out would be coming back in. My father was always very worldly about money and much concerned with expenses incurred when I took care of him in his old age. The funeral expenses I had laid out did indeed come back soon after through a Social Security payment and a small bank balance he had had!

Turning to my wife, Betty announced that an "Alex" had come "in" to greet her and that a Fedor was with him. Betty Ritter did not know that Catherine's father was named Alexander and that her late brother Teddy was called Fedor by the family.

In another sitting requested by me on December 22, 1966, Betty Ritter remarked: "Your father stands with Max. A lady stands with your mother on her side of the family, close, Martha and J."

My father's brother was Max, who had preceded him by several years into the world of immortality. My mother's name was Martha, and her mother's name was Julie.

On May 7, 1967, Betty Ritter "contacted" my brother-in-law, Fedor. Word came that he was pleased the car was in working order. My wife and I had bought his old car from his estate after his death. The car turned out less than satisfactory and was a source of worry to us. Finally we exchanged it for a brand new Citroen, and of course the new car was working perfectly.

Perhaps the most publicized contact with a dead person was the late Bishop James Pike's dialogue with his deceased son Jim. The bishop himself wrote about these remarkable séances, and there were some exciting accounts in the daily press concerning his experiences. The personality of his son, who had committed suicide, manifested at first directly to the father in what had been their apartment in England. Later Bishop Pike consulted with several distinguished professional mediums, including Ena Twigg and Arthur Ford, under cautious conditions making fraud completely impossible.

One of the séances took place on Canadian television, in full view of millions of viewers. In discussing his experiences with me, the bishop made it plain that they were not his first contacts with the nonphysical world but that he had been encountering psychic phenomena for many years. These included the presence of a dead predecessor with whom he had disagreed in life over church matters, and the restless spirit of another clergyman who came looking for his jeweled cross that had somehow disappeared. But these contacts were more in the nature of hauntings. After his son Jim died, a number of evidential contacts were made between the two, always in the presence of competent witnesses and churchmen. The material obtained includes much that was private and known only to the bishop and his son. Some of it was of the kind that could not have come from bishop Pike's own unconscious mind, had this been possible, because he was not aware of it.

"At first they complained I didn't believe enough," the bishop said to me with a wry smile when I last saw him in Santa Barbara, "and now they think I believe too much." He was referring to his doctrinal doubts, which had brought about a quasi heresy trial. The bishop had tried to bring ancient faith in line with modern factuality and research realities.

On August 5, 1967, I went to visit Ethel Johnson Meyers at her house in Connecticut. It was quiet and peaceful outside, so the perfect setting for a conversation with the dead was established. After a moment, and before trance had come, Ethel reported the presence in the room of her control, Albert, a sort of telephone operator between here and there. Albert was Ethel's first husband, and it was his apparition many years ago that talked her out of a state of despair after his passing, preventing thoughts of suicide and convincing her that life did continue after death.

This happened many years ago, when Ethel knew very little about spiritualism or psychic matters. Only after this personal experience did she take an interest in the field. At the beginning she frequented the good mediums of her day, trying to learn more about the other side and trying also to establish contact with her Albert. Then one day she was told that she herself was a fine trance medium and should develop her powers by using them regularly.

By profession a voice coach, after a brilliant career with the San Francisco Opera and later on concert stages, Ethel pursued the side of her personality involving mediumship as a sideline until the clamor for her services became so loud that she decided to turn professional in this field as well.

I had first met Ethel—and Albert—at the New York headquarters of the Cayce Foundation, where she "sat" for a study group. We became friendly then and later worked together at various times. Ethel Johnson Meyers had a triple gift, actually. She was, first of all, a fine medium and could "get out" of herself to allow a ghost or "regular" discarnate to take over her speaking faculties and thus communicate with the living directly. This phase of her ability was always controlled by Albert, so that no unwanted or deranged personality could take over and harm the medium. I worked with Ethel in this area for many years and through countless cases of hauntings, always establishing afterward that the personality manifesting through her entranced vocal chords was indeed a real person who once had a body of his own and lived a real life. Ethel's other talents were the gifts of clairvoyance and clairaudience, in which she was able to see or hear of events at a distance or in the future. Sometimes she added the tool of psychometry to this: that is, she touched an object once belonging to a person whose story or problems she wanted to read and explore.

Her ability to serve as a link between the living and dead employed both of her gifts—conscious transmission and trance takeover, with Albert controlling.

Usually the conscious state precedes the trance condition, and the door to the other side is kept open by what seems to be a rigid and well-supervised system of access and control.

I was facing Ethel in her home now, and I had just been told that Albert was already present and that my parents were with him. The purpose of my presence was an attempt to link up with them, of course, or with anyone else who knew me and wished to use the facilities to communicate.

"There is a woman with them, with a longish face, hair pushed up, and her initial is E. She resembles you, more or less. The name's something like Edith or Evelyn . . . can't quite make it out."

My father's only sister, Ella, looked a lot like all the Holzers, including myself. Her appearance *with* my parents was significant for another reason. My father had several brothers who had predeceased him. Ella and my father had been at odds for many years and did not see each other for a large part of their lives. Only in the last few years of Ella's life had a reconciliation taken place, through my efforts. During those years when they were again writing to each other, Ella deeply regretted the long periods when they were estranged and wanted somehow to make up for them but never could.

Ethel went on to describe my father standing very tall and erect, wearing a gray suit with a red tie. One of my father's regrets during his last years had been his inability, due to crippling arthritis, to "walk straight" and tall, as he always had before. A gray suit and "Sunday" tie were his favorites.

"I see a darkish man next to E., with dark hair," Ethel said, "rather square forehead, initial L. I also get the initial M. with them. Does it mean anything?"

I nodded emphatically. L. was Leopold, Aunt Ella's husband, and Ethel had described him very well indeed. Max was Ella's favorite brother, who passed a short time before she did and with whom she had shared an apartment in Vienna for many years. Apparently the family had started to assemble around her. As Ethel rattled off their initials, they waited to be acknowledged, one by one.

"There's a G.," she began, and I said a mental hello to my cousin Gustave.

"Your Uncle Otto stands here now, and there is an E. with him this time." E. might be his brother and my uncle, Emil.

"Your father is doing something very peculiar now," Ethel reported; "he's taking your mother by the hand, and they are waltzing!"

In his youth my father had been an excellent dancer. In later years, however, he and my mother had had difficulty with their legs. But over there, one is as young as one wishes to remember oneself.

"Did your aunt with the initial E. have a small dog named Peggy?" Ethel suddenly asked. "It's a small dog, very low slung, not a dachshund but a dog not high above the ground."

At the time, I could not confirm this. Later I recalled that my Aunt Ella had indeed had two small dogs, Boston bulls, and one was named Peggy. As she had not had any children, Aunt Ella treated her dogs like babies, and they were very dear to her.

"I also see canaries with her." Ethel continued.

How I remember the canaries! That was when I was a little boy, before Ella and my father became estranged. Ella had been very fond of all animals.

It was time for the trance to begin, and I settled back in my chair to await the coming, first, of Albert and anyone he could bring to the "psychic microphone" through Ethel's help.

After the usual few moments of deep breathing and "total dissociation of personality," when Ethel's own self had withdrawn, Albert assumed control of her body. He expressed pleasure at meeting me again, as we had not spoken for several months. After a brief exchange Albert withdrew and turned the instrument—the medium—over to my late father.

At first he had great difficulty making himself heard, and the sounds emanating from Ethel were inarticulate. Gradually the voice emerged. At the same time, he attempted to get up to show me that he could walk easily *now*. I had a devil of a time restraining him, as I did not want the medium taken out of her safe chair. But my father was stubborn even in afterlife, and it took some doing to make him stay put.

The medium was standing up now, exactly as my father had stood before arthritis had severely crippled him. When I prevailed on him to sit down again, he did so, and the medium sat down in the characteristic posture of my father. The movements of the hands, the expressions of the face, despite the closed eyes, all resembled my father's. Ethel had known my father, but she had not seen him in the last years of his life—the last time was in a crowd at my wedding.

The voice sounded excited and emotional. He was laughing with joy at being able to talk to me, his favorite son. "I came through, I came through!" he said, hoarsely but clearly. Then he added, "I can stand!"

I assured him I realized it but to stay seated so as not to upset the instrument.

"Putzi is big," he said next, which is exactly what my father would say. His granddaughter, our little "Putzi," was the apple of his eye, too, and her size was always the first thing he mentioned when we visited him at his apartment.

"I can dance now," he said, and again it reminded me of an expression he sometimes used when he had recovered from one of the many falls he had taken in his last years. It was his way of saying, I'm better than OK.

"I'm sorry I was not here when you passed over," I said. He had passed unexpectedly before I could get to his bedside in the United States.

"I was with you . . ." he replied, "Deutsche. . . ." Although my father died when we were in Ireland, his illness had started while I was lecturing in Germany, and he lost consciousness about the same time, although I did not know this until afterward. Thus his last recollection of me would have been that I was in Germany at the time of his hospitalization.

Then he said he and my mother were together now.

"What are you doing?" I asked, somewhat uncertainly.

His voice chuckled, as it often had in life.

"None of your business," he said, an expression he liked to use in jest. He added that my mother had prepared a house for his coming over there.

"Who is with you?" I asked.

He moved his hands in the characteristic manner I remembered. There was no mistaking it—*this was my father!*

"You have many enemies, . . . but we will help you tell the truth. . . . The Indians will help, too . . . never saw so many Indians." And then he laughed—a characteristic laugh, loud and uninhibited.

He explained that he had to get used to the thought world in which he now lived and that at first he was bouncing around in it until he learned to control his thoughts and thus his movements.

"I was *sehr dick,*" he remarked, which means very stubborn. That was an understatement. My father had not accepted the possibility of survival after death and in his earlier years actively fought any mention of the subject. "I know I'm here, and I know I'm alive. Ma has gone further, and she's taken me like a schoolboy. . . . I've got so much to learn."

My mother passed twelve years before my father did. I questioned him about "the doctor you mentioned," referring to Betty Ritter's reading without telling him so.

"Don't want any doctors now," my father replied, and that too was in character. My father had been very suspicious of the medical profession, except for Dr. K.

"Anything I can do for you?" I inquired.

"Keep seeing me."

"I would like to—" I began, but he interrupted: "No, wait a minute, wait a minute. I want to say see me like Ma, . . . see me leading her instead of her leading me! I've got to go to school again."

His expression, "Wait a minute," was also very characteristic of him whenever he wanted to make a point. Power seemed low at this point, as his voice faltered.

"September 23rd . . . I'll try . . . I'll find you. . . ."

We made it a "date." Later I learned it was Albert's birthday. What happened on that day, when I sat with two different British mediums, we shall learn presently.

For the moment, my father was ready to leave again. A moment later Albert was back in control. After some more discussion of the life beyond, Albert took the instrument out of trance, and Ethel assumed once more control over her physical self, remembering absolutely nothing about the hour or so she had served as the intermediary between the two worlds.

When September 23 came, my wife and I were in London. It was a rainy day, and I had not yet seen my father's spirit. But the day was still young, and something might yet happen.

I had a sitting with Roy Morgan at the headquarters of the Spiritualist Association of Great Britain, where one can book sittings at a nominal fee with about a dozen reputable professional psychics. The little Welshman was a gentle, erudite person who started to talk to me in a rapid-fire monologue, rattling off conditions around me, future entanglements and hopes and desires in a fabulous conglomeration of fact and not-yet-fact but highly-likely-to-be-fact, interspersed with some statements of events to come that were, at least at the moment, most unlikely. As he got my bearing or "vibration" better and, presumably, I his, he brought in other elements.

"Your father's passed over," he said; "your father is here. He was a good-looking man, not a handsome man but tall. Full face, and you are like him in some way, around here." He touched his nose and forehead.

Now my father, *in his prime*, was tall and good-looking but certainly not handsome in the usual sense. And I am very much like him in appearance, especially the nose and forehead.

"He didn't understand you, only that which was solid; he didn't realize about this other sense. There is a dog that comes running toward you, . . . and then there is your mother. She is here. There was a parting when one of them went. Your father went rather quickly. Your mother was ill for a time; she was in the hospital. Cancer. She was thinner then."

All this was entirely true. Yet here was a medium whom I had met only briefly several years earlier. He did not know my name or who I was, then or now. He had not been expecting me. I had not said a single word to him except hello. Several years before, I had had a brief sitting with him, but I cannot believe he remembered me after all this time and out of the hundreds of people he sees week in, week out. Why should he? The fee he received for his time, or rather his share of it, was around $2.

" 'I knew that I wouldn't get out of this bed,' she says," Morgan continued, "and I think she realized what she had toward the end." This was entirely true. My mother knew only in her final week that she had cancer.

"She suffered a little, then stepped out of her body and went out on the other side of life; she saw no change in her physical being. She saw she had a body, but she realized it was an etheric body. There was no change, but she was free from pain. She certainly felt younger and lighter and much freer. She says she is with you a great deal."

"I see music. . . . Your father says you were always musical." He then elaborated on my future success in music. At the time there was nothing to indicate any interest of mine in music. I was known for my contributions to psychic research, not for music. But to my father, my greatest talent had always been musical, and his greatest regret was that I had not yet been successful in that art.

"Your grandmother has been over for some years. Did they

come from abroad? Not American. The Continent, Polish or German—no, Austrian. Vienna. You will be successful in music; it's in the blood." I could only nod assent. Vienna was right. Also, my Uncle Otto was one of Germany's leading composers in the 1930s, a very successful writer of songs and musicals.

"You'll be astounded in your future career how the spirit world will step in," the medium asserted.

"Nothing astounds me," I replied, but I gleefully welcomed the promised help. Any kind of help is welcome in our century.

I asked if anyone else of my family was present.

"There is a grandfather," Morgan replied after a moment, as if he were looking over there. "Then there is an Anna who is linked with the family. I'm getting some names, Hans and Carl and Kurt. And Oscar. And with him Melenne or something like that, and Helga, no, Olga. And Brno."

I was taken aback by this wealth of loved ones! Anna was our old family factotum and cook, truly "linked with the family." Hans and Kurt are myself and my brother, and Carl is our uncle. The family came originally from the city of Brno, in Czechoslovakia. Very few people know of Brno outside central Europe, I would think. Oscar was a cousin with whom I had a close relationship, as we shared an interest in the classics. His cousin, Marianne (not Melenne), and her mother, Olga, have been over there for some years. How could a stranger link these names unless they were truly present and manifesting?

Morgan continued to "present" my dead relatives! "I'm also getting a name like Nasher or Tasher, . . . and then I get Marie, or rather Mahrie. . . ."

I have a cousin by the name of Marketa Ascher, who now lives in Brno. Her late husband, Dr. Ascher, was a lawyer. When my grandmother passed on, her cook of many years went back to her village. But years later she returned to the city of Brno and served my cousin, Mrs. Ascher. Her name, strange as it may seem, was Mahrie with the accent on the broad a, not the usual form of Marie.

"Someone keeps saying Max, . . . there is also Stephanie, . . . also a Hildegarde and a peculiar name, Gina or Tina or Nina. She's a very autocratic old lady with white hair. She's linking with your mother's side."

All this was very interesting. Max was my father's brother, and his widow, still living, is named Josephine. But her husband and the rest of the family always called her *Finie*. To an Anglo-Saxon ear, Stephanie would be more logical, of course.

While I was still trying to figure out who Hildegarde was and the Italian-sounding Gina or Nina, Morgan added: "Who is Gustave? She is with Gustave. Also Olga."

Gustave was a cousin of mine whose first wife had been an Italian lady from Florence. I know nothing about her family; thus I can't confirm or deny whether anyone named Gina or Nina formed part of it. But Olga was Gustave's own mother.

"Who's Martha?" Morgan asked. I acknowledged my mother.

The day was still young, and I had another appointment, this time with a lady named Ivy Jaggers. Miss Jaggers greeted me in another room upstairs a couple of hours later. A quiet-spoken lady in her forties, she went right to the job at hand. This time my wife was with me, helping me to tape-record the reading.

There was a good deal of character analysis at first. Miss Jaggers showed an astute sense of appraisal and some psychological insight in describing us. And yet there were elements far beyond this in the reading, elements that could not possibly be inferred from merely looking at us.

"There is a gentleman who passed through a heart condition, on your father's side of the family," she suddenly said, turning from prognostication of my future to the presence of "spirits" in the room.

Pretty vague, I thought, although my father's father did die of a heart condition, rather suddenly, many years ago. I never knew him myself.

She next explained that my grandmother on my mother's side was present, and described her as a very definite forceful personality who thought that I'd inherited all my good qualities from her side of the family. However, she did not give me her name or anything else. But as I accepted this news with mixed feelings, she volunteered that an anniversary was near for my wife and me—according to my grandmother. That was perfectly true—our fifth wedding anniversary was six days off! Still, that could have been ESP.

But on another occasion, the first time I had ever met Ivy Jaggers, she had been a lot more evidential, that is, as far as the contacts with dead family members were concerned.

The date had been May 17, 1964. Miss Jaggers had never met me before, nor I her.

Hardly had I sat down when she announced that someone was present who wished to make himself known to me. She described him as a man with a beard and thought he was German. I could not place any such person, so I asked that she identify him further.

"He's a teacher . . . a professor."

In my Austrian *gymnasium*, we referred to our teachers always as *herr professor*, although the title was really honorific. Some of the teachers were Ph.D.'s, some were merely mister, but all had to be addressed as "professor."

While I was still groping in the dark, the medium placed her finger on her lips in a peculiar gesture and said in a voice not quite her own: "Think . . . think hard!"

I thought hard, and still nothing came to mind that would identify the man.

"He taught languages," Miss Jaggers said. "He was a wise man."

"Did he have any other interests or hobbies perhaps?" I asked, still not sure who he was.

"Yes," Miss Jaggers replied immediately, "his hobby was chess. I also see his apartment. It is filled with books."

Something within my memory began to stir. "Quickly," I said, "what was his name?"

"J," Miss Jaggers replied, and waited for my reaction.

All at once I knew who the stranger was. One of my favorite teachers, Professor J. K., had taught languages and history at my school. He was a European chess champion, and his greatest love was collecting books. His apartment was literally lined with books from floor to ceiling. His favorite expression had been the command, "Think . . . think hard!" He would put his finger on his lips to emphasize the remark.

I had not had any contact with Professor J. K. for many years. If he were still alive he would be in his eighties. In 1965 I happened to be in Vienna. Just as soon as I could, I went looking for Professor J. K.'s old apartment. The superintendent had never heard of him. Nevertheless, as if driven by an inner force, I mounted the stairs and walked up to what had once been his apartment. On the chance of being mistaken for a panhandler, I rang the doorbell. A young woman answered. Uncertain, I asked whether she had ever heard of a professor named J. K. who had once lived in the apartment she now occupied. To my surprise, she did not throw me out or slam the door in my face.

"Come in," she said. "This used to be his place, all right. I knew him."

Encouraged and at the same time puzzled, I asked whether she could direct me to his current address.

"Hardly," she replied. "I doubt that you will be able to locate him. He died six years ago."

How could Ivy Jaggers know so much about me, a stranger walking in from the street, whom she had never seen, as to be able to bring me a contact with a schoolteacher I had not heard from in many years? Very unlikely that a fraud could be perpetrated even if there had been such an intention. Miss Jaggers, like the other spiritualist mediums at the center, received about $2 for her hour's reading.

It is the little private facts in a person's life that make interesting links from the beyond. I think these little facts are chosen deliberately to emphasize the authenticity of these contacts. Take, for instance, my postmortem contact with Danton Walker, the late *New York Daily News* columnist, whom I knew in life although not intimately. For one thing, the period of his youth was totally unknown to me or, of course, to my medium, Ethel Meyers, when we made an attempt to contact him a few months after his passing. The séance took place next door to his old home in what had been the apartment of his valet and sometime confidante, Johnny.

Even Johnny did not know much about his onetime boss when it came to Walker's early years. Danton never liked to discuss anything personal, especially anything pertaining to a period of his life when he was not yet the glamorous, successful columnist of his later years.

After about fifteen minutes of conversation with the alleged spirit of Danton Walker, I requested some sort of identification. Not that I doubted that the person speaking to me through Ethel Meyers was anyone but my old friend, but I wanted to hear something none of us knew at the time that I could later check out as genuine. He mentioned a place called Craybill, where he had been happy. I found out that Danton's boyhood home, where he had indeed been happy, was called Carabell.

One of the obvious tests of authentic communications with the departed is the securing of matching information about the same people from different and totally unconnected sources. On September 13, 1964, I sat with Magdalene Kelly, a portly lady who works for the Spiritualist Association of Great Britain. This was our first and only meeting at the time, and I sat in front of her, waiting.

"There is a man who has passed on with a heart condition, on your father's side of the family," she intoned. That could be my grandfather, and it is interesting to note that Ivy Jaggers, the other London medium, also saw this gentleman when I came in for possible contact. Since neither of these mediums knew of my coming or anything else about me it is very unlikely that they exchanged information about my dead relatives just to please me!

On September 29, 1967, I visited Magdalene Kelly again. Both my wife and I recalled her, but she did not and could not recall us, since she sees perhaps a hundred people a week and has deliberately trained herself to forget her sitters the moment they walk out of her door. Most mediums work this way, because the burden of remembering so many people and relating to them would destroy their aloofness from the problems of the sitters, and aloofness is a very necessary condition for successful and continuing mediumship.

Only a handful of frauds practicing at the spiritualist camps in the United States use index cards, on which the particulars of regulars among their gullible clients are noted. But they are not genuine mediums to begin with and owe their continuing existence to an incredible leniency on the part of the spiritualist organizations in the United States, who like to ignore the very well-grounded objections to some (but by no means a majority) of their members.

"Your father from the spirit side of life is here," she said immediately, "and he is very happy to come. Since he passed, he has recognized in many ways how he failed a little. He is now trying terribly hard to make this up. He is trying to help you build up best conditions in a material sense."

My father's prime worry had always been the financial drain his support in the later years meant for me. He was always concerned about my material welfare and frequently inquired after it.

Mrs. Kelly then informed me my late mother was also present and proceeded to describe her, pretty accurately I thought. She then turned to my wife and said: "There is a gentleman on your side of the family who passed rather quickly."

I tried to get her to be more specific, but it did not sit well with the medium.

"Let him come through," she admonished me sternly. "You cannot ask questions like on the telephone!"

We both laughed, and let her resume in her own way after that. "He was well known in his field, well liked and respected," she added. "Was there anyone linked with you who married twice?" My wife nodded. Her father, a respected architect, had married her mother in a second marriage. He passed suddenly.

"He brings a fatherly feeling to you," Mrs. Kelly added.

The late Carolyn Chapman, whom I have called "the dean of American mediums," saw me on November 3, 1960, during a survey of psychics I had undertaken under the sponsorship of the Parapsychology Foundation. Mrs. Chapman did not know me. She mentioned a number of names of deceased persons somehow connected with me. She remarked that my mother, Martha, was present and could hear me. Then, to satisfy my curiosity as to the genuineness of the contact, she added: "It's right after the anniversary."

My mother's birthday had been two days before.

A Mrs. Donaldson, from outside Edinburgh, gave me some interesting messages during an impromptu sitting on August 3, 1964. She knew nothing about my wife or me at the time. In looking at us she mentioned a Henry, Mother, and Mary. Somehow I had the feeling this was a family group.

My late Uncle Henry had always called my grandmother "Mother"; their cook for many years was named Mary, pronounced however, Mahrie, with the emphasis on the broad *a*.

A little later she mentioned a Joan, who sent love to her mother. She further identified this Joan as having passed suddenly. Now the interesting part is that the message was for someone other than us, but somehow we were to be the intermediaries. I instantly recognized the originator of the message. A dear and close friend named Joan, who had passed away unexpectedly some years before, was linked with her mother in this sense only through me. Her father was unreceptive to the idea of spirit communication, and her mother was at least open-minded enough to listen, although not really convinced that it worked. The message did not fit any other situation, and I know of no other Joan whose mother I also count among my friends.

Sometimes mediums are the bearers of code messages that they themselves do not understand but that make sense to the proper recipient. The value of coded messages is in their specific content, and the fact that the medium's unconscious or even conscious mind is not involved prevents distortion. The disadvantage is, of course, the need to find the right person to decipher the code.

In the case of the late Clara Howard, sister of the even more famous California medium Sophia Williams, finding the right person was not a problem, as the message concerned me and I was present. The sitting took place at her apartment in New York on July 21, 1960. After she had named several dead relatives of mine correctly by name and even described my late grandmother "Strauss" (real name Stransky) as having had "mouse-gray hair"—something my grandmother would not have enjoyed although it was perfectly true—she paused as if to recharge her psychic batteries.

"*Kennst du das Land wo die Zitronen bluehen?*" she suddenly exclaimed in German. This was the second German phrase she had used that evening. Half an hour before, she had said out of a clear sky, "*Es war so schoen gewesen, es hat nicht sollen sein.*"

Now, the preceding sentence means, "It was so beautiful, it was not meant to be," and it was an expression my father used at my mother's funeral, indicating that it was meant for her to go first.

The other sentence, meaning "Knowest thou the land where the lemons bloom?" is a poetic expression from the popular opera *Manon*. It so happened that *Manon* was my mother's favorite opera, and she would frequently hum that particular aria to herself.

In a prior visit with British medium Roy Morgan on September 24, 1966, I was actually a substitute for someone else. A cancellation had come in, and he was able to take me unexpectedly, without of course knowing my name or anything about me. Some of the interesting contacts that day were the kind no amount of "coincidence" explanations would account for.

I went, hoping some of my loved ones would wish to answer my call. My father and mother, according to Morgan, did just that. He described my mother as sixtyish and dressing very nicely and referred at once to my father's rather prominent nose, remarking that at one time he had had a mustache but had shaved it off.

My mother was sixty-eight when she passed on, and she always wore elegant clothes. My father had a prominent nose, and during his World War I Army service he did sport a mustache, which he later removed. I hardly think that my father's mustache is the sort of thing hanging on in my unconscious; in fact, until Morgan brought it up, the mustache was not even significant to me, and only after some thought did I recall the business with the mustache. But there was more to prove the presence, though unseen, of my loved ones from beyond the veil.

Ray Morgan mentioned my father's name, Leo; our cook's name, Anna; and both my own and my brother Kurt's names correctly; then he went on to say a Peppi was also present. Peppi was one of my late father's best friends.

"A young man is here who was killed accidentally in a car crash," he suddenly said. "Is he a brother? Thirty . . . he was on the verge of a divorce, thought his wife was selfish. . . . He has a fair complexion and dark hair. He was killed instantly, through injury of the head."

I recognized my brother-in-law, who was indeed on the verge of a divorce from a selfish wife when he was killed in a car accident exactly as described, at not quite thirty years of age. I asked what my brother-in-law wished to tell me.

"I'm all right now," Morgan reported. "There are great opportunities here. I was disturbed before I passed, but now I can move on, now I'm free. . . ."

Chapter Ten

The Laws of the Next World

BY NOW IT MUST BE CLEAR TO MY READER that communications with the dead are not only possible but frequently highly evidential. Only a firm nonbeliever with a mind already made up that such things *cannot* possibly be could reject the evidence. To do so requires mental gymnastics at times, for it is not easy to twist facts around so that they will fit into a theory excluding the possibility of personal survival. ⟩

The question of some sort of law and order in the specific area of "death" has of course occupied the minds of scientists and philosophers, of medical doctors and laypeople, for many centuries. From the volume of observed material and cases I am personally familiar with, I have come to certain conclusions about this matter. This is not jumping the gun on the evidence but evaluating it by the standards of today's scientific methods of inquiry. Perhaps tomorrow we shall learn some other method. For the present, this is what I find to be factual, because it is drawn from a great many cases, cases observed and examined separately by a variety of people and involving no cross-communication between the subjects of the cases involved. That is, the subjects and the observers did not tell each other of their experiences or results in order to create a unified picture. The unification of the situation is my own contribution, arrived at only after the examination of many separate, independent, and unconnected cases.

Some years ago a book by Anthony Borgia entitled *Life in the World Unseen* caused a sensation in the world of ESP research. To some, this book was mere fiction. To others, it represented the first rational description of life in the spirit world. The book was soon followed by a second volume called *More About Life in the World Unseen.* Neither book was a commercial success, but in psychic research circles the books were discussed a great deal. Anthony Borgia, a British medium, claimed that he had served a dead Catholic priest, Monsignor Robert Hugh Benson, as a spokesperson. Mainly through automatic writing, the dead Monsignor, son of a former archbishop of Canterbury, wants to make up for his misdeeds while alive. These errors consisted in a negative attitude displayed by him toward survival after death and those asserting its truth. Having found his medium, the monsignor then proceeds to describe his own passing and the details of the life beyond the veil. He finds guides in the nonphysical world who take him around and explain the facts of afterlife to him. In these two books, we learned amazing details of an orderly world in which everything is regulated by laws, although the laws differ somewhat from our physical laws.

My first reaction to the Borgia books was one of doubt. But I later ceased to doubt. Much of what Borgia described may also be found in the classic *Heaven and Hell* of Emanuel Swedenborg. Though the eighteenth-century language and Swedenborg's own poetic style tell the stories of the world beyond somewhat differently from Borgia, the basic facts in both accounts are identical. Additional descriptions of that other life can be found in various chapters of other psychic books. *The Search for Bridey Murphy,* for instance, has an interesting account of a priest's first encounter with after-death life. This is a book, by the way, that has survived malicious and slanderous attacks through a complete defense and supporting evidence researched by the *Denver Post.*

Many of the cases I have worked on contain elements of description pertaining to the other world. *This, then, is what happens when you die.* As death approaches, relatives or friends who have gone on before gather around the dying person to assist in the imminent transition from the physical to the non-physical state. Frequently the dying can see them already, for at the time of imminent death the bonds between conscious and unconscious are very loose. Dr. Karlis Osis of the American Society for Psychical Research did some valuable studies on bedside observations of the dying in various hospitals. In these reports, mention is made frequently of the alleged presence in the hospital room of a long-dead relative or friend whom only the dying person can see or hear. In the past, such phenomena have been brushed aside as "hallucinations of the dying," implying that *all* patients in their terminal stage are mentally incompetent and therefore their testimony is not to be taken at face value.

Today some psychic researchers are taking a second look at this material. Personally I have no doubt that the dying do see their dead relatives and friends. When the body gives up the struggle, the "silver cord" is cut between the physical body and the finer etheric, or "inner," body that now contains the personality, mind, and memory, and the bedside has to be left as quickly as possible. With the help of the more experienced discarnates, the "newly arrived" individual is taken out and brought over into the nonphysical world. Ordinarily the person is conscious when this happens, except in cases where the nature of the disease precludes this. Unfortunately, modern doctors like to administer great amounts of narcotics to the dying; often they do this to overcome great pain, but sometimes they administer narcotics just to calm the dying. The narcotics make it necessary for the newly dead to be brought to the equivalent of our hospitals "over there," where discarnate physicians minister to them until the effects of disease *and* treatment wear off. Then the person can continue the voyage into the area where he or she now belongs.

Unless one is a spiritualist, which I am not, it is difficult to visualize this journey. I think the nonphysical world is composed of energy particles moving more rapidly than the particles making up our physical universe, and this nonphysical world coexists in the same general spatial area as our physical world. Since the two "trains" travel at different speeds over the same track, they never collide or meet up with each other. The faster "train" has no trouble crossing ahead of the slower one, but not vice versa. In all cases known to me, the dead speak of their world as being far from earth. When they mention a number of planes, or spheres, inhabited by different types of people according to their spiritual and personal development, it is at first difficult to visualize these planes as solid places the way we might think of the floors in a building. But again dismissing our notions of space and three-dimensional things and assuming that in a thought world all thought is also tangible and real, I find that the planes must be the sum total of similar attitudes or development stages of large numbers of individuals rather than purely solid places in our terrestrial sense.

For instance, if we place twenty classical musicians in a garden with their instruments and allow them to play, rehearse, and talk with each other or just sit there and think, we will have created a garden filled with the atmosphere of a concert world. Walking between the individuals as an outsider, we will nevertheless sense the overall tonality of their world, as they all have much in common. Each individual reaches out to the others, and some tiny part of each flows out into the atmosphere and imbues it with the tonality of the world to which these individuals belong. If you take them out of the garden, there will soon be just an empty garden. But as long as these people are in the garden and interact with each other, the garden itself becomes transformed into a specific world, a *plane of existence.*

Now if a rock and roll artist arrived at the garden entrance and wanted to enter, the others would quite rightly reject him as being not of their kind and possibly harmful to the harmonious atmosphere around them. If he nevertheless gained entrance, the rock and roll artist would find himself in alien territory and quite ill at ease. He would soon make his departure and gravitate toward a world of his own kind, where he would link up with similar people who together would again form another plane of existence of their own.

In the nonphysical world, like gravitates to like. This does not refer to race, religion, age, or economic status, of course, but to the *essential* thing in human beings: their spiritual selves.

What survives physical death is not the entire personality. Strictly speaking, what survives is the whole *emotional* self. Routine matters unpossessed of emotional associations are soon left behind as unimportant. Memory of what your telephone number was five years ago is not worth "taking with you." But the moment of great happiness, your wedding, an encounter with a dear friend, a beautiful trip, or, conversely, a great tragedy or perhaps only a small amount of despair—these are all remembered and remain part of your spiritual self.

When death occurs normally or more or less in an accepted routine fashion through illness, old age, or weakening of the body, then the transition is reasonably quick and unhampered. One "wakes up" over there amid one's dead relatives and friends—not all of them but those one is spiritually close to—and life continues. At first, this is life modeled on earthly life habits. Since you are exactly what you bring with you, much of your continuing life is built up from those memories, habit patterns, and other emotional stimuli accumulated during your tenure on earth. Gradually you acquire new knowledge and new concepts of yourself and the world around you, and as you incorporate them into your way of thinking—which is what you are now—other and less useful traits of yourself will fall by the wayside.

Your physical appearance will closely resemble what you were in the physical life. Some who arrive over there revert quickly to the prime of their lives—what they, individually, consider their best years, not what some "government spirit" tells them! In fact the nonphysical world is free of all coercion such as we know and dislike on earth. Laws are administered through moral pressure rather than force. Some newly arrived people may be unable to revert immediately to their best years, and others really prefer to be their old-age selves. Some may wish to appear as mere youths.

All these wishes are granted since the process is entirely voluntary and controlled by the individual. As you appear to yourself, so you appear to others, of course. The question of clothing naturally puzzles many who question me on this. How is it possible for a person in a thought world to wear clothes? The answer is not difficult. In a world where everything consists of thought-created matter, there is no difference between creating a youthful body and a nice suit or dress. As long as you are capable of thinking up the clothes you wish to wear, you will wear them, and that is how you will appear to others. You may even appear in them for the benefit of your earth relatives on the occasions when you pay a return visit, through a medium or directly to a former abode. The degree of similarity between the clothing worn on earth and the replica worn in the world of spirit depends only on the individual's own ability to visualize the old clothes. The better one is at visually recreating the image of oneself wearing those clothes, the more accurately they will be recreated on one's etheric body, and they will stay that way indefinitely as long as one does not wish to undo them again, also by thought processes.

As for persons killed traumatically, who are unable to move into the world of spirit and instead are earthbound individuals known as ghosts, they do not have this freedom to be their former selves or to wear the clothes they would like to. They are not yet inhabitants of the realm of the spirit, either being caught in the world between the two stages of being or, even worse, being held in the physical world in which they exist like fish out of water, out of their true element. I have written several books on this subject and have told how, with the help of a good trance medium, I have been able to help many of these unfortunate ones across the threshold into the land of spirit.

Based on my findings and my own interpretations, communications received from discarnates by myself and by unimpeachable researchers, either directly or through mediums, it appears that the system prevailing on the other side is something like this: Having arrived over there, the newly dead, surrounded by some relatives or friends, are then led to a reception center, or so it would seem from available testimony. There they are either checked out for further travel or sent to a hospital or rest home for a period of adjustment.

Although time as we know it does not exist in the nonphysical world, the equivalent in our time of two weeks or more is often spent in the preparatory stage after death. This is especially necessary when long illness has preceded the dissolution of the body. Although bodily destruction does not hurt the condition of the etheric body or spiritual self, prolonged disease can create anxiety states affecting the emotional part of the personality and therefore does create problems for those who come across the border in a very weak condition. For them, the period of adjustment is a must, and it is similar to deep sleep during which the individual is not conscious of anything. They do not dream or partake in any way of the world around them. Afterward they are allowed to proceed, usually with the help of an assigned guide. This need not be a relative or friend but may be anyone who has been given the job of helping them adjust to their new surroundings.

I wondered who handed out these assignments, but despite much questioning I never got knowledge of the real boss. It was always a business of getting one's orders from the masters, these being merely people of greater advancement or skill than oneself. But these masters are not superbeings or saints, and they were human at one time just like you and me. Who gives the masters their orders I was never able to find out, and for want of a better term I called the system "the boys upstairs" or the "board of directors" in the world beyond.

The law is very efficient, I found. You attract what you are at the moment. If you wish to improve your image, you can do so by studying in what seems the equivalent of our schools. Especially the vast majority of people who come over without any conviction that life continues must learn new sets of facts and adjust to a totally different concept of life from the one their churches and scientists taught them on earth. Advancement in the spiritual sense is always possible and desirable. But it does not seem feasible for a lower-development individual to go hobnobbing with more exalted ones merely by desiring to be in their presence. Apparently when such individuals try to leave their plane and attempt to enter the next higher level, they will find themselves out of breath and unable to continue. On the other hand, a higher individual who wishes to visit the lower one can do so without difficulty. This does make sense to me. After all, the faster-moving particles of the etheric personality can penetrate the denser, slower moving particles representing the physical life, while it is not quite so easy to do this the other way round.

A medium who wishes to walk amid the spirits must first get out of the physical body in order to be of "their kind" temporarily. Stepping down the "vibrations" (particles on the move) is easier than stepping up. The only way the lower element can move up to the higher world is through such auxiliary tactics as "raising vibrations" through community sings, breathing exercises, elimination of inhibiting white light, and well-disciplined thought concentration. Even then, success is spotty.

Unless there is some unfinished business or inability to accept the separation of death, temporary though it is, desire to communicate immediately is not always present in the newly arrived. This is due of course to the overpowering elements of the wondrous new world one has just entered and the need for a lot of learning and sightseeing, which deflects the individual from any thought of contacting the old world left behind. Gradually, as individuals get used to the new surroundings and learn to live a new life in them, their attention may return to the earth world left behind. Only some maladjusted, negative individuals regret their new status. The majority, it seems, enter with joy and exultation into what religion justly calls heaven. These include former priests, ministers, rabbis, and monks who now have to unlearn a lot of old fairy tales. For one thing, this heaven is not populated by angels with goose feathers on their backs, flitting to and fro playing on golden trumpets. There is no old man with a white beard on a throne surrounded by twelve apostles just back of an entrance gate at which St. Peter divides the arrivals into heaven types and hell-bent types. Hell, incidentally, is not what it has been pictured to the faithful of many religious persuasions. No mean-looking fellows in red underwear driving pitchforks into sinners, no sulphuric caverns where the bad types suffer physically for the wrongs they inflicted on others while in the flesh.

Instead of these fantasies of sexually maladjusted medieval monks, there are many heavens and hells, depending on the individual reviewing his or her own past. For it is true that you create your own heaven or hell in your memories, and if there is guilt left at the time of the great transition, then this guilt becomes part of your own torment, your own private and individual hell. The sum total of people with lots of demerits, living in their own private hells without knowing how to get out of them, may create the illusion that there is a physical place called hell. But it is merely one of the multitude of "states of being" into which surviving souls congregate or are drawn by their individual stage or lack of spiritual progress. This, too, is part of the other side of life. The dividing line between the heaven-type groupings and the hell-type groupings is indistinct. You take with you what you are, and if in life you have lived at peace with yourself, you will most likely find a peaceful, beautiful world awaiting you.

But if your conscience has long been racked by the uneasy

feeling of having done wrong to others, you will find those feelings assuming the touch of reality in a world where thoughts are physical things. Thus the only consolation I can offer humankind is to live a life of spiritual values. Not necessarily a religious or sanctimonious or even a moral life. Kissing the neighbor's wife in an outburst of admiration is hardly reason enough to find yourself in a hell-type place after you pass over. Nor does a regular contribution to the Sunday morning plate in church assure you of a place next to God.

Man-made concepts of good and evil are not necessarily equal to the natural law that alone determines one's status over there in the world of spirit. But taking another human being's life, for instance, is always a sin. Even if you do this during a war and for what you thought was a just cause, you will find yourself regretting it when you arrive over there. For one thing, you realize that killing for any cause whatever is contrary to humans' purpose on earth. For another, you may very well run into the fellow you killed, who has preceded you across the border. Having been over there longer than you, he naturally will be ahead of you in spiritual attainment. How any human being taught the essence of spiritual truth—the nature of humanity, its purpose and destiny—can still go out and kill, no matter who orders him or her to do so or for any cause whatever, is beyond my ken.

I condemn killing; I find it repugnant. Exceptions are so few that we can easily dismiss them. If you are threatened by an evil man and must defend your life and in self-defense take his, you may be excused but not forgiven. The natural law does not require you to be a martyr and be killed rather than kill. But the natural law demands that you exhaust all possibilities of nonviolent escape from the killer before turning his own weapons against him.

Accidental death may result in your being exonerated legally and even morally, but over there the guilt of having made a mistake will still haunt you, no matter how innocent you may have been in the actual deed. As highly evolved spiritual beings we have the responsibility and duty to weigh very carefully all our actions. Far too many hurts are the result of improper thinking.

The natural law not only makes you pay for your mistakes

but also rewards you for your good deeds. This is not through some kind of prize-awarding jury handing out laurels, of course; payment and reward happen far more directly.

For every unselfish or spiritually proper action or attitude, you have the deep sensation of having done something *right*. This inner knowledge is reward in itself. But as thoughts over there are equivalent to reality, the achievement of such sensations automatically propels you into higher levels of consciousness. Thus you advance yourself by your past deeds and attitudes.

If you desire, and as you learn more about the nature of life, you can add to your "credits" even after the physical body is no more. Advancement—and downfall—is always possible. The law is in operation, it would seem, invisibly and all-present at the same time. Because it is automatic and immediate in its application, your own actions bring it into play. Thus, ultimately, you as an individual control your own destiny on the other side of life.

You have arrived in the world of spirit; you have met your people and exchanged small talk with them; you are shown to your new quarters and discover how much like your house on earth this one is—quite naturally, since it is created by thoughts drawn from your experiences in the physical state. You can build your own house, if you wish, in the same way you create your clothes, or it might be that a loved one who has preceded you has done this for you and you are now led into it, all prepared and ready.

Gradually, as you become more highly evolved, the need for the physical elements in your house becomes less and less, and a divine simplicity of design takes their place in your home. Your clothes too become impractical and outmoded as you accept your new world as your proper home. You will then replace them with the "spirit robe," a garment or gown of white material created in the thought way. It is totally functional and serves your needs. You can go nude if that is your bent. There are no moral offenses on the other side. There are only spiritual shortcomings that are self-adjusting. It's really all up to you.

Having adjusted to the new world and being unaware of the passage of time, you begin to wonder what comes next. The absence of time is difficult to take at first. Instead you find that you measure your existence by states of being—so long for the state of being with such and such individuals. Then, as you move into higher spheres—if you wish and qualify—another period, or state, begins. It is only when you return to earth to have contact with a living person in the denser world that you become again conscious of time. To some this presents a problem during these communications, since the whole time concept has become alien to them. They may experience difficulty in expressing themselves in such matters as the prediction of events to come concerning a loved one they have made contact with.

There is neither day nor night in the nonphysical world; there is a glow shed over it quite different from the sunlight of our world. Those requiring the rhythm of sleep and wakefulness can induce it by merely desiring it. In fact, *desire is immediate action* in many ways. The thought, for instance, of wanting to be with another individual is immediately followed by your being swept up and transported through space to the side of that individual. Thus, proper controlling of one's natural thoughts is essential for the newly arrived personality if one does not wish to be bounced around mercilessly by one's own wild thoughts!

Sooner or later you find yourself drawn to the many activities taking place in the world around you. As there are no inhibiting factors over there, every individual is able to realize his or her ambitions, many of which may not have been practicable in earthly life. Thus an artist who could not get a hearing on earth but who strove hard and honestly, though unsuccessfully, will now suddenly find she can conduct a spiritual symphony orchestra for the benefit of like-minded individuals. Everything exists in duplicate over there if humankind has created it at one time. The duplicates are more nearly perfect, more radiant than their physical counterparts, as they do not fall under the restrictive laws of material and human failure.

You will find that some of the leisure-type forms of expression attract you, and you satisfy long-held desires in some areas of your personality. Then, too, you discover that there are many varied jobs to be done to help those in the physical world attain higher grades of spiritual attainment prior to coming over.

If you yourself were one of those who did not know that life continued after death, you would naturally wish to help prevent this sort of ignorance in as many worthwhile individuals as possible. In helping them as far as you are able, not only do you perform useful and therefore spiritual deeds, but you automatically create a higher "rating" for yourself at the same time.

Thus many of the dead become links to the living. They may be guides or merely friendly influences, working with mediums or directly to help the living find better ways of expressing themselves within the framework of a spiritual concept of the universe. This does not mean that the dead are actively trying to run the lives of the living. Every soul must work for its own salvation, so to speak, and cannot delegate the power of decision to another. But the dead can and do provide hints and nudges to make the task a little easier, if the living are receptive and willing to live by the thoughts reaching out to them.

Chapter Eleven

How to Prepare for Life After Death

AFTER EXAMINING THIS MATERIAL, we have reached the point where we must ask: What are the implications of these phenomena, if they are authentic?

First of all, the phenomena, both spontaneous and induced, *exist*. Nothing can make them go away, even if *some* scientists with materialistic concepts wish they would. We have to grant that there is no longer any question of the genuineness of the reported incidents and experiences. There is no loophole for the doubter. No way out. No alternative explanation. Nothing has been overlooked, underexamined, or neglected. This is a tremendously important statement. If the experiences herein reported are true, then the world that average people know is not the world that awaits them after death.

However, the cases cited in this book are a mere fraction of the available material. I have reported only what I myself know firsthand. Other investigators have had similar, parallel experiences. The literature of psychic research contains many additional valid cases. They are not isolated oddities easily set aside until "further research" will cast light upon them or, some would hope, invalidate them. They rather are typical cases involving evidence of personal survival after death. Now if they be typical, then the position of the materialist concerning the existence of the soul and the hereafter must be atypical or incorrect. The evidence and the materialist position cannot be reconciled.

The problem rests perhaps in the general attitudes of average people when dealing with religious concepts. Very few take their religion literally. Religion speaks of the hereafter as a world existing somewhere out there but restricts itself to its acceptance by faith alone. Religion does not wish to come to grips with objective proof that such a world does in fact exist. If it did, it would have very little left of its substance. The morality of religion perhaps, the ethical concepts, and some historical traditions would remain, but nothing basic would.

But if religion has of necessity avoided the matter of proving or disproving the existence of a hereafter world, science has no such problem. To the contrary, science has the obligation to delve into this subject with all its tools. Unfortunately most representatives of empiric science are incapable of dealing with the subject on its own terms. Instead of exploring the nature of and laws that regulate the nonphysical world, both within human beings and without, and arriving at a set of laws that correspond to the evidence at hand, they try to establish a prior framework of laws, drawn from physical science, and force the evidence of survival after death into it. In the process of squeezing the evidence through this filter, most of the valid material remains outside; what comes through is merely a small part of the truth.

A small and fortunately increasing number of scientists with psychic research interests do apply the methods proposed by me here and get much better results. In studying the available evidence free from all prejudice and preconceived notions of methodology and then evaluating it at face value, one arrives at some startling discoveries. For one thing, the nonphysical world obeys nonphysical laws and not physical laws. That should come as no surprise to anyone but hard-core materialists, but it still puzzles some researchers who cannot conceive of a more nearly perfect or different set of laws than the physical ones.

There are certain recurring patterns running through many cases. In sorting the cases by type and then comparing the similarities, one arrives at certain conclusions regarding the laws under which such phenomena exist and operate. At first, one does not question the probability of such events in terms of ordinary physics, because in doing so one would automatically have to exclude the bulk of the material. But ordinary physics does not apply to extraordinary sets of circumstances, just as terrestrial navigation does not suit a celestial voyage around the moon or the stars.

Each set of laws has its own area of usefulness and reference. The problem with the nonphysical world is to locate the point of reference and then explore the laws converging on it, or from it, depending again on the observer.

In my view, this point of reference is the duality of human personality. Man consists of an inner body and an outer body. The inner body is the seat of personality, and it outlives the outer body at physical death. It in turn is recast in the process of reincarnation. Thus the energy field that each personality represents is forever on the move, never dissipated entirely and continually changing form.

In my view, the duality of the human being is the reason for the dual set of laws: physical and nonphysical laws governing the two areas of personality. As the physical laws govern the outer, or physical, body and all that is material or of substance in our ordinary physical world, so the laws governing the nonphysical body apply only to the psyche and its manifestations via the mind, emotions, feelings, and thoughts and its final extension into the thought world beyond the grave.

Perhaps the medieval concept of a macrocosmos and a microcosmos hinted at this duality. At the macrocosmic level we humans are all part of one and the same existence, in which we are subject to one and the same law or set of laws. On the microcosmic level, we are as different from one another as our human frailties and foibles make us. We obey the physical laws of the universe we know and have learned from observing.

In speaking of a dual structure in humans I do not mean to imply that the two halves are equal in any sense. The kernel of a person's true self is the personality imbedded in the inner body. It exists without difficulty independent of and without the outer body, both incarnate and discarnate. But the outer body not only disintegrates promptly at the moment of separation from the inner body; it is subject to many weaknesses and imperfections while still covering the inner body. Thus by its very nature, the outer body is vastly inferior in importance to the inner body, although a necessary adjunct to it primarily for the acquisition of life experiences in the concept of reincarnation and karma.

Even while the two bodies are connected in the physical lifetime of a person, the seat of personality is in the inner body and not the outer. The brain is not the center of man's thought activities, but the mind that operates the brain is.

The Russian scientists who first examined the functions of ESP proposed a physiological origin for this strange power in humans. Although I hold that duality is the intent of nature, I also feel that there is nothing in the universe that is *totally* "nonphysical." Everything that exists has some substance. The nonphysical world is merely a world consisting of a finer substance than the physical world; ESP is a mental and emotional activity. But the energies necessary to operate the nonphysical world have physical properties; they are particles of electrically charged matter traveling at high speeds. Thus the physiological aspects of a person's nonphysical self are by no means as farfetched as a first glance at the Russian findings would lead one to think.

If one is an unbiased observer or researcher in this field and realizes the reality of the psychic phenomena indicating personal survival after death and communication with the so-called dead, the philosophical concepts required by this view will immediately become a major issue. For if people have a nonphysical part, perhaps animals have, too, and even flowers might exhibit such amazing nonphysical tendencies. The evidence to support such a view is just as strong as the evidence for personal survival in humans. But animals and flowers do not speak to us in words; consequently they cannot sound or appear so convincing as can the living dead.

I will go even further: everything in nature, not only the organic but even the inorganic, and perhaps even that which is created by humans, has some sort of counterpart in the nonphysical world. Of course it has. That is, if a human can *think* of a thing, it exists. In recreating the world they knew, people create a facsimile of the world to surround them in the new dimension into which death has catapulted them. Many of the communications from the dead, and some from people who have been "over" and had to come back, speak of beautiful country vistas and colors and nature at its best. It would seem that everything over there is as it is here, only better and more highly developed.

Some of the most interesting testimony comes from people who "died" on the operating table in a hospital, or in an accident, and then were brought back by the skill of the medical profession. Or perhaps they came back because they had not yet been expected in the land of the spirit. The orthodox medical profession will bury these experiences under the label of "hallucination due to shock or anesthetics," but the description of the views seen by such cases is startlingly similar and quite logical in its details.

For instance, a woman whose heart had stopped during an operation saw herself walking in a beautiful landscape like a park. At the end of a winding road she noticed some people in white gowns who waved at her to go back, calling out to her, "Not yet, go back. . . ."

Next thing she knew she was back in her own body. The surgeon had been massaging her heart, and she was back in the physical world. The experiences of the dying who don't die at the time always include some suggestion of being told "to go back."

❮ Suicides are dealt with sternly on arrival over there. They are treated the way we treat unwanted immigrants without proper passports. Invariably they are forced to rest and go through a reorientation program in which the futility of suicide is explained to them. Moreover the karmic law points at suicides with a shrug: they merely have to do it all over in the next incarnation. Nobody can cheat or escape earthly commitments. What this implies, to my mind, is a very strict law dealing with the time of arrival for each and every one of us. *I don't know who sets up the timetables, but I do know there is no way to change trains.* ❯

In a way, this is comforting, for it eliminates fear of death, if one's spiritual knowledge has not already done so. For surely I cannot die a moment before I am scheduled to go and not a moment later. To try to change this concept would be tantamount to defying the laws that govern all life. This too is one of the important philosophical implications one perceives when one accepts the scientific evidence for survival.

❮ One must enlarge one's thinking to a life span that extends beyond the physical. Certain things one will accomplish during one's physical life, others in the next place, and still other things never. But the comfort of being reunited after a comparatively short period of separation with those one has lost to death should more than compensate for this view of an inescapable fate.

Other implications of this evidence involve the motivation for practically everything one does. From study and professional life to emotional life and pleasure, the question of another world intrudes. Surely, if death is not the end, then that which one does before death counts all the more. One's morality, one's thoughts, suddenly become matters of great concern.

Some will wish to embark on a personal adventure into the world of the psychic to find out once more for themselves if these great truths apply to them as well. In doing so, they invariably become converted from the concept of pure materialism, tempered perhaps by a vague religious consciousness allowing for "something" within a person beyond the physical, to the duality view in which one's spirit is the dominating factor.

Others will put the whole question aside and refuse to look into it at all, preferring to be surprised by the new reality that awaits them after death. By doing so, they merely express their doubts that the "old order" of a single materialistic universe has all the answers. In refusing to look into the evidence of the kind presented here, they forestall their spiritual development, but ultimately they too must learn the truth.

Certainly additional studies should be made of the evidence, and scholars in many fields should be drawn into the investigation. New evidence should be looked into even though so much already exists. This is the scientific way, and I cannot accept the view of some spiritualists who feel their case for personal survival has been proved and that there is therefore no further need to duplicate the efforts.

There is always need to continue the quest for more knowledge in far less significant areas than human nature itself. How much more important is the continuing accumulation of material proving time and again that we do have an immortal portion within ourselves and that there is indeed the liveliest of lives awaiting us after death!

Part Two

Returning to This World

Introduction

THE PURPOSE OF THIS SECTION IS TO ACQUAINT my readers with material pointing in the direction of reincarnation and to analyze this material in terms of some sort of system that would allow us to understand the phenomenon better than we have in the past. Furthermore, it is my intention to delineate a system under which reincarnation and karma seem to work. The purpose of this is to allow my readers to come to some conclusion concerning their philosophy of life; for it is my contention that the system involving reincarnation and the karmic law is the only plausible explanation for our world, the universe of which it is a part, and the seeming contradictions found therein.

As far back as the Stone Age, the ancient Celtic religion of witchcraft, or Wicca, held that humans' ultimate goal is to return again and again in reincarnation cycles to fulfill that which they were unable to fulfill in an earlier lifetime.

Even Christianity, at least in its early forms, has overtones of rebirth, but we must speak of this at the proper time.

Reincarnation, then, as a subject at least in the western world, somehow has always been linked with the East, and to this very day there are serious scientists who think that all examples of reincarnation (that is to say, all those cases that seem to have the ring of truth about them) must of necessity come from India or, at the very least, the East.

It will therefore come as a shock to those who think this way that not a single case in this book occurred in the eastern part of the world. To the contrary, every single one is of western—mainly American—origin and, of course, is factual as far as I am able to determine.

Religious philosophy has played absolutely no part in my work. The purpose of this book is not to reaffirm any religious concept but to determine by analysis whether reincarnation is a fact or a fallacy; to establish whether there are sufficient grounds, sufficient material, and evidence to support a conviction that people are reborn into other bodies, that life does not end at death's door but that all of us do return to continue the cycle of life and rebirth.

True, there are many books dealing with the subject, some of them in a philosophical manner, others quite factually. The problem is not so much to write a book that will present facts never discussed before but to present them in such a manner that an open-minded person can accept them as true. By open-minded, I mean neither committed to reincarnation nor dead set against it. Open-minded people are those who have not yet made up their minds and who are willing to examine the evidence at face value.

The difficulty is in defining not only what reincarnation is but also what constitutes *proof* of reincarnation. First of all, reincarnation is not a return in an animal's body but a return in human form. This may occur at various times in one's life cycle, and it does not follow that everyone reincarnates in exactly the same manner. Far from it! The variety of reincarnation material suggests that each case is different and must therefore be examined on its own merits.

To define my quest scientifically, then, I would say first that reincarnation is the return of a human being in another life. Proof must be of a kind that cannot be explained away by ordinary means. It cannot be vague or subject to another explanation, such as having read books dealing with a particular period or knowledge of the person one feels one has come back as because of some family connection. All these things have to be taken into account when one weighs the evidence, of course, for proof must be absolute, or reasonably absolute. Human beings are fallible, and nothing is 100 percent correct in our lives, but one must strive to attain at least a reasonable amount of evidence before one accepts reincarnation as a fact.

Reincarnation, if generally accepted as factual, would of course greatly influence our personal conduct. I am referring especially to the conduct in times of war, under conditions of violence, or whenever there is a possibility of taking another person's life. Whenever a man or a woman is faced with the commission of a crime or an evil deed (I mean evil in terms of contemporary morality), there is the possibility of "accumulating karma"; that is to say, of mortgaging one's future lifetime in a negative sense. Now, if reincarnation is subject to a universal law of retribution and justice, then an evil deed committed in one lifetime may very well have dire consequences in the next one. The knowledge of this might influence people toward a better life, toward a more moral existence. It may prevent crimes of violence, perhaps even war. This may only be wishful thinking on my part, but it stands to reason that a universal and scientifically accepted conviction that reincarnation is factual would have deep and long-lasting consequences in our entire way of life. The common attitude toward death, for instance, would undergo rapid and profound changes, for if there is more than one lifetime to live, surely one would not fear death as the inevitable end. One might even welcome it at times if the existence one suffers could be exchanged for a better one within a short time. The hopelessly ill might very well welcome the continuing life cycle.

Let there be no mistake about this: Reincarnation is a very important subject today. It may very well be *the* most important subject tomorrow.

Chapter Twelve

What Exactly *Is* Reincarnation?

WHAT EXACTLY IS REINCARNATION? Derived from the Latin, *reincarnation* literally means "to enter the flesh again." The equivalent term in German, *Wiederverkörperung*, means reembodiment. Other descriptive terms include *rebirth, to be born again*, and, in German, *Wiedergeburt* (rebirth). In French, the word *renaissance* has the same literal meaning (rebirth) but is not used in the same way. Renaissance simply means a renewal of life or interest in life, a rebirth of productivity. Capitalized, it refers to renewed interest in classical art. The number of incarnations is not defined in any term; it merely indicates that one has been born at some other time.

In the world of parapsychology we speak of discarnates and incarnates, meaning dead individuals and living individuals. A reincarnated individual has been born again in a physical body, with the understanding that some sort of memory or proof lingers on from that earlier lifetime. Basically, the idea of reincarnation involves the conviction that one may die and lose one's physical body and then return in another physical body, live another lifetime, and presumably die again in the same manner, only to return once again for any number of times. This system involves either no memory of previous lives or only partial memory of the so-called karmic law governing it. This will be discussed in detail later.

Reincarnation concepts should not be mistaken for two other ideas with which they are frequently confused. *Anabaptism*, meaning to be baptized again, is purely a religious concept prevalent among certain Protestant splinter groups. In the sixteenth century a group of religious fanatics called Anabaptists even seized the city of Münster in Westphalia, Germany, and held it for awhile, establishing a religiously oriented state. This state was eventually destroyed by the bishop of Münster, and the Anabaptists were mercilessly suppressed. The French composer Giacomo Meyerbeer wrote a celebrated opera, *Le Prophete*, based on this event.

In more recent times, certain U.S. fundamentalist communities have also practiced anabaptism. The idea behind it is to be baptized again, usually after one has reached adulthood, as a declaration of faith in Jesus Christ; the original baptism, undertaken when the subject was a mere baby and therefore unable to grasp the significance of the act, is thus reinforced by a conscious baptism at a time when the individual is fully aware of the implications and thus can make his or her declaration of faith that much stronger.

Another idea frequently confused with reincarnation is *transmigration*, which refers to the passing of the soul from one state to another at death. Actually, to transmigrate means to journey through an area. Transmigration signifies a possible incarnation of a human soul into animal form and, conversely, the rebirth of an animal soul into a human at a later stage of development in order to purify the soul. This philosophy, basically of oriental origin, is based on the idea that all life must undergo a gradual development up the ladder of existence. It was part and parcel of the Egyptian religion in antiquity; it is still considered a valid belief by the Vedic religion of present-day India. To date I have not found any strictly scientific evidence to support this contention. This does not mean that the concept is impossible; it only means that no factual evidence has yet turned up to support it. Probably the most valid parallel to the concept of transmigration can be found by observing the stages of the human fetus. It undergoes a rapid passing through various stages of development, including a number of animal-like stages. Some warm-blooded animals also undergo changes from a lower order of existence to the final, higher state into which they are born. No doubt future research will enlighten us further on this aspect of soul travel.

Reincarnation has always been viewed differently in the West than in the East. By West I mean Europe and the Americas—to the extent that they were colonized by European people. By East I mean the Near, Middle, and Far East and Africa. Western society has generally viewed reincarnation as a subject not fit for logical discussion. Only in recent years has it become acceptable in the West to consider the possibility on a scientific basis. Western civilization, therefore, has nearly always avoided considering the impact of such a system upon its development. When there was material pointing in the direction of reincarnation, it was considered an oddity or an exception to an otherwise perfect system. If avoidance did not lead to a total sweeping under the carpet, then the problem of explaining the "unusual phenomenon" of reincarnation was relegated to religious and philosophical authorities. Most of the great philosophers of the nineteenth century viewed reincarnation with little respect. Even in our century, men who were friendly toward psychic research, such as Dr. Carl Jung, did not go far enough in accepting the probability of reincarnation. If anything, the idea of "coming back as someone else" was a subject for popular jokes; in particular the idea of coming back as an animal was held up as punishment for misdeeds in another lifetime.

A kind of transmigration is a frequent subject in western mythology and in the wider realm of fairy stories. The idea of the enchanted prince who must live as a frog until some fair maiden saves him from his fate by being faithful runs through most western societies. But the change from one form of existence to another was not a matter of advancing development. Rather, it was a fiat of some supernatural authority, such as a sorcerer or a deity. Changing a human being into an animal or vice versa was reserved to those possessed of magical or superior powers.

No attempt at verification was ever made of these myths and stories. The stories were taken at face value by children but regarded as symbolic or merely charming tales by adults. One might possibly consider them as indicative of turning the inner being into something more valuable, but I doubt that many adults look at fairy tales with such far-reaching and analytical eyes. The idea of changing a human being into something else or an animal into a human being is not so much an expression of the desirability of the altered state as an expression of power; that is, the power of the one who does the enchanting. Sometimes the power to change is inherent in the position the sorcerer holds. A great magician, a wise man, a powerful monarch perhaps are expected to have inherent powers to do all sorts of wondrous things. An evil witch—standard character of the western European fairy tale—also has the power to do terrible things to human beings and to animals. In her case, the power comes with the job. Others may obtain the power temporarily or on special occasions: the little boy who overhears a gnome speak the magical formula that opens the mountain, imitates it, and also succeeds, only to be tripped up later by the very fact that his magical knowledge is incomplete. Or the power may be conferred on an ordinary mortal by a superior agency, such as the good fairy granting someone three wishes.

In most fairy tales, magical formulas or words are used. The power inherent in *words* goes back to the very dawn of humankind, when nearly all religions considered the name of the deity sacred and possessed of great powers. When the name of the deity (or deities) was pronounced in vain, that power was dissipated, and consequently the name was not spoken but covered up by the use of another term. Word magic rests largely on the belief that it works; changing from one appearance to another—from human being to animal and vice versa—is possible instantaneously, provided one knows the right words. They have to be spoken in just the right way or at a certain time or in a special place, of course. Ancient magical manuscripts supplied the necessary details. In many fairy tales such special books form part of the lore.

Although the concept of transmigration as such is not anchored in western philosophy, the idea that one might change shape under special circumstances runs through all of it. In addition to the fairy tale, there are of course the horror tales, such as the werewolf traditions of eastern Europe, and vampirism, said to originate in Romania but also strongly entrenched in western Europe. According to these beliefs, man can change into a wolf or vampire—a bloodsucking animal—at certain times, especially when the moon is full. (Actually, *lycanthropy* is a real disease, in which an individual displays animalistic behavior due to certain disturbances of the nervous and vascular systems.)

In the East the idea of transmigration is much more firmly anchored. Even with religions in which it does not form part of the dogma, the idea of being changed into an animal at the discretion of the supreme power occurs from time to time. Messengers from heaven or hell or their equivalents appear in various disguises and are capable of changing back and forth with the greatest of ease. Anyone who has ever read the *Arabian Nights* knows of the jinns, or little devils, and of course of the genie, another form of the same word. In the Tibetan pantheon alone there are several hundred demons or demigods, many of them part animal or all animal in appearance and representing various forces of nature. Similar interweaving of the worlds of man and of animals occurs in the Vedic religion. Animalistic forms occur on occasions in Buddhism and Shintoism as well. In these cases, however, there is no well-ordered system whereby every soul goes through various states—from low animal to human being and beyond into a divine form of existence—such as we find, for instance, in the ancient Egyptian religion. Orthodox Hindus hold such beliefs, it is true, but the caste system is still tied to individual effort and does not work equally for everybody. Just the same, in the Vedic religion we have the closest approach to orderly belief in reincarnation as we understand it in terms of western research. Although the Hindus accept reincarnation as part of their religion, and on faith alone, it gives them the same comfort a westerner might derive from scientific evidence pointing to the existence of the reincarnation for all.

In the East, especially in Africa, we find the belief in the return of souls into the bodies of their own descendants, such as the souls of important warriors or kings returning in the bodies of their children. These beliefs are not based on any objective research but are more in the nature of political stratagems. Similarly, the Tibetan search for the next incarnation of the Dalai Lama immediately following the death of the previous Dalai Lama is motivated not so much by objective research methods as by considerations of state and religious beliefs.

When we leave the area of religion and philosophy, where, after all, everyone may have his or her own ideas—ideas with which one can scarcely argue since they are essentially personal—we come face to face with the public acceptance of and attitude toward the reported occurrences of seemingly valid reincarnation cases. In the East, such matters are still reported in the press and in books with very little public attention, almost with public apathy. This isn't because the public lacks interest in such matters but because, by and large, the people of the East have lived with the concept of reincarnation, and frequently also of transmigration, for so long that any reports bearing on such subjects seem anticlimactic to them. Only among revolutionary societies and certain government circles in present-day India do we find active resistance to reports dealing with reincarnation material. But even in modern India, there are several universities studying phenomena of this kind in much the same way universities study them in the West; Professor H. N. Banerjee is probably the best-known authority in this area.

Although the former Soviet Union and its satellites until recently looked with jaundiced eyes upon all psychic phenomena, research projects into ESP phenomena and all related subjects are now going on at more than a dozen universities in those countries. When reincarnation material occurs, it is treated with respect, although they do not necessarily reach the same conclusions a western researcher might.

But in the West, which includes, as I have already pointed out, the Americas, reincarnation as a serious public issue dates back only a few decades. True, Swedish researchers regressed subjects with excellent results many years before the Bridey Murphy case burst upon the public scene. But it was Morey Bernstein, with his book *The Search for Bridey Murphy*, who acquainted large sectors of the general public with evidential material pertaining to reincarnation.

Bernstein is the son of a wealthy manufacturer of plumbing, heating, and electrical supplies in Pueblo, Colorado. In 1953 he became interested in hypnosis and started to experiment with various subjects. As a young man of means, he did this solely out of curiosity and not because he hoped that his research would yield anything of commercial value. In his home in Colorado, and later in New York City, he pursued his studies of hypnosis and regression into former lives with a zeal that overshadowed all his other duties. Shortly after Bernstein concluded his first experiments with a housewife from Colorado,

Mrs. Virginia Tighe, now known as Mrs. Morrow, he played the tapes for me in his New York City apartment. I was impressed with both the sincerity of his efforts and the quality of the tapes, which contained much regression material concerning an alleged former life of Mrs. Tighe in Ireland.

Under hypnotic regression Mrs. Tighe recalled in great detail her life as Bridget, or Bridey, Murphy, giving so much in the way of names, dates, and places (Bridey Murphy was born in Cork in 1798 and died in Belfast in 1864) that Bernstein felt sure he had stumbled upon an authentic case of reincarnation. He told his findings for the first time in *Empire Magazine*, the magazine supplement of the *Denver Post*, in 1954. The response to his article was so great that he decided to put it all into book form, and in 1956 *The Search for Bridey Murphy* was published. In the book he protected Mrs. Tighe by giving her anonymity. This was a wise move since the book became an immediate bestseller. Despite the attempt to hide her name from public knowledge, entrepreneurs managed to get through to Mrs. Tighe and offered her all sorts of opportunities, ranging from nightclub appearances to franchising automobile agencies. Despite the documented findings, however, Mrs. Tighe does not believe in reincarnation to this day. Both she and Mr. Bernstein refused all kinds of offers, preferring the rational, scientific approach to the problem. They did, however, permit Paramount to make a movie based on the book. In the motion picture Teresa Wright played Mrs. Tighe and Louis Hayward played Bernstein. Part of the payment received for the motion picture rights went to the subject. The motion picture was a flop, perhaps because it treated the book with less than sincerity and respect.

Today, if you were to ask the average person whether he or she remembers Bridey Murphy, the most likely answer would be, "Yes, but wasn't that proved to be a hoax?" This proves, if nothing else, the old Roman saying *semper aliquid haeret*, meaning "something always sticks." No matter how great a lie or smear, no matter how unfounded, people will remember it even if it has later been proved false. Thus it was with the book. Although it is not generally known, a major picture magazine tried to buy rights to the story from Mr. Bernstein. The author did not like the terms and refused the offer. Shortly afterward, the same picture magazine sent a team of investigators to look into the background of Mrs. Tighe. In the Middle West they came up with what they claimed to be proof of Mrs. Tighe's Irish background. From bits and pieces, neighborhood conversations, hasty conclusions concerning her acquaintanceship with an Irish priest, the picture magazine constructed the story that the "reincarnation memory" was actually due to her childhood memories of Irish people in her immediate environment. So contrived was the "explanation," and so patently motivated by the earlier rejection of a sale to the same magazine, that Mr. Bernstein's hometown paper—the respected *Denver Post*—found the money and personnel to put together an investigative team of their own. The *Denver Post* team, however, went all the way to Ireland to check out the original story in painstaking detail. The result was that the *Denver Post* published a six-part series concerning the Bridey Murphy case, in which not only were all of Mr. Bernstein's original findings corroborated but much new material was added to it, upholding the reincarnation theory.

Later on, the new material was incorporated into a reissue of the book itself and in the paperback version, which came out in 1970. At that time, Morey Bernstein spent part of the year in Miami. As a result of the renewed interest in the story, Bernstein and his star subject were interviewed again in the press and on television. "Writing *Bridey* was the most important thing I've done in my lifetime," Bernstein was quoted as saying. "Today the book is taken seriously by psychic researchers and enjoying a new popularity. It has been called a parapsychological classic, and its principals are finally able to laugh at its debunkers," said Bob Wilcox, the *Miami News* religion editor. Nowadays, Morey Bernstein commutes between his winter home in Colorado and his summer home in Florida, is knee-deep in the investment business, and is planning to write two more books.

Chapter Thirteen

The Scientific View of Reincarnation

"THE EVIDENCE INDICATES THAT REINCARNATION is a fact. I think it likely that people have been born before and that after they die will be born again on this earth." This was the headline-making quotation in an article on reincarnation in the popular weekly *National Enquirer*. This weekly newspaper is not known for its subtlety of approach nor for the reliability of its information. But the above quotation is not from some metaphysical believer or astrologer or amateur investigator. It was the expressed opinion of Dr. Ian Stevenson, head of the Department of Neurology and Psychiatry at the University of Virginia's School of Medicine. Dr. Stevenson has for many years been the champion of reincarnation research in the United States. His first book on the subject, *Twenty Cases Suggestive of Reincarnation*, was soon followed by additional material that he published through the American Society for Psychical Research. Stevenson has investigated cases both in the West and in the East and has done so on a careful, scientific basis. No one can rightly accuse Dr. Stevenson of being a charlatan or of jumping to conclusions. His language is careful, and he makes no unjustified claims. The difficulty toward total acceptance of his findings and the findings of others like myself that parallel them lies in the stubborn insistence on the part of most orthodox scientists that laboratory experiments are the only way of proving reincarnation. "Nobody has as yet thought up a way that reincarnation could be proved in a laboratory or a test tube," the professor is quoted in his interview. In studying hundreds of valid reincarnation cases, he combined the methods of the historian, lawyer, and psychiatrist. Gathering testimony from as many witnesses as he could, he and his staff sometimes interviewed as many as twenty-five people regarding a certain case. Sometimes, if the original talk was not satisfactory or conclusive, he went back for further interviews. Everything was taken into account: the behavior of the person who claimed to have lived before; the environment in which he or she lived; background, education, and general knowledge; and even personal habits. "Many of those claiming to have lived before are children. Often they are very emotional when they talk of the person they used to be, and they can give minute details of the life they lived," Dr. Stevenson added.

Dr. Stevenson, just as any responsible parapsychologist does, always looks for alternate explanations before he accepts reincarnation as the answer to a puzzling case. Everything is considered: early experiences, accidental information, newspaper accounts—anything that might have been forgotten consciously but can be brought out under hypnosis. Fraud, memory lapses, fantasy, and wishful thinking are considered and eventually ruled out before a valid case for reincarnation is established, according to Dr. Stevenson's method of inquiry. But that is by no means the end. He explained that he also considers and excludes telepathy as a means of obtaining unusual information. "Extrasensory perception cannot account for the fact that the subject has skills and talents not learned, such as the ability to speak a foreign language without having had the opportunity to learn it in this present life."

Most of the cases investigated by Dr. Stevenson were in India and the East, but he also looked into some interesting situations in Alaska and Europe. This is not because fewer cases occur in the West but because the prevailing attitude of the public traditionally made discovery of such cases difficult. In the East the climate is favorable toward a free and open discussion of such matters; in the West only very courageous people dared come out with statements that they may have lived before.

Old-line scientists prefer to regard reincarnation research as exotic and reject the evidence out of hand without ever examining it. Some parapsychologists, even conservative ones, are eager to examine the material there is, especially since Dr. Stevenson opened the door to such investigations. The acceptance of reincarnation as a reality, however, is a hard nut to swallow for some. Inevitably, it also means acceptance of survival after physical death. Some parapsychologists still cannot accept that probability simply because they have been weaned on laboratory research methods and cannot or do not wish to understand that the evidence is in the field among spontaneous phenomena, or actual, unplanned occurrences.

The material for the survival of human personality is overwhelming, far more so than the evidence for reincarnation. Strangely, though, some support for reincarnation research can be gotten among scientists who, on the surface, would be the least likely to be interested in such a subject. I am speaking here of physicists and physical scientists. The reason is that in learning about the nature of energy and mass and in dealing with the electromagnetic forces in the universe, many of these scientists have come to realize that energy is indestructible. Basing their views to some extent on Albert Einstein's pioneering opinions, they too feel that energy may be transformed into other forms of power or into mass but can never by dissipated entirely. Since the life force—the human personality—is an energy field, they argue that such fields cannot be dissipated either and must therefore *continue to exist in some form*. Experiments involving the discovery of energy fields in so-called haunted locations and of significant changes in the atmosphere of an experimental chamber, such as ionization, have been going on for some time. It is therefore not too surprising that such strong centers of technical learning as the New York Institute of Technology (where I teach) should be interested in parapsychology and, within that field, reincarnation research.

Medical science has been more hostile toward reincarnation material than has any other branch of science. This may be due to the fact that medical science relies heavily upon the assumption that a person is essentially a physical being. As Dr. William McGary, the brilliant physician working in conjunction with the Association for Research and Enlightenment in Phoenix, Arizona, pointed out to me, the basic difference between orthodox medical science and medicine based upon such knowledge as the Edgar Cayce records lies in the way they regard the human being. To conventional medicine the human being is structural; that is to say, the physical body is the essence of being, and mind is merely a subdivision thereof. To the esoterically oriented person the human being is functional, not structural. The physical person is a manifestation of spirit, or mind, which came first, and represents the outward expression of the soul that governs and determines everything from within. Such thinking is at variance with conventional medical procedure, of course, since it necessitates the treating of illness from a total point of view rather than from the usual sectional or physical viewpoint.

For medical doctors to accept reincarnation as a reality requires changes in their medical approach as well; except for the psychiatrist, the conventional physician has little to do with the nonphysical aspects of human personality. The general practitioner and the specialist both leave mental problems to the psychiatrist, concentrating on purely physical problems. Thus the question of reincarnation research becomes essentially one of acceptance or rejection by the psychiatrist and psychoanalyst. Today the majority of psychiatrists explain any valid reincarnation material as malfunctions of personality, ranging all the way from mild neuroses to schizophrenic conditions. Just as the conventional analyst will regard *all* dream material of the patient as purely symbolic and representative of suppressed material in the unconscious part of the mind, so the psychiatrist will explain reincarnation memories either as aberrations of the mind or, if the particular psychiatrist is a Jungian, as racial memories, or archetypes.

But these scoffing psychiatrists and analysts seem to forget that Dr. Sigmund Freud, the father of modern psychiatry, himself leaned toward parapsychology in the later years of his life. He made the statement in print that he would want to study parapsychology if he had to do it all over again. One of his star pupils, Dr. Carl Jung, who contributed as much to psychiatry as Freud, was not only firmly convinced of the reality of psychic phenomena but possessed ESP himself. His discovery or, if you prefer, invention of the *archetypes* as a symbolic expression of "original concepts" does not militate against genuine reincarnation experiences, in his view. At the Jung Institute in Zurich, much research went on in this area in the 1930s and 1940s. In his important work *Acausal Synchronicity (The Law of Meaningful Coincidence)* Jung postulated that there is a superior order of things connecting events and people. This superior order lies beyond the law of cause and effect and must be dealt with on different terms. What Jung is hinting at in this precedent-shaking work is the existence of a law of fate; by trying to explore the ways in which this noncausal link seemed to work, Jung approached the question of fate, free will, and reincarnation (which is intimately connected with them) in a modern, scientific way for the first time.

Chapter Fourteen

The Religious View of Reincarnation

THE RELIGIOUS ESTABLISHMENT HAS VIEWED reincarnation with various attitudes. In the past any deviation from the norm was considered heresy. People were persecuted for it more in the West than in the East, but in essence no established churches like their followers to have doctrinal ideas of their own. In the West, early Christianity contained elements of belief in reincarnation. This may be due to the Essene influences that showed in the teachings of Jesus, due to his background as a student at the Essene monastery at Qumran.

When Christianity became a state religion and the early concepts were edited to fit in with this new view of the faith, much early material was deliberately omitted or suppressed. Not only were several books of the Bible removed, but also passages intimating belief in reincarnation were taken out or rewritten in subsequent translations. From about A.D. 300 onward, Christianity was no longer identical with the early teachings of Jesus but had become a combination of his teachings with later religious philosophical thought and the necessities of an emerging state religion. The medieval church had no use for reincarnation. Belief in the final judgment, a moment when the dead are called to account for their sins on earth, is a cornerstone of

Christian dogma. If man were to go through a succession of lives without that final Judgment Day, much of the power of the faith would have been lost. The Church needed the whip of Judgment Day to keep the faithful in line. It was therefore a matter of survival for the Church not to allow belief in reincarnation to take hold among its followers.

For somewhat different reasons, the Jewish religion does not like the idea of reincarnation either, even though there are hints of it in scriptures. Notably the prophet Elijah was always expected to come again, and this idea can even be found in early Christianity. But the Hebrew faith rejected the idea of reincarnation, since it would indicate a system that was not wholly dependent upon the grace and will of a merciful God. A personal God was very much at the heart of both Hebrew and Christian faiths in the beginning. Only in later years did the moral concept of religion become a stronger focal point.

Some Protestant faiths, especially the Fundamentalists, emphasized Jesus Christ as the personal savior of mankind. Consequently a law that applies universally to all people and gives them rebirth regardless of this personal savior is particularly odious to the Fundamentalists.

Some great religious leaders say one thing, but their followers understand another. Emanuel Swedenborg was an eighteenth-century scientist, philosopher, and seer in Sweden. Among his proven accomplishments is a detailed description of the great fire of Stockholm, which he described to a number of witnesses while some seventy miles away. Swedenborg did not found a new religion in his lifetime; his many books, among which *Heaven and Hell* is perhaps the best known, were later used as the foundation for a religious faith called simply the New Church. It has many followers in Scandinavian countries and in this country, especially in Minnesota, where many immigrants from northern Europe settled, but also in various other parts of the United States. A cornerstone of this religion is a belief in the coming of a "New Jerusalem."

The writings of Swedenborg indicate quite clearly that he had visions in which he saw "the other side of life" very much the way spiritualists do and almost the same way scientists feel who follow the "survivalist" line in parapsychology. The terminology may differ, but in essence Swedenborg spoke of a number of "societies" where people live after physical death. Depending upon the state of consciousness prior to death, one joins a particular society and advances to a higher one when one is ready to do so. The Swedenborgians in the United States are, by and large, a peaceful lot and not given to missionary efforts. It was therefore with some surprise that I received a note from Duncan B. of Minneapolis, an avid Swedenborgian, wondering how I could possibly lean toward reincarnation. "Swedenborg proved reincarnation to be an error once and for all for those who have eyes to see," Mr. B. complained. He sent me a little pamphlet entitled *Reincarnation—the View of the New Church*. As far as rebirth is concerned, the Swedenborgian church accepts only spiritual rebirth, and during earthly life, for the most part, the individual is not even aware of it.

Among modern churches the Episcopal Church and some of the liberal churches, such as the Unitarian faith, have been most receptive to material hinting at the reality of reincarnation. They see no conflict of insurmountable proportions in the teaching of reincarnation and their own concepts. As long as people accept the teachings of Jesus, these churches feel, it does not matter whether they lived once or several times. Very few Catholic priests and laymen will commit themselves on the subject of reincarnation. Those who are open-minded toward it are quite unusual. The problem here lies with fundamental issues: if psychic phenomena are accepted as natural and realistic happenings, the entire basis of the miraculous story of Jesus could be explained entirely on the basis of psychic research. This would, on the one hand, make the miraculous side of it far more acceptable to sophisticated individuals who do not accept their religion on faith alone. But, on the other hand, it would deprive the account of the Resurrection of its uniqueness. It is precisely that uniqueness that the Church needs so sorely to build her entire edifice upon.

Nothing reported about Jesus, both while in the body and after his physical death, is inconsistent with the findings of modern parapsychology. As a matter of fact, parallel happenings have been reported from many other quarters. Perhaps none of them were quite as spectacular or had such fortuitous dissemination, but psychic healing, materialization and dematerialization, levitation, and, finally, the appearance of a person known to have died after physical death are well-attested phenomena that have occurred from time to time in the annals of psychic research all over the world. What makes the position of Jesus unique, therefore, is not the phenomena as such but the *implication* of the phenomena and, of course, Jesus' teachings and views. The phenomena themselves, in my opinion, were used by Jesus consciously and deliberately to underscore his belief in the continuance of life after death. Whether Jesus was, in fact, a believer in reincarnation cannot be ascertained with certainty, especially since so many of his sayings and teachings have been lost, or were perhaps eliminated at later dates. But there was a belief among Jesus' contemporaries that he had come as the reincarnated prophet Elijah, and a much-quoted exhortation "to live, you must be born again" may be a hint at reincarnation beliefs. Much of Jesus' philosophy was misunderstood even at the time when he promulgated it. His references to his "Father," his assertion that his kingdom was not of this world, "judge not lest ye be judged," are all indications of symbolic language and were, I think, not to be taken literally.

Although we are moving toward greater enlightenment in religion and a much more flexible attitude on the part of the various religious establishments, we have as yet not come to grips with the problem of integrating scientific findings into the religious edifice, especially when such findings go counter to traditional doctrine. When the various religious establishments realize that there lies strength in incorporating scientifically supported findings of this kind into their philosophies, they may very well regain their following, especially among the young.

Chapter Fifteen

Regressive Hypnosis as Evidence for Reincarnation

To BEGIN WITH, no one should undertake regression experiments who is not fully qualified to do so. By qualified I mean
not simply possessing a knowledge of hypnosis—that, of course,
is necessary—but also having a deeper understanding of the
problems involved in bringing a person back, through childhood and the threshold of birth, into an earlier lifetime. Only a
trained psychic researcher and hypnotist should undertake this.

When *The Search for Bridey Murphy* was a bestseller, a
great deal of attention was focused on this technique. Morey
Bernstein had come to the field as a novice, and hypnosis to him
was nothing more than a hobby at first. That his book was
honest and authentic is the more to his credit. Despite those who
tried to discredit it, it was later fully exonerated. But there is the
danger when those unfamiliar with the technique are involving
themselves with it that a person may have unresolved psychiatric problems in this lifetime that can become acute or aggra-
vated by simple hypnosis. If such is the case, the operator—that
is to say, the hypnotist—must be qualified to deal with them so
that no damage may result to the psyche of the subject.

Assuming then that those who wish to regress another
person are fully qualified to undertake this task, I will proceed

to explain the techniques I find most useful and successful in obtaining the desired information.

To begin with, the majority of individuals who feel they might be good subjects generally are not. Just claiming that hypnosis would yield good results with oneself doesn't mean that this will be the case. Many people harbor resentments and other forms of resistance, usually on an unconscious level. They cannot be hypnotized even though consciously they are willing to go under the hypnotist's spell.

I find that no more than one-fourth of those who are willing subjects can actually be brought under hypnotic control, and only one in ten people makes an excellent hypnotic subject. There is no rule as to the kind of person who can be easily hypnotized. Generally women are easier to hypnotize than men. But there are exceptions even among women, who may have difficulty letting go control over their bodies and personalities, something absolutely essential if genuine hypnosis is to take place. Emotional people are probably more prone to be good subjects than logical and reserved individuals.

A positive attitude toward the experiment is valuable but not essential. On the other hand, a negative attitude, which includes unwillingness to let go of one's self-control, may frequently thwart the efforts of the operator. I usually suggest that subjects make themselves comfortable on a couch or in an easy chair, remove shoes if they are too confining, and relax for a few moments before beginning the actual verbalization. I then suggest that people close their eyes and listen to my voice. I will usually count from one to ten and suggest that at the count of ten the person be fully relaxed. This is followed by instructions to the various limbs of the person's body, saying that the limbs are becoming heavier and heavier and that the whole body finally feels as if it were sinking down into the couch.

I then proceed to suggest that the individual is quite alone and can only hear my voice coming from a distance but that no extraneous noises will be heard. Again I count to ten, suggesting that at the end of the second ten the individual will float out into the distance, far away from the usual surroundings, but that my voice will always be heard.

Depending on the success of the first stage, I then suggest that individuals will be able to hear everything I say and will not awaken until I awaken them; that, however, they will answer all my questions without awakening.

All this time I observe very closely and carefully whether hypnosis is in fact taking place or whether the person is still fully awake. I do not test my subjects with needles or in any other physical manner. This is strictly for stage hypnotists, and I view their work with both alarm and disdain, for hypnosis is too serious a subject to be used for entertainment purposes.

To reach the third, or deepest, stage of hypnosis I will suggest another ten steps down an imaginary staircase, toward the sea or toward some pleasant open area such as a meadow. I suggest conditions symbolizing freedom from all problems, total aloneness, and a happy climate such as a blue sky, clouds overhead, a sunny day, or some other form of atmospheric condition symbolic of well-being. At this point, most subjects are indeed under hypnotic control. I test this by asking individuals for their name and age; if they are not hypnotized at this point I will be told, "But I am not under yet, Mr. Holzer." In that event I have to start all over again, and if I do not succeed the second time, I generally dismiss subjects and ask them to return some other time, for it can very well happen that a subject feels tense on first meeting me and may be relaxed a second time. If after the second visit no hypnosis results, I regretfully dismiss the subject and turn to another person for further research.

People cannot be hypnotized against their will or without their express wish to go under—at least not in the total sense in which I use hypnosis. People have fallen under spells through repetition, through advertising, or through slogans that they may hear or see on such mass communication media as television or the stage. But specific personal hypnosis, especially the kind needed for regression, is possible only with the cooperation of the subject.

Assuming that my subject has now gone down to the third, or deepest, stage of hypnosis, I will suggest age regression. This means that I will say, you are now so many years old and so many years old, and gradually will suggest the person is at a younger and earlier stage of life. Having suggested a specific date in the person's lifetime, I will then request information about the circumstances he or she lived under at that time. I will ask for the name of a schoolteacher or an address where the family lived at the time, the sort of information that one would only know if one were indeed at that age, and the kind of information that one is prone to forget at a later stage in life. This, of course, proves that under hypnosis one remembers a great deal more than one is aware of in the conscious, or ordinary state.

Gradually I will then regress the person back to childhood and to the moment of birth. After this I suggest crossing the threshold of birth into another lifetime. Sometimes I will give a figure, such as fifty years before birth or a hundred years before birth; or at other times I will simply direct the person to go back until he or she meets an earlier incarnation, another person in another lifetime. When this happens, I ask for specific details and a description of the person, the period, and the circumstances under which the scenes now described take place.

Having obtained information of this kind, I then bring individuals back into the present by easy stages, making sure that they are not taken out of the hypnotic stage too quickly. Just before bringing them back to ordinary consciousness, I will suggest that nothing be remembered from the discussion or conversation held between myself and the subject under hypnosis. I will then add that a feeling of well-being will be experienced immediately upon awakening. If individuals have requested that I help them fight against abuses or bad habits, such as excessive smoking or drinking, I will at that moment insert a message to the unconscious to the effect that the person will not be able to smoke or drink as much as before, or not at all, depending upon the desire of the individual. After that I will count to ten once again, instructing individuals that at the second count of ten, they will be fully awake and in good spirits.

This happens quickly, and individuals generally do not remember much or anything of the conversation that has taken place between us while they were under hypnotic regression. If some parts are remembered, this indicates that hypnosis was not as deep as desirable and that on future occasions I must correct this condition. However, even a full remembrance of everything said under hypnosis does not prove that the state of hypnotic regression was not in fact successful. Some individuals have total recall even when instructed not to do so.

A few minutes later, the subject will be allowed to get up and go home. Generally I need between one and five sessions to establish full character in the case of previous lifetimes. On occasion a single session has done what four or five sessions might do in other cases. This all depends on the depth at which the earlier lifetime material is buried in the unconscious of the subject.

I never do any corroboration or research while still working actively with a subject but begin my conscious research only after I am satisfied that I have obtained all the possible material that I can from this particular subject.

There is, of course, the problem of fantasy, which one must always reckon with. Some researchers feel that reincarnation material in general consists only of fantasy manufactured by a willing unconscious to please the researcher. I do not for a moment accept this version, but there are cases where fantasy may play a part. In my many years of reincarnation research, I have never encountered a seemingly genuine case where fantasy played a significant role, but I have encountered cases of hypnosis in which subjects related fantasy stories in order to work out some repressed material or some unattainable goal in real life. These, however, pertain solely to the present incarnation and not to earlier lifetimes.

When one deals with genuine or seemingly genuine material, it is always imperative to try to corroborate as much of it as possible. Only when at least a portion of the information can be traced and is not due to other factors can we assume reincarnation to be the explanation. Then, too we must realize that reincarnation does not work, apparently, in the same way for everybody and that it is a highly individual and sophisticated process in which each case must be taken on its own merits. There are rules, but they do not apply to everyone in exactly the same way. How the law works is still partially a mystery, but that it *exists* I do not doubt in the least.

Chapter Sixteen

Recurrent Dreams Indicative of Reincarnation

SINCE A PERSON'S UNCONSCIOUS MIND CAN BE entered more easily during the sleeping state, a large number of psychic experiences take place while the individual is asleep. It appears that the communications, such as they may be, can be implanted in the unconscious of the sleeper with less resistance from the conscious mind than would be the case if the communication were attempted during a wakeful state.

The majority of dreams, however, do not fall into this category. There are four different types of dreams. The first type of dream may be caused by physical discomfort; the second type may contain suppressed emotional material, frequently of a symbolic nature and furnishing the basic material for the psychoanalyst; a third type of dream contains psychic material if the individual is sufficiently advanced in ESP development; and the fourth type of dream corresponds to what is now called "out-of-body" experience, in which the etheric body of the individual travels to places outside of the physical body. Recurrent dreams fall into the third category and consist of precise, frequently emotionally tinged dreams that repeat identical or very similar scenes more than one time. The more frequently the recurrent dream occurs, the stronger the emotional memory seems to be. This does not mean that potential reincarnation material cannot also be found in single dreams but suggests that recurrent dreams are inevitably connected with some sort of reincarnation remembrance. In the recurrent-dream phenomenon the dream is usually well remembered on awakening, to the point that it is hard to shake even during the course of the day. When it reoccurs it is usually identical to previous incidents and in some cases may advance the action, as it were, of the previous dream, generally slightly but significantly.

It is the nature of dreams to be condensed versions of actual occurrences. Consequently we find that even ordinary dreams are very short representations of what under ordinary logical conditions would be extended periods of time. In the recurrent dream episodes the number of facts pertaining to a given situation are also strongly condensed; that is to say, only the key words or facts are flashed into the unconscious mind of the sleeper, much in the nature of a telegram. On awakening, the key words are easily remembered and can be written down, if necessary, in order to be followed up. Recurrent dreams are generally very emotional and frequently deal with situations involving death or tragedy or, at the very least, highly dramatic conditions. It is also significant that such dreamers always see themselves in the dream not as an outsider but as a participant. If the physical figure of the sleeper is not actually perceived, a sense of presence is nevertheless felt.

In this respect, recurrent dreams differ greatly from ordinary psychic experiences, even those that may be ascribed to intervention from deceased individuals trying to communicate with the sleeper and using the sleeper as a medium for their unexpressed communications. This is an important point, since those not too familiar with reincarnation research but otherwise cognizant of ESP and psychic phenomena tend to substitute ordinary ESP communications for genuine reincarnation explanations. The difference between a psychic experience where the sleeper merely acts as the *receiver* of information from a deceased individual and those where the sleeper is involved as a *principal* is very important: In recurrent dreams containing reincarnation material, sleepers see or feel themselves in the scene. Where the sleepers merely act as mediums, they never put themselves into the scene but feel very probably, that they are an observer, standing on the outside, as it were, looking in.

The people to whom events of this kind happen come from all walks of life, all social backgrounds, and all ages. There is nothing specific about them, nothing that would single them out as being prone to reincarnation memories or even to psychic phenomena. Having ESP or experiencing something along psychic lines is in no way unnatural or supernatural, and people who partake of these experiences can be any kind of people—you and me included.

Diane R., a Chicago housewife and mother in her early forties, works as a film laboratory technician. Her husband is a supervisor, and she has two children, ages ten and fifteen. When she first contacted me, it was because reincarnation memories and other psychic experiences had disturbed her. She wanted to know what they meant and if necessary how to cope with them. Her interest in the occult was practically nonexistent at first, and she had only once before been hypnotized, three years prior to our meeting when she wanted to stop smoking.

When we met in Chicago, she was visibly nervous. Her face was pale. She smoked one cigarette after another, since the attempt to stop smoking had evidently not been a success. "I have had numerous dreams and feelings, and most of them involve my husband or close friends," she explained. "One dream involved my husband and another woman, and in it I actually saw them on the street in front of a restaurant in the town where I was then living, Harvey, Illinois. Her face was not clear, but on her sweater was the initial *J*. In the dream I was very upset, and I remember stamping on my husband's foot and kicking him in the shin and then walking away. A few days later I learned through a friend that my husband had indeed had an affair with a young lady whose initial was *J*. She worked in the restaurant I had seen in my dream. I confronted him with the evidence of the dream, and he admitted it. But he wanted to know how I knew about it." Telling her husband that she had dreamed the information would not have done any good, so she simply told him that a friend had given her the information. Since Mrs. R. expressed a desire to be regressed hypnotically in order to learn about any previous lives, I wondered whether she had ever had any indication that she had lived before.

"I've always had a strong interest in the pre-Civil War South," she explained. "I read everything and anything I can get my hands on, and I am very interested in the period but only until the middle of the war, and then I don't seem to care any longer. Coming back from Florida in 1968, I was going through Georgia and admiring the countryside. My father-in-law was driving, and we were just passing through a wooded area. Suddenly I had a strong impulse to go down a certain side road, but I am sure if I had gone down that road I would have discovered something about a previous life in Georgia. I have a feeling that I lived as a slave."

"Have you ever had any specific dreams in which you saw yourself as someone else?" I inquired.

"I've seen myself wearing long dresses, but I couldn't see the face, just the clothes. I've seen myself drowning. It is always dark in those dreams, and it seems to have something to do with a wooden bridge. I have a recurrent dream about being in the water and it being dark."

Karen M. contacted me in New York because of what seemed to her a puzzling experience. Consequently I met with her in October 1972 when I visited Houston, Texas. The attractive young woman had had some premonitory dreams most of her growing years. About five years before we met, she began to feel that she really belonged in the France of about 1740. She kept seeing herself dressed in long, fluffy dresses. In another scene she saw herself in what she considers the early eighteen hundreds, somewhere in an area that had not been fully settled as yet. She and her husband were living in a little log cabin. She remembers that he had asked her to go out and get something from outside of the cabin near a ravine. When she went out, she saw an Indian standing beside a tree. Frightened, she yelled for her husband to come out. She remembers her husband telling her not to move, and then she saw him shoot the Indian in the stomach. It was a horrible dream but very real to her—she even felt the leaves crunching under her feet.

Although the conscious material was not overwhelming in terms of evidence, I decided to hypnotize her to see whether additional evidence might surface under hypnosis. Karen was fairly nervous but eventually calmed down sufficiently for me to be able to put her under. When I reached 165 years prior to her birth, she reported seeing a little boy with red hair but did not know who he was. At minus 200, however, she described a village and someone named Molly. Molly was a four-year-old girl she knew then, she explained in the hypnotic state. I took

Karen, or Molly that is, back to age eighteen, and now there was also a boy named John Bradbury. The scene, according to the hypnotized subject, was England in the seventeen hundreds, and the location was called Abanel. Karen now became someone else, even to her facial expressions. Under questioning she disclosed that her name was Barbara and that her father was dead and that her mother was named Margaret. She was fifteen when I "found" her, but I quickly advanced Barbara to age twenty-five and discovered that she had had several children in the meantime, being now married to the aforesaid John Bradbury. At age forty, Barbara was still alive but "very tired," a grandmother now. Eventually she "just lays down and dies."

"After she dies what happens to her?" I inquired of the hypnotized subject.

"She just watches things and everybody."

"Where does she go?"

"Into the air."

"Does she meet anyone there whom she knows?"

"Papa."

"How long does she stay up there?"

"Until somebody needs her."

"Does Barbara get born again?"

"She just keeps looking around from there, looking at things."

"What is she looking for?"

"Probably John and her children."

I suggested that the subject follow Barbara forward in time until she reached another incarnation. "Where is Barbara now?"

"She's me, her name is Karen L., but they call her Kay."

"Does she know she's Barbara?"

"She could if she wanted to."

"Was there anything Barbara didn't finish that Kay could finish?"

"No, but she just shouldn't be unhappy. She's unhappy not knowing if she'll ever see her kids again."

I then changed my line of questioning, asking the subject to describe Barbara more closely.

"She has pretty hair in curls, green eyes, and they sparkle when she smiles. Some women don't like her because of John Bradbury. He was Molly's boyfriend originally, and he married

Barbara. Molly married somebody else." Shortly afterward I brought Karen out of her hypnotic state. On awakening she remembered absolutely nothing of what she had said while hypnotized. "I don't remember any Molly" she said firmly.

Juanita T. is a housewife in California. When she was about ten years old she had a vivid dream that she never forgot. She was easily able to draw a picture of the vision in this dream. The road curved to the right and then led into town. There were hills on both sides, and in the center of the town there was a corner with a drugstore on it. In the dream Mrs. T. had no idea why she was in that particular town, on that particular street. It reoccurred very vividly between ages sixteen and seventeen. In June 1961, when she was eighteen years old, she was married. A few months afterward her husband and she drove from Springfield, Missouri, to southern New Jersey. They took the northern route (Route 66) that led through parts of Ohio. When they neared the town of Zanesville, Mrs. T. seemed to feel that she had been there before; the road fit her dream experience. She did not make a point of it, and they did not stop. But as they drove through town, she was suddenly thinking, "There are a lot more houses now." Since this was a unique experience, Mrs. T. wondered what it meant. "I have no idea what this is all about, since I have not been east of Missouri except as an infant when my father was stationed in South Carolina."

A good case in point where great contrasts are obvious is the case of Helen J. of Philadelphia, Pennsylvania. She had a dream that was neither very long nor mysterious, except that it involved her being in a place unknown to her in her present existence. "The place is a big house with a large number of rooms. There is a part of it that I keep locked up and do not use. Although I live in this place, there seems to be some anxiety, unhappiness, and even fear. In each dream it is exactly the same place, the same feeling. I have never lived in such a place and could never afford the furniture, such expensive furniture as it had. I am not interested in finding out whether I was great in another life. I would like to know what the dream means. I am an African American of modest means, and I consider myself intelligent, with some education."

Sally S., a housewife in Pennsylvania, has had various psychic experiences all her life, mainly precognitions. But the most disturbing event in her life was a dream that used to occur to her many times as a child, all through high school. Eventually it faded away and has not come back to her since. To my knowledge, she never has understood its true meaning.

The dream always started out in the same way. She saw herself as a small girl running, full of terror, down a redbrick road. She knew that this little girl was herself. As the girl looked behind her, she saw a man swinging a rope with a noose on the end. He was chasing her, and she ran and ran and finally came to a bush. The bush had no leaves at all. The little girl could see straight through it. She hid behind the bush, and the man kept coming after her. When he came upon her and was ready to put the rope on her, Mrs. S. would wake up. Was she reliving death at the hands of an evil person? Every time this dream occurred to her, she found herself in a state of absolute terror upon awakening. It would be easier to dismiss this as merely a symbolic dream capable of the usual psychoanalytical interpretation were it not for the fact that all her other dreams were totally dissimilar to this one.

Mrs. Lois S. of Arkansas is married and has five children, one deceased. Their eight-room house is in the country, and she leads an ordinary middle-class life. Yet, since age five or six, strange things have happened to her. She would say things that were out of context for her age and surroundings, which amazed her elders. Ever since then, she has developed precognition to a high degree, has been able to foretell future events, and has practiced extrasensory perception in many other forms. There are witnesses to every one of her predictions that have come true, but I am not concerned here with her psychic experiences as such.

There are two dreams she has had repeatedly. The first recurring dream concerns an event in which she sees herself alone in bed at night, and she then sees a man come in and stab her with a knife in the left side. At this precise moment, she feels exactly where the knife goes in. It stings her, and there is much pain after that, for she is dying. This dream has come to her many times.

Another dream is more detailed. In this she sees herself on a ship she describes as a clipper ship. Mrs. S. has no knowledge of boats or ships, but the ship she sees in these recurring dreams seems to be of an earlier age. She remembers men wearing

Taken at the allegedly haunted Winchester Cathedral in southern
England, a site of religious persecution in the sixteenth century,
this photo shows several hooded monks walking in the aisle. One
hundred years after the monks were either killed or driven out, the
cathedral floor was raised. These spirit monks, however, are still
walking at the level of the original floor.

Dr. Holzer and his former wife, Catherine, in a photograph taken by the late medium Betty Ritter. The picture shows the outlines of a psychic figure beginning to form.

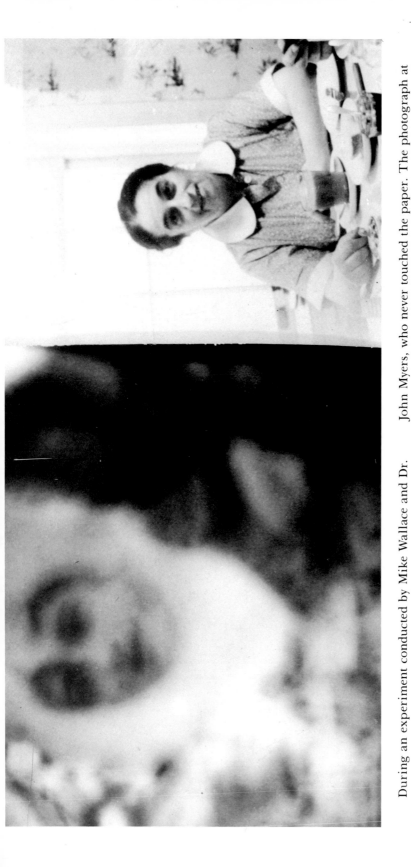

During an experiment conducted by Mike Wallace and Dr. Holzer and broadcast on New York television, unexposed photographic paper—purchased by Mr. Wallace and handled only by him—was "exposed" in the presence of medium Dr. John Myers, who never touched the paper. The photograph at left is one of several that resulted. The photo at right matches it very clearly—it is Holzer's late mother, who was totally unknown to either Wallace or Myers.

Dr. John Myers, a London dentist and medium, was the catalyst
for this spirit photograph of Holzer's late aunt Irma (left). No
camera was used to produce this, and Myers never physically
touched the photographic paper. A photograph of Irma, taken
when she was alive, appears right for comparison.

During a visit to a psychically active Hollywood house where a young girl had allegedly been killed and buried, Dr. Holzer took this photograph on high-speed film, showing what he came to call "the girl in the negligee" near the window.

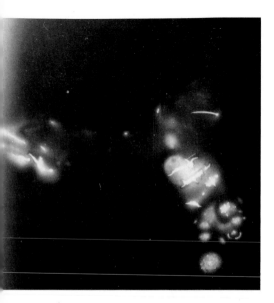

A Vineland, New Jersey, house, formerly owned by a woman named Emma, was the scene of continual psychic disturbances. Dr. Holzer visited it and took several high-speed photographs. Taking the picture of the main staircase in the house, Holzer instead got this eerie photograph of ectoplasmic matter; Emma's face, black hair and all, appears within the mass in the center.

In the Old Town section of San Diego stands the Whaley House, probably the most haunted house in America. The famous dwelling is now a museum. Dorothy, a staff member, took this photograph of an entity, a ghost, reclining on a bed in one of the more psychically active rooms.

Here the photographer captured ectoplasmic mass in formation, indicating a presence. No accidental exposure, reflection, or trickery was involved.

r. Holzer's former wife, Catherine, in a Polaroid portrait
ken by Dr. Andrew von Salza. Next to her appears the
:toplasmic portrait of Catherine's direct ancestor, Empress
atherine the Great of Russia. Dr. von Salza was totally
naware of the relationship of the two Catherines.

A print of the Great
atherine as she appeared
when living.

At the little-known resort of Aetna Springs, California, Dr. von Salza took this photograph, which shows a row of monks walking on what was, at the time the picture was taken, an empty golf course at four o'clock in the afternoon! Research disclosed that centuries ago there had indeed been a small band of Franciscan monks who had incurred the wrath of the Spanish government and were exterminated by the Dominican Order, the "executive arm" of the Spanish Inquisition, in 1532. Below is another picture of the monks, who were known as the Jeronomite Fathers.

ruffles, and she remembers a number of children and turmoil. She has the feeling of a robbery and an exchange of riches for the lives of these children. One of the children reminds her of her own five-year-old daughter, Linda, but she's not sure of the resemblance. She sees the child playing under a blanket with her head covered. She describes the riches as being in brown or gray bags and very heavy. A passage on this ship is quite vivid in her memory. She describes it in great detail, even including the wooden paneling.

"The place seemed quite roomy and comfortable," she explained. "It was lit by some sort of light enclosed in a glass globe that hung on the walls here and there, but mostly it was dimly lit, which led me to believe it was nighttime. The color was amber, because it reflected off the wood of the ship. This gave the wood a soft, reddish color. At shoulder height there were strips of wood going around the boat's walls. The children," she explained, "were in another place on the same ship. This was located near a doorway. They seemed happy and contented and unafraid." She remembers having to stoop a little when entering through a curtain. She didn't feel frightened, and she remembers only being annoyed at having to be there at all. The strange thing was that she didn't feel as if she were participating in this event but rather that she was watching it, as if she were outside.

There were men coming into the ship from her left. An exchange was made, and the men were forming some kind of relay with the heavy sacks. They wore ruffles on their sleeves, while others were in odd clothing. She recalls thinking that they were peasants because of this and their very bad smell. They smelled of fish and oil. One of the men had a long knife stuck through his belt. The belt was like nothing she had ever seen before. It was more like a piece of material tied around the waist, and the knife was stuck through it. It was a curving knife, with twine around the handle—very big, perhaps thirty inches long, It shone brightly, and she remembers being fascinated with the shine. She also recalls being repelled by the dirty appearance of the man who wore the belt and knife. He was bald, and the shine of his head was almost equal to that of the knife.

She recalls that the robbery was very quiet, and she had a feeling that the entire transaction had the cooperation of someone aboard the ship. Finally she recalls that the men taking the heavy sacks upstairs were all wearing gray cloths wrapped around their heads—not Turkish style but so that they had a bald look at the top of their heads.

Now, Mrs. S. has had no interest in pirate stories or ships or anything pertaining to the events depicted in her recurrent dreams. The vivid impression left each time she dreamt this— and she dreamt it many times in exactly the same fashion—did not fade as time went on. She got to wondering what it all meant. Eventually she read books dealing with extrasensory perception, and eventually also she thought that it might indicate some kind of reincarnation memory. Only then did she decide to read books dealing with the subject of reincarnation, and she read several. But at the time when the dreams occurred to her, there was no knowledge of the field or what it might mean to her.

Chapter Seventeen

Déjà Vu Experiences as Possible Evidence for Reincarnation

ALMOST EVERYBODY HAS AT ONE TIME OR ANOTHER had a sudden short experience called déjà vu—a distinct feeling that one has done something before, has been to a place before, or heard something said before that is now being enacted. Logical thinking tells one that this cannot be so because the event is just taking place, but there is a very strong feeling nevertheless that the scene one is just experiencing has been experienced before. This is generally followed by a nagging doubt as to whether one is correct about the situation, at the same time that there is a certainty that one is familiar with what is being said or done at that precise moment. Orthodox psychologists and psychiatrists have long explained this as a trick of memory. They say that people sometimes open a "false memory door" and thus experience a feeling of previous knowledge when in fact there is no such knowledge. But the same psychiatrists fail to tell us how the mind accomplishes this marvelous trick of "false memory doors." In this case the commonly heard explanation for déjà vu is simply not sufficient. Déjà vu means "already seen," but it covers experiences of "already heard" and "already known," as well. Foreknowledge without a logical base might be a better way of describing the phenomenon.

Hardly anyone goes through life without having at least one or more such experiences. They are probably among the most common forms of ESP phenomena. Undoubtedly the majority of these déjà vu experiences can be explained on the basis of precognition. An experience is foreseen and not noted at the time. Later, when the experience becomes objective reality and one goes through it, one suddenly remembers "as if in a flash" that one has had knowledge of this particular experience before. In other words, the majority of déjà vu experiences are nothing more than forgotten precognitive incidents. However, there is a residue of such experiences that cannot be explained on this basis. Among them are such cases as people coming to a town or a house for the first time and having exact foreknowledge of what the house or town looks like—even to the point of knowing specific rooms, furniture, and arrangements in rooms and other details that are far beyond the scope of ordinary precognition. There is a thin line where the precognitive experience must end; precognitive experiences do not contain exhaustive details, including names, dates, arrangements in rooms, and so on, to the point where the details are so specific and so numerous that only a person who would have been familiar with the arrangements could have remembered them. In general, precognitive experiences are partial and stress certain salient points, a few details perhaps, but never the entire picture. When the number of remembered details becomes very large, we must always suspect reincarnation memories.

A young man in upstate New York went to a house he had never been to before in his lifetime. Upon arrival he became very excited and suddenly remembered every detail about the house he was about to enter. When he reached the upper story he told his companions what lay around the corner and what the room to which they would next come would look like. All this was confirmed. Had this merely been a precognitive experience, he would have had a flash of himself coming to this house and might see himself enter it, but the foreknowledge of details would have been absent.

It would be erroneous to assume that all such déjà vu experiences have deeper significance or that they even represent important memories. Quite the opposite is true; the majority of such remembrances seem to be everyday details of no particular significance. They are, however, important in an indirect way;

by heaping a number of commonplace memories one upon the other, a continual basis for remembering is established. As with all other psychic experiences, there is always an emotional base present. Purely logical or mechanical details are never remembered.

Mary C., the youngest of four children of a dairy farmer, lived in Missouri for twelve years before moving to California. Married, with six children—three boys and three girls—and living in a small town in the San Francisco Bay area, Mrs. C. has had various ESP experiences throughout most of her adult life. On June 9, 1970, she and her daughter Linda Gail were on a shopping expedition to the nearby town of Vallejo. Somehow she felt the urge to go back home by way of Sonoma, where there are a number of historical landmarks. They decided to stop at the old San Francisco Solarno Mission and tour it, especially General Vallejo's home. They followed the directions leading there:

"The oddest feeling came over us as soon as we got out of the car," Mrs. C. explained, "A feeling that we had been there before, but of course neither of us ever had. As we walked through the gardens and the house, we could sense someone right at our shoulders, but no one was to be seen. It wasn't a scary feeling but a warm feeling, as if someone were saying, 'Welcome back, where have you been?' " Mrs. C. then continued her account: "The objects in the room seemed familiar, especially a piano in the living room and one of the upstairs bedrooms. It was all we could do to drag ourselves away, but we felt a pull back for months. Finally we were able to go back on October 18, 1971. The feelings were stronger than ever; in fact we even had tears in our eyes, tears of joy at being there again.

"While on this same trip we stopped at the Petaluma Adobe near Santa Rosa, another place that had belonged to General Vallejo. The same feeling of being home hit us, and we knew what was in some of the rooms before looking in at the doors. While we walked on the upstairs balcony, the years seemed to melt away, and we could sense how things had been a hundred years before. Also, throughout the hour we were there we could smell flowers in bloom, although it was mid-October and there were no flowers around." Salvador Vallejo was a young officer in the Mexican army serving in California. In 1833 he was sent to inspect Russian activities at Fort Ross near Bodega Bay.

Eventually the region became part of the United States, with the blessing and the advice of General Vallejo.

The curious thing about these short flashes from another existence is that they occur not only to people who may have an understanding of such previous situations but also frequently to people to whom such earlier existences would be totally alien. When the information from a possible previous existence contains cultural, social, or historical information not available to the person in the present, the evidential value of the observation is of course that much greater. Naturally there are just as many cases where individuals experience a reincarnation flash from a lifetime in surroundings similar to their present ones.

Mrs. Helen F. of Macon, Georgia, is a housewife. Her husband is a well-to-do businessman, and she has two grown sons. She has always been interested in ESP, because she found that she possesses this power herself. On a number of occasions she knew about events that were happening at a distance, and she has a very close telepathic relationship with both her children. But the experience that shook her up most happened in the summer of 1966, when she and her husband were in Europe, traveling through Italy. They were leaving the Trevi Fountain in Rome during a light rain, crossing a narrow street, and hastening toward their waiting bus. Her husband was pulling her along, holding her by the hand so she wouldn't slip on the wet sidewalk. Suddenly she happened to gaze fleetingly at one of several small, enclosed gardens. Peeking through one of the wrought-iron doors, she saw a place that she instantly knew that she knew well, though she had never seen it before. "I felt as though I were home. I knew that if I cast my eyes around to the right I would see a statue of a mother and child. If I looked to the left, there would be an old tree with a bench around it. I did, and *they were there just as I knew they would be.*"

But her husband was hurrying her back to the bus, so she could not stop and go in, though she wanted to very much. As he pulled her away, she recognized even the doorway of the house. Unfortunately they could not go back because they left early the following morning. When she explained her startling experience to a friend, the friend kiddingly called her "another Bridey Murphy." Until then Helen F. had never heard of Bridey Murphy, but eventually she caught up with the book and understood the reference. That was all she could consciously remember. Nothing like it ever occurred to her again, nor had anything like it happened to her before the incident in Rome. Under the circumstances, I suggested regression through hypnosis, and on my next visit to Atlanta, Georgia, we met for that purpose. That was on November 8, 1968, and after some initial conversation we went over the matter of the courtyard in Rome once again.

"All the houses were enclosed with high fences," she explained. "You could see through a gate into the yard, and I was glancing at them as we went by. Suddenly I recognized the lintel over the door; that is the top part. I glanced at it, and it looked very familiar. So I stopped, and although my husband was pulling me and said, 'Come on,' I said, 'Wait just a minute,' and I stopped completely at the gateway and looked in, and I recognized the whole yard. I didn't look at the house; somehow or other it didn't occur to me to look at the house, but the doorway in the yard I recognized immediately. I knew I had been there. I knew that there would be the statue and over to the left an old tree with a bench of some sort around it and *I knew that I used to sit on it.* I looked for it and there it was."

"Did you see yourself in the picture?" I asked.

"I guess so," she replied, "but it was that courtyard that attracted me most strongly."

An excellent case in point, and perhaps a typical déjà vu experience, involves a young man from upstate New York by the name of Del C., who was a senior in high school, going on to college. Here is Mr. C.'s report:

In the spring of 1965 several friends of mine, Joseph D., Christy D., Peter P., Margaret P., Joanne B., and myself, Del C., were on our way to a Christian camp at Beaver Falls, New York, accompanied by Father George K., our group supervisor. We were going to visit this camp to inquire about spending two weeks there. Upon arriving, it occurred to me that the main building, which was four stories high, was familiar to me, but at that time we went to see the director of the camp so I ignored the impression. After meeting the director, we went to look around the area. Then the feeling that I had been there before began to increase, but I didn't tell the others. We went to the side of the large building. There was a pool there, but it was relatively new, and I didn't recognize it.

As time went on I felt more and more that I had been there before, even though I had never been in the area. I told the others to follow me around to the back of the house. Just before going into the door I realized it was the door to the kitchen. We went through the kitchen, but it was not very familiar. At this time I didn't think much about it being unusual that I recognized the area. Then we went through the dining room to the stairs, and I told the others that I had seen the place before, even though I had never been there. I told them that I would show them around, so they agreed, but were a bit hesitant. Next I showed them the second and third floors, recognizing the rooms as we went. While on the third floor I told them that I would then show them the next floor. They asked where it was, as no stairs were apparent. I told them that the door to one side was the one that led up to the attic. They asked how I knew, and I told them that I remembered it from somewhere. We opened the door and there were the stairs. We went halfway up, and I told them that as they went through the door at the top of the stairs they would see some old pictures, and to the left there would be two trunks placed end to end. The first one had china, and the second had clothes in it. Then we went up the rest of the way, and the room was just as I described. The trunks were there containing the china and the clothes. All of this was out of the line of sight of where we were on the stairs when I told them there was a door at the top of the stairs as well. Then we went through a bit more of the house and went out. Outside I saw a dog, a Russian wolfhound, and I remembered its name. I can't remember the name now, though. It began barking, and a lady came out of the house and called it by the name to stop barking. At this time I was fourteen years old.

Sometimes the line between prevision or clairvoyance and later verification in objective reality is very thin, and the memory of the earlier impression is not entirely erased or suppressed.

There is, then a vague or uncertain feeling of having heard someone say something or having seen something or someone before, and when the event actually takes place, one realizes that this has not really happened until this very moment. A good case of this kind occurred to a colleague and friend of the previous communicator. John L. was also a senior in an upstate New York high school and would later attend the University of Notre Dame. Here is his report:

> Del C. and I were in English workshop on May 15, 1969. For several days previous to this particular afternoon, I had been thinking that something Del had said to me was very unusual. This thing that he had said was, "Did you know that gluttony was a moral affection?" I didn't give this too much thought during these days, except that it was such an unusual thing for him to say. Also, I had a mental picture of him turning to a certain page in the book and then saying that. Then on the fifteenth I was sitting at a desk in the English room, when it seemed as though I had seen the whole scene, with the people in exactly those positions, before. Then Del said, "Did you know that gluttony was a moral affection?"

Now, a phrase of such unusual connotation is certainly not explicable on the basis of coincidence—if there is, indeed, such a thing as coincidence. Here we have a similar experience to déjà vu, except that it is the reverse—the confirmation follows the impression that it has already happened.

Ilsa B. is a librarian in Mansfield, Ohio. All her life she has been having psychic experiences. When she went to boarding school in her native Germany, in Dresden, she went to the so-called English garden, where she had never been before. Immediately upon arriving at the garden, she knew her way around and knew that she had been there before; yet she was unable to pinpoint the time or occasion. Since then she has had many experiences in which she would arrive at a town or place only to recognize the place as something she had seen before. In her case, certain smells seem to evoke certain memories. In other cases, it is sound or a pictorial impression that seems to stimulate the faculty of recalling an earlier impression.

Betty F., a Los Angeles housewife with many years of psychic experiences, has now read a great deal on ESP and other forms of psychic consciousness, but in previous years when the bulk of her experiences took place she had no knowledge of parapsychology and was stumped by the things that happened to her. Of interest here is an incident that occurred to her in a German restaurant in La Jolla, California. The restaurant had been open only a few years when Betty F. and her husband paid it a visit. Upon seeing the German owner of the place, whose name was Ernie, she instantly felt that she had known him before, and he felt the same way about her. Now, to be sure, this did not have a romantic connotation at all. They glanced at each other casually, and they knew each other. This went on for the several visits that the Fs. paid the restaurant afterward. The entire thing troubled her so much that she tried time and again to figure out where she had met him. At the same time, he was trying to figure out where he had met the strange lady before. Finally she had enough nerve to go over to him and ask, "Where have I ever met you before?" and it developed that they had, indeed, never met. He had come from Europe recently and gone on to Chicago and from there to his present place.

During World War II, a soldier found himself in Belgium. While his buddies were wondering how to enter a certain house in a particular small town in Belgium, he showed them the way in and went ahead of them up the stairs, explaining as he went up where each room was. When he was questioned after this about having been there before, he denied ever having left his home in the United States, and he spoke the truth. He could not explain how he had suddenly found himself possessed of knowledge he did not have in his normal condition.

Chapter Eighteen

How to Prove Previous Lives

IN CASES INVOLVING REINCARNATION, an author should not rest with the presentation of the story alone but should verify at least a substantial amount of the material obtained, either in flashes of conscious knowledge or through hypnosis. When the story is presented without the proper verification, it becomes nothing more than an interesting account. Such, in my opinion, is the case with much of the material to be found in *Here and Hereafter*, by Ruth Montgomery.

A different slant is taken by Joan Grant's account of her research, especially when it involves ancient Egypt. Here we must consider Miss Grant's own involvement with Egyptian archeology and the possibility that the material rose from her own unconscious mind. But if this were not so, the need to verify some of the material involving Egyptian archeology is very great and, in my opinion, entirely capable of producing information, data, and details that could be considered genuine only if they were indeed stemming from the communicator or from the previous incarnation claimed. Surely, in delving into the mystery of a previous lifetime, one is allowed to ask certain test questions in order to establish identity beyond a shadow of a doubt. If such questions are not asked and the proper research not undertaken, then the case becomes weak and, while it may be genuine, lacks the necessary convincing elements.

The cases I am presenting in this chapter are not lacking in research where research was possible but are incomplete in other ways. Either there is not enough material available on the case in point or the material is of a kind that rings true but cannot be verified, no matter how much one would like, due to lack of research sources or to other technical reasons. Even though in these cases I was unable to present a completely convincing picture, all the cases here discussed are incapable of alternative explanations and therefore fit in with the concept of reincarnation memories as I have established it earlier. In some cases, additional sessions with the person involved might have yielded additional results, but this was not always possible. Reincarnation is a not a matter of life or death to the one to whom the memories occur, and researchers such as I may not always be free to travel to distant cities to follow up on each case, much as we would like.

I am presenting these partial or fractional cases here to show how common among all of us is the fleeting glimpse into a previous lifetime—that it is not a freak experience that happens to a few but is indeed far more common than is realized by most researchers, let alone the ordinary person in the street.

Whenever people have flashes of memories pertaining to earlier lives, these flashes are generally brief and are often confused and out of context. It is sometimes years before these people realize that what appear to them as either waking visions or strong dreams are actually part of an earlier lifetime. Frequently the puzzle doesn't seem to work out and the pieces do not fall into place, but occasionally people do realize that what appears to them in this form has some meaning and is not merely a figment of their imagination or just another dream.

In a number of cases there seems to be a relationship between psychic ability and reincarnation memories, although this does not mean that only those who have ESP have reincarnation flashes or that those who have reincarnation flashes are also psychic, but there are a number of cases in which both abilities coexist.

Rosemary B., a twenty-eight-year-old housewife in Massachusetts, remembers far back, even as far back as when she was only one year old. Today she wonders whether she has lived before. Often she would sit knitting a sweater, which is a job needing some concentration, when suddenly there would be a quick flash, and before her eyes, before her mind's eyes, she would see a vision of two girls coming home from school and a driveway of a house—a house she had never seen before except in these visions. All of a sudden she would remember this as if it were a dream from long ago. She didn't know where this place was, but she knew that she had been there.

What she saw involved a black car parked on a hill. A man was in the driver's seat, a man she instinctively knew to be her father. She hugged him, and it was nighttime. The car was standing on a dirt road. There was a large pine tree just next to where the car was parked and a log cabin below. They were waiting for someone. Her father wasn't the father she has in this lifetime. He was a strange man, and yet she knew he was her father. She herself was in the back seat as her father got out of the car. Next she saw herself out of the car also, playing with the bark of a tree—peeling it. Then someone called to her, and she ran down the hill behind some older children. The name Edwina flashed through her mind. Consciously, she does not know this name, yet in the vision she felt she had been there— that she was young and that it was she who ran down that hill. She clearly saw this girl running last among the children—a girl with long hair, in a plain dress with a ruffled hem and a ruffle bodice. The hem was just above the ankle, the dress had some red and white on it, and she also wore long, white stockings.

She began to wonder, Who was Edwina? The name sounded strange to her. Of course, she felt that perhaps this was something from her own childhood memory. She thought about it consciously, and she asked questions of her relatives. The name Edwina did not occur in her family. No such scene had ever taken place in her own lifetime, and yet she is possessed of an extraordinary memory going back to age one.

When I questioned her about details of this vision, she recalled that the car was one of those that were in style perhaps in the 1920s or early 1930s. She remembers seeing similar cars in old movies or on television, especially those dealing with Al Capone and his days. The windshield had a bar in the center; the interior was brown, perhaps leather or suede. Beyond that, she cannot recall any details, but there is a haunting feeling that she was Edwina running down a hill in another lifetime.

Ouija boards are the least likely tools to obtain verifiable information in psychic research, and yet, once in awhile, a Ouija board can be useful in research. Now, a Ouija board is nothing more than a piece of wood inscribed with the letters of the alphabet, numerals, and a few simple words such as *yes*, *no*, and *maybe*. Upon it is placed a contraption, usually very light-weight, made of wood, glass, or plastic, called the indicator. Upon this indicator rest the hands of two or more people partic-ipating in the experiment. These hands must be applied lightly. Naturally the movements of the indicator across the board are not due to any spirit action per se but are due to the muscular action of the hands, or rather the *persons* whose hands are placed upon the indicator. But the motivation in moving the indicator to certain letters and thus spelling words and sen-tences may be due to another control than that of the person operating the board.

I have pointed out earlier in this book and in many of my previous books that I do not advise the use of Ouija boards by the average person, because it presents certain dangers to those who have deep trance mediumship and are not aware of it at the time they first use such a board. But I do feel that occasionally this board my be an instrument for tapping the unconscious in a verifiable manner.

A strange case in point is the case of Mr. and Mrs. A., of Columbus, Ohio. Fascinated with extrasensory perception for some time, the couple had acquired a Ouija board and were trying to communicate through it with certain deceased entities. Having considered it merely a toy at first, the As took their board somewhat more seriously when it started to give them information pertaining to the husband.

It all started one evening in 1968, when they used the board to amuse some of their guests. After the guests had left, Mrs. A. and her husband sat down alone and tried the board again. This time the communicator, whoever it was, had immediate refer-ence to the husband. The communicator in this case was a woman named Rochelle, who claimed to have been the wife of Mrs. A's husband in a previous incarnation. "Did you know Pete in his lifetime?" Mrs. A. asked. The board indicated assent. "How long ago?" "One hundred and five years ago," said the

board without a moment's hesitation. Stimulated by this exchange, Mrs. A. then pursued the question. It developed that her
husband, Pete, had been known as Robert Hinis and that he had
lived during the Civil War. Rochelle claimed to have been his
wife at that time. At the time of his death, the board explained,
Mr. Hinis had been twenty-five years old.

"Where was your home?" asked Mrs. A.

"Blacksburg, Virginia," came the answer.

"Where was Rob born?"

"Patascala, Virginia."

"Where were you born?"

"Blacksburg."

"What year was Rob born?"

"Thirty-eight."

"What year were you born?"

"Thirty-eight."

"How old were you when you died?"

"Twenty-four."

Mrs. A. stopped the board and did a quick bit of arithmetic.
If Rob had been born in 1838 and died at the age of twenty-five,
he had died in the year 1863. Now, Rochelle said she had known
him a hundred and five years ago, which also gets us back to
1863. The Civil War lasted from 1861 to 1865. It would be very
difficult to do such quick arithmetic without time to think.
Besides this, Mrs. A. knew that her husband was not making
this up or trying to play a practical joke on her, and as far as she
was concerned she certainly had no knowledge of either the
character of Robert Hinis nor of the dates mentioned by his
alleged wife, Rochelle. She questioned the communicator
further.

How had her husband died? It turned out that he had been
shot. He had been a scout and a colonel at the same time. This
threw Mrs. A. off, for she could not conceive of a scout being a
colonel also. However, there were scout regiments in the Civil
War with all the necessary ranks among their officers. A scout,
in terms of Civil War history, does not mean a Boy Scout but
simply a regiment of advance troops.

It developed further that Rochelle and her children had all
died together in a fire and that this fire had been due to war
action. Pete, as Rob in previous lifetime, had killed many men
in defense of the United States government. The Confederate

soldiers had burned down their house. Somehow the attachment Rochelle had had for her husband, Robert, in the nineteenth century had carried over to this new incarnation as Pete, and she felt she still should help him and his new wife get on as best they could.

After the sessions with the Ouija board, Mrs. A. felt sort of foolish about the whole thing. She really did not believe that the communication was genuine, but to assure herself that there was nothing to it and to end the matter once and for all, she did write some letters about the period and people involved to what she considered the proper sources of information. These included the attorney general's department in Roanoke, Virginia; the General Services Administration at the National Archives in Washington, D.C.; the clerk of the County Court House of Montgomery County in Christianburg, Virginia; and the clerk and treasurer at Blacksburg, Virginia, a Mrs. Rochelle Brown. Mrs. A. managed to find that there was, indeed, a Blacksburg, Virginia, in existence, although she could not locate Patascala, Virginia. However, she found there was a Palasky near Blacksburg and wondered if the communicator on the Ouija board had misspelled the word, as she had misspelled many other words. This, Mrs. A. soon found out, is par for the course when you deal with a Ouija board. Strangely she could not get anything else out of the communicator, who had called herself Rochelle, beyond this material—at any rate, nothing that proved to be of much value.

When replies came to her inquiries she felt differently about the matter, however. There was a Robert Hinis from Christianburg County, Virginia, who died in the Civil War at about the time the Robert Hinis whom the communicator, Rochelle, had spoken of had died.

One might go though life without ever remembering anything from an alleged previous lifetime until something starts one to thinking. Frequently these are parallels to what one might have experienced in a previous incarnation, and it is the similarity between the two events or places that causes the recall.

Mrs. Betty J., a horse breeder in Pennsylvania in her late thirties, is the mother of two lovely daughters and college educated. Her interests in life are varied. In addition to caring for her family, she does volunteer work for the Red Cross, works with the handicapped in nursing homes, and is generally active in the community.

Early in her childhood she frequently had the feeling that something, or rather someone, was missing in her life. Although she was happy with her parents and her many friends, the feeling persisted. She often felt out of place among her family and friends, somehow vaguely searching for someone who wasn't there.

When her oldest girl was in college, some friends of hers were having difficulty in caring for their aged father. She decided to spend two days each week with them in order to care for this elderly gentleman until he passed away. For some strange reason she could not understand, there was a change in her attitude toward her own family. Whenever she left in the evening to come home to her own family, whom she dearly loved, she felt as if she were leaving her true home to spend the night and the remainder of the week with strangers. Every day when she returned to the home of the aged man for whom she was now caring, she felt as if she were coming home to her own house. As soon as she crossed the threshold of this man's house, she felt complete—like a whole person. No longer did she have the feeling that someone was absent, but a sense of peace and serenity came over her just as soon as she entered the old man's house.

What confused the matter was the fact that she had several dreams while sleeping in the house. In one of them the deceased wife of the old man took her on a tour of her home in another town. Afterward, Mrs. J. asked his children whether the descriptions she had of their mother and their childhood residence were correct. To her amazement she was informed that they were.

In another dream, she saw a woman whom she had never met in life; and when her daughter showed her a picture of this same woman, she almost fainted, for it was the woman she had seen in her dreams. Could it be, then, that this old gentleman so near death was thinking of his earlier life and in some way his thoughts had become transferred to her? she argued. But this would not explain the reason for the deep sense of fulfillment she had every time she set foot into his house.

Life has been good to Mrs. J. in many ways. She has been happy all her life, and yet the peace and the feeling of having come home that she experienced when going to the old man's house was something beyond her comprehension. After the period of caring for the old man ended, she felt more miserable and discontented than she had ever been in her life. Returning to her own home, she lost that precious sense of fulfillment and contentment she had had for a short time in someone else's home. Mrs. J. cannot help feeling that she knew this man in a previous lifetime and that perhaps she was discharging some form of karma.

Ellen was born in New York City. When she was ten years old, she became aware of another young girl, who appeared to her in visions and daydreams. Somehow she knew that the young girl used to be herself, even though she did not look like Ellen. A certain scene kept impressing itself upon her mind over and over. In this scene the young girl was riding a horse, and the horse jumped a hurdle and fell, and when the girl fell off the horse, she died.

Ellen saw very clearly how the little girl was dressed. She wore a red jacket and riding pants. There were large tracts of land around, and Ellen had the feeling that this was somewhere in the United States. She also felt that this was in an earlier century, and at one point she got the feeling that it was around 1881. The girl had dark hair and didn't look like the present Ellen at all. There were other scenes: She would see this girl in a kind of library wearing a long dress—a dress going down to the ankles—and the library was lit by big white, bubbling lights. The bubbling lights Ellen described as clusters of what she thought were bulblike crystal containers. She wasn't sure whether they were gaslights or electric lights. In this scene the girl was reading a book. The book was open in her hands, and then the scene just faded out. Somehow Ellen felt very emotional about this other girl. Somehow she felt she liked her and felt sorry for her. She had a strong feeling of emotional attachment for this other girl—a feeling as if she knew her.

Over the years, these two scenes stayed with her. The last time she had experienced these daydreams was only a few months before she met me. Then, a few weeks before she came to seek my help, she had a terrifying experience. She woke up in the middle of the night, sat bolt upright in bed, and started talking, and yet she felt as if it wasn't she talking at all but some other person speaking through her. All the time, she heard every word she was saying, unable to control what came out of her mouth. By this time she was fully awake and realized what she had said. What she had spoken was one sentence: "Clara J. Wiston, Clara J. Wiston is coming for me."

She was surprised at herself. She had never heard that name before. What did it mean? Who was Clara Wiston? At that moment she was fully awake and thought it was all nonsense and foolishness. For awhile she entertained the notion of looking up whether there was indeed a Clara Wiston somewhere, but she really didn't know where to begin to look, so she dropped it, and the matter was of no further interest to her. Then she read one of my books and decided to question me about it. When she came to see me, we went over the entire incident carefully.

It developed that she wasn't sure of the girl's age. Perhaps she saw her at various times of her life; that is to say, first as a child of ten and then later as an adolescent. I sent her home with the request to try to return, as it were, in her daydreaming or even in the nocturnal dream state to the period in which Clara Wiston lived and to try to get additional information. On the night of July 3, 1967, she started to work on herself. "Who is Clara Wiston, and where was she born?"

That night Ellen had a dream, and although she could not remember all its details, she was able to write down quite a bit on awakening. In her dream the girl was talking socially to a gathering of people and kept mentioning two places—Cresskill or Crestmont and another place called Crow something (she couldn't quite get the word that followed Crow). Subsequently, research in local libraries yielded some results.

There isn't a Cresskill or Crestmont anywhere in New York State, including Long Island, but there is a Crown Point, which dates back to 1755. It is located near Ticonderoga, on the neck of land connecting Lake George and Lake Champlain. During the Revolutionary War this was a location of some importance, as it fell to the American troops in 1775. Of course, the place might also have been Croton-on-Hudson or any name beginning with a syllable like Crow.

What interested me more was the name Clara Wiston. Wiston seemed to me a very uncommon name, and so it turned out to be. My own research in genealogical sources confirmed my suspicion that the name Wiston was indeed a rare name, but finally I discovered in a book called *The Pioneers of Massachu-*

setts, by Charles H. Pope, published in Boston in 1900, that a Wiston family did indeed exist in New England as early as 1665. John Wiston, father of Joseph Wiston, lived in Scituate, Massachusetts, in that year. Evidently the name is of New England origin, for I also discovered in *Massachusetts Soldiers and Sailors of the Revolutionary War* (Boston, 1908), on page 660, that one Edmond Wiston lived in 1778, a Joseph Wiston in 1778, and a Simon Wiston in 1776. Was Clara Wiston a descendant of that New England family?

Mildred C. grew up in Whittier, California. Her family—Mildred, both parents, a brother, and a sister—came from Ohio in 1901 and settled in southern California. She says she was a lonely child despite her brother and sister—always playing alone or being with animals. She married for the first time at age eighteen and had three children—two boys and a girl—but her husband passed on in 1931. Later she married again, but that marriage did not work out, and she has since remained divorced. Her husband held the rank of major in the air force.

Of average height, she had dark brown hair and sparkling blue eyes. She was far livelier than her years would suggest, but all in all was a typical upper-middle-class lady with average interests.

The event that amazed, if it didn't upset, Mrs. C. happened in July 1956. At that time she was living in Modesto. One afternoon Mrs. C. decided to go shopping to Stockton, which is about thirty miles away. She asked a friend by the name of Greta B. to come along for the ride. Her friend readily agreed. To make the shopping expedition more interesting, she asked her friend whether she had ever seen the University of the Pacific. Greta said she hadn't, so they decided to drive past it to look at it.

It was just about four o'clock in the afternoon, and the two ladies were talking of nothing in particular and laughing, "for we were both in a very relaxed mood. Shopping does bring out the best in women sometimes." They were winding their way through the afternoon traffic when all of a sudden Mrs. C. felt very strange.

"I had the oddest feeling, as if something had washed over me," she said.

All of a sudden she was no longer on the road, driving her car through the city of Stockton. Instead she seemed to be in a different place. She saw a path in front of her, flanked on both sides by several large, white, old-fashioned houses with trees. The houses were two stories high and were set back from the street a little bit with picket fences, and there were no sidewalks in front of them—only a kind of dirt path and rows of trees on what she knew was the parkway.

Suddenly she noticed a woman walking up the pathway, with her back toward her so that she could not observe the woman's face. The woman then stepped to the left and walked off the side of the road. At this instant Mrs. C. knew that this woman was she *herself*. Although she did not know the age or period this woman lived in, the woman seemed grown up.

Then, ahead of that alter ego of hers, Mrs. C. noticed a fence and a small hill. The woman kept walking toward that hill with a picket fence around it, and then the whole vision vanished. Mrs. C. found herself back in her driver's seat. The car was still running through traffic, and she felt rather strange, as if she had just been deflated.

"Is there anything wrong with you?" her friend asked, worry in her voice. Apparently Mrs. C. had suddenly become very quiet and looked odd. Her friend thought she had been taken ill. The odd feeling stayed with Mrs. C. for about an hour, and then it slowly went away. Yet the impression was so vivid she could never forget it. She thought about it many times, realizing full well that she had never been to this place in her life. To her it did not look like California but someplace "back East." Although the incident felt as if it had taken a long time, it was actually only a second or two. She had never lost control of the car.

I questioned Mrs. C. about the appearance of the woman she had seen in her vision. "She had on a light skirt, and it was down to here," she said, indicating her ankles, "and either a jacket or loose top, but that is about all I can remember." She was equally sure that the houses she saw were not of a kind that have ever been built in California but reminded her of houses in the eastern part of the United States. No further visions of this kind ever occurred to her.

Mild incidents involving ESP, such as knowing who might be calling before the telephone rings or having a feeling that a dead relative was present in what used to be his house contributed somewhat to Mrs. C.'s understanding, if not acceptance, of psychic phenomena. The only other incident tying in with her amazing experience in Stockton happened in the summer of 1967.

Not far from her present home is the old capital of California, Columbia. One afternoon she decided to take a ride up there with her dog. She had been there before many times, and she had a feeling of belonging there. This time it was particularly strong.

Columbia is a small gold-mining town that the state has turned into a national park. Mrs. C. was walking along the main street and looking at the restored buildings when all of a sudden it seemed to her as if there weren't any buildings there at all, and again she saw a woman walking ahead of her. The woman was the same person she had seen before in traffic at Stockton, when her first vision overcame her, but this time the woman wore different clothes. The old-fashioned clothes she was wearing were not the kind the people in Columbia put on for tourists. The woman walking ahead of her wore dark gray clothes, a big bonnet, and some very high, heavy shoes, but even more interesting, she seemed to be floating ahead of her rather than walking on the ground. All at once Mrs. C. realized it was she herself who was walking ahead of her in the road, and that she saw a vision of something that had happened in the past— *her* past.

Again the woman did not turn around, so Mrs. C. could not see her face, but the certainty that she was looking at an earlier incarnation of herself remained with her. The feeling did not leave her for several hours. Although Mrs. C. was sure that she herself was the woman she had seen, there was no physical resemblance between the apparition and her appearance at that time. But as she grew older, a vague and yet persistent feeling came back to her again and again. She saw in her mind's eye trees, a stream, a quiet place somewhere in the country, and she knew at the same time that she had been there. Every day she yearned more for it, wishing she could be there again.

Chapter Nineteen

Reincarnation Memories
in Children

IT IS NOT UNCOMMON FOR A YOUNG CHILD to speak of places, situations, and people that a child couldn't possibly have known. Those unfamiliar with the record of reincarnation research are quick to attribute all such unusual utterances to childish fantasies. But what is one to make of entire sentences formed by a two- or three-year-old child, using words the child could not possibly have heard or absorbed even if they had been spoken in the immediate family? What is one to make of complicated, even sophisticated, descriptions of places from the historical past in households where history is not a household word? The number of cases where small children, even as little as one year old, speak in coherent and intelligent fashion of places and people they could not possibly know, apart from the fact that they could not possibly speak in such a fashion anyway, is impressive. Some of these cases have been called "miracle children," or *Wunderkinder*. With very rare exceptions, however, they are not miracle children but children who remember something from their earlier lives. Even those few who are genuine miracle children are likely to be in that position not due to some special talent within themselves but because of what they have brought into this life from another one.

In the majority of cases that have come to my attention the ability to recall seeming bits and pieces from an earlier lifetime gradually fades out toward the time when the child goes to school. In some cases, the memory returns around the age of seventeen or eighteen, and then usually with a vengeance and in greater detail. But at that point the rational capacity of the person as well as some educational background must be taken into account when evaluating the evidence. With a little child below the age of five such problems are of less impact. On the average a child begins to speak in coherent sentences after age two, in many cases only when reaching age three. The ability to describe places and situations outside the immediate family does not usually begin until age four or five. Even if one takes a certain amount of fantasy into account, and many children refer to invisible friends as part of their development, there remains a hard core of evidential cases where all these explanations must be ruled out.

"Had I not been familiar with the theory of reincarnation I would have ignored Amy-Kay," stated Diane L. of Indiana. The unusual incident she was reporting to me concerned her two-year-old daughter by that name. The family had spent the day with friends out of town; the little girl had missed her afternoon nap, and her mother knew that she would soon be asleep on the ride home. As they were riding, the mother noticed the little girl swaying from side to side in her seat and slowly getting a certain look in her eyes that came just before the child fell asleep. They were passing a familiar road now, and Mrs. L. said casually, "There is the road to Nonnie's house." The word *road* somehow must have jogged the little girl's memory. Suddenly she started to mumble: "He killed me . . . that man killed me . . . that man killed me *in the road* . . . he killed me. . . . I was born in the road and that man killed me, he stomped on me. . . ."

After this outburst, and ignoring her mother's questions, the child went back to sleep.

For a two-year-old child, such expressions seem out of place. Mrs. L. also noted that the child had been using strange words ever since she began to talk. For instance, instead of saying "blanket" she would say "cover." On one occasion at the dinner table, she informed the family, "I picked cotton . . . I and Mommy." Mrs. L. quite rightly points out that a two-year-old simply doesn't know words like *born* and *stomped,* let alone *cotton.*

Mrs. Raymond K., also of Indiana, contacted me to tell me some amazing things about her son Larry. "When he was around two, he would react to small, one-engine-type airplanes by lying down spread-eagled on the ground. There is a small airport near our house. Whenever my husband or I were taking him for a walk and one of those small planes came overhead, Larry would react this way and then get up and resume his walk, as if nothing had happened." Apparently the little boy only reacted this way with small, one-engine planes; ordinary large airplanes, jets, did not disturb him in the least. He would merely point at them and say "plane," like any other little boy.

However, by the time Larry reached age three, things crystallized somewhat more. "He started to talk about the war with Germany, about the soldiers in their green uniforms," Mrs. K. explained. "He told us, at age three, how he killed his best friend by not helping him, and how he broke his leg on a large rock. He said he was taken away in a four-passenger ambulance. One evening we had pumpernickel bread at supper, and Larry pointed at it, saying it was black bread and that they ate it with fish soup. Periodically he brought up different things and made comments. We never prompted him or started deliberate conversations about it." Mrs. K. had no idea what color uniforms the Germans wore in World War II. One day she read a book about the war and learned that the Germans wore green uniforms.

Mrs. K. also noticed that whenever the little boy played war, as other children do, it was always the Germans and Americans. As Larry grew older, he did not refer to the things he "knew" but behaved more and more like any average boy his age. The Ks. assumed quite correctly that the four-passenger ambulance referred to by the little boy must have been a military one and that the small, one-engine planes reminded the little boy of fighter planes.

Gloria S., who lives in New York State, has a twenty-year-old daughter. When the little girl was three years old an incident occurred that made Mrs. S. wonder whether her child wasn't speaking of reincarnation memories. The family was watching television at the time, and it so happened that a program dealing with Pilgrims was on the screen. Unexpectedly the little girl said, "My other mommy wore clothes like that." Mrs. S. was quite surprised and asked her daughter to repeat the statement. Firmly the little girl replied, "The mother I used to have wore dresses like that." There wasn't anything else Mrs. S. could get out of the child, but the little girl insisted again and again that she had had another mother, and that the mother was dressed in clothes similar to those she was seeing on television.

Mrs. H. P. Z. of Ohio is now well into her eighties. When she was a little girl, she frequently broke into tears and asked to go to see her other parents. This was a repeated occurrence, and the child, at the time, insisted that she wanted to go back to the parents *she knew*. Eventually the desire faded as the child grew older. But to this day Mrs. Z. can draw a picture of her previous home and its surroundings and the little girl she used to be. Connected with this is a strong feeling of having lived in the Old South. "I can't drive through certain portions of the South without looking for the one I used to live in," Mrs. Z. explained. "Also, one day I was standing on our porch looking out, enjoying the trees, when all at once I was standing in the doorway of a little log cabin, looking across a tiny clearing at a primeval forest and smelling the fragrance of the trees. It was a brief flash, and then I was back on my own porch."

Ordinary memories fade in time, and so it is not surprising that reincarnation memories might also fade as time goes on. It is therefore rather interesting to study the cases of young children who have such memories, which in later life will disappear from their conscious minds. A good case in point was brought to my attention by Mrs. Carole H., in Montana. Mrs. H. lived with her husband, who worked in one of the local mines. She was an art student by correspondence, and they were people in the middle-income bracket—ordinary people, I would say, living in an eight-year-old country house. They had four children—nine, seven, four, and three years of age—representative of an average middle-class family. Mrs. H. had a crippling condition that prevented her from writing in longhand. Other than that, there really wasn't anything extraordinary about them. There is, however, a great deal to be said about one of their children, Brenda, aged four.

Nothing very special happened with little Brenda until Good Friday of 1969. On that day Brenda sat up, awaking from a sound sleep, and started to talk about a previous life. She had spent the night in the home of Mrs. H.'s sister, Mrs. P.

"I have lived in the country once," the little girl said, "in the South, in a big white house." She then went on to describe it as having had a big porch with white pillars and a big green lawn. She referred to a pet horse named Hooper John that she seemed rather fond of. Her aunt asked her if there were any other children. "Yes," the little girl said, "a lot of little darkies." She spoke with a strong accent, apparently French, and even gave her name, which was also a French name. Her aunt couldn't even pronounce it. Finally the little girl added, "But I died." Her aunt thought she had misunderstood her and asked what she had said. "I died," the little girl repeated somewhat impatiently, "I fell off my horse, Hooper John, when I was sixteen, and died." She then lay back down and went back to sleep. The little girl's uncle, Mr. P., who was present throughout this amazing conversation, attributed it all to the child's lively imagination, but the following morning the aunt again spoke to little Brenda when she awoke.

Present this time was her daughter Sharon, aged fourteen. Together the two questioned the little girl further: Did she live on a farm when she lived down South? "Of course not," the little girl said, "it was a plantation." She then went on to describe how they raised tobacco, speaking of cutting the tobacco and sheaves. When asked what it looked like, she said, "You know, like crimped tobacco." Brenda then repeated the same account she had told for the first time the previous night. She spoke of a fire wagon and described a firebox and the purpose it served, but as the day wore on she forgot about this, being, after all, only four years old. By evening she had completely forgotten the incident. However, a few days later she referred to a toy horse as "Hooper John" for just a moment, finally saying, "Oh, no, you're not my Hooper John." She put the toy down and has not spoken of it since.

Now, this is an extraordinary thing for a four-year-old girl to use phrases, language, and information rarely, if ever, possessed by someone that young; especially so since Brenda had had no occasion to visit the South or to learn about the tobacco business. At age four most children do not read books, nor had Mrs. H. read any such stories to her at any time.

Chapter Twenty

The Perfect Case for Reincarnation: Scotland 1600

ONE DAY IN OCTOBER 1967, I was going through my fan mail, which had been piling up for a few weeks. I get about three to four hundred letters a week from readers all over the country, and even from abroad, and I cannot devote as much time to these letters as I wish I could, but on this brisk October morning I felt compelled to go over the mail and to try to pick out the most urgent letters for an immediate reply. Somehow my hands picked up a letter from Harvey, Illinois. It looked just like any other letter that I might get from a reader, but I proceeded to open it and read it. I read it three times, and then I wondered what had made me open this particular letter of all the hundreds that lay on my desk that morning.

Dear Mr. Holzer,

I am writing to you about an experience I had, which may not really mean anything. I have seen what looks like a Scottish girl, standing at the foot of my bed, three times. I don't know if she actually talked to me, but after I'd seen her, these words keep coming back to me: "castle," "perch" or "purth," "Ruthvin," "Cowrye," "sixteen," and "towers." Also, something

214

which sounds like "burn night." I've never mentioned this to anyone, because they probably would not believe me. If you can make anything out of this, I would appreciate it if you would let me know.

Sincerely,
Pamela W.

What puzzled me about this short letter was the fact that the words mentioned by Miss W. had no immediate meaning for me either. It didn't sound like the usual ghost story or the usual psychic experience relating simply to something left behind in the atmosphere of a particular room or house. It didn't sound like an ordinary dream either, since Miss W. was not precise in mentioning what appeared to be place names.

I was intrigued by her letter, and I wrote back requesting additional information, asking her whether she could remember any more details about this girl or any further communications from her.

The lady from Harvey, Illinois, answered my letter immediately. I had asked her whether there were any witnesses to the experience she had reported in her first letter, but apparently there weren't any, since she was asleep at the time.

I have no witnesses to the Scottish girl I see, because no one else has seen her. The girl I see seems to have red hair and seems to be very elegantly dressed, with long white gown and gold braid. I saw her the other night. It seems she said to me the word "handsel." It seems as though she's lost. She keeps saying "ruthven," "gowrie," "sixteen hundred," "two towers." She also said, "glamis—angus." She also said, "I leaped." I don't believe I have any Scottish background, but it's possible, because on my mother's side they are all English. On my father's side they are all German. I do not know if I have ESP, but I seem to see some things before they happen.

I hope this will help you.
Sincerely,
Pamela W.

The matter rested there for awhile, but I was determined to go to Scotland in the future and investigate this material. It meant nothing to me at the time, but I knew some research historians in Scotland and thought that perhaps they might be able to shed some light on the mysterious words of Miss. W.'s letters.

We had no further correspondence until I was able to go to Scotland in the summer of 1969. I took the two letters with me, although I really didn't know where to begin the search. One of my dearest friends is a writer named Elizabeth Byrd, author of *Immortal Queen* (a history of Mary, Queen of Scots), who then resided in the Scottish Highlands. I thought that perhaps Elizabeth could shed some light on the material I was bringing along with me. She read the two letters but could not offer anything concrete except the promise to look into it further.

We were luncheon guests of Mr. and Mrs. Maurice S. at their castle, called Muchalls, in northeastern Scotland. The occasion was a casual invitation from Mr. and Mrs. S. to visit their castle because of a possible haunted room. It turned out that there was no such room, but Mr. and Mrs. S. were amiable people, whose hospitality we enjoyed.

For no reason in particular, I mentioned my letters from the lady in Harvey, Illinois, wondering whether Mr. S. had some idea as to the meaning of those letters. To my amazement, Mr. S. caught on immediately and seemed to remember a legend or story involving "a maiden's leap" in one of the castles in Scotland.

"You mean, there is something to this?" I said, getting more and more interested. Evidently fate had destined us to come to Muchalls not because of a haunted room but because of a link supplied by the owner, leading me to an understanding of what Miss. W.'s letter was all about.

"I think I have a guidebook here, a book dealing with Scottish castles," he said. "Let me look for it."

A few minutes later he returned, triumphantly holding what seemed to be a slender booklet. The booklet was called *Huntingtower Castle* and was the work of J. S. Richardson, formerly inspector of ancient monuments for Scotland. As I leafed through this booklet I realized that we had discovered the key to Pamela W.'s strange dream/vision.

What is now called Huntingtower Castle was originally known as Ruthven Castle. The name goes back to the first half of the thirteenth century. The third and fourth Lords Ruthven apparently had some part in the murder of Rizzio, Queen Mary's favorite. The father subsequently died, while the son eventually returned from England, whence he had fled, and received a full royal pardon. This fourth Lord Ruthven, whose first name was William, was created the first Earl of Gowrie by King James in 1581. The king was then still legally an infant, and his regents actually created the title.

The following year the newly created earl repaid the favor in a rather peculiar fashion. He and some associates captured the young king and held him a prisoner for almost a year at Ruthven Castle. The reasons were political. Gowrie and his associates disapproved of the government of the earl of Arran and the duke of Lennox, who were then running Scotland. They took power away from those two nobles and into their own hands, with the young king unable to do much about it. They forced the king to listen to their complaints and to sign a declaration denouncing the former government. When the young man remonstrated against this enforced order, the master of Glamis, who was among those detaining the young king, is reported to have said, "Better bairns greet than bearded men," meaning "Better a boy weeps than a bearded man!" Allegedly, King James never forgot those words.

This "Raid of Ruthven" was an important event in Scottish history; that is, important to those who specialize in sixteenth-century Scottish history and do research into this turbulent era.

Eventually, it appears, when King James found his freedom he returned under the sway of the earl of Arran, so the detention at Ruthven really didn't change anything, except perhaps the king's feelings toward the man he had just created the first earl of Gowrie.

At first he showed a forgiving spirit to those who had been connected with the raid, for he issued a proclamation offering them all a full pardon. But two years later the earl of Gowrie was ordered to leave the country. Having retired only to Dundee, he was arrested by one William Stewart, taken by ship to Leith, and thence to the royal palace of Holyrood. There he stood trial on the accusation of being implicated in a plot to seize Stirling Castle, was found guilty, and was beheaded at Stirling on May 4, 1585, his property being forfeited to the crown.

A year later the estates and honors of the first earl were

restored to his son James, who died shortly thereafter. James was succeeded in 1588 by his brother John, the third and last earl of Gowrie. All the Gowries, incidentally, had the reputation in their time of being adepts of necromancy and witchcraft.

Evidently King James's revenge did not stop there. The last earl of Gowrie and his brother Alexander Ruthven were killed on the king's orders in the Perth town house in August 1600. The reason given at the time was "an alleged attempt on the life of the King," which was apparently without foundation. No details are known of this so-called Gowrie conspiracy, but contemporary reports speak of some papers taken from the belt of the dead earl that contained magic spells no one but an adept in the black arts could properly read. The dead bodies of the two brothers were then carried to Edinburgh, where indictments for high treason were read publicly.

Not satisfied with having executed the two Ruthven brothers, the king ordered their bodies to be publicly hanged, drawn, and quartered, and the remnants to be distributed to various parts of Scotland, thus ensuring, according to the belief of the times, that their souls could not rest in peace.

The early seventeenth century was a hard and rough period in history. People were not gentle to each other, and political tempers rose high at times. Religious differences had not been settled, and Scotland was torn by the Protestant and Catholic factions. The king's continuing vengefulness must be understood against this violent background. The Parliament of 1600 abolished the name of Ruthven, ordering that the castle change its name to Huntingtower and remain a property of the Crown of Scotland. Finally, in 1643, the castle passed into the hands of William Murray and was generally known from that time onward only as Huntingtower Castle.

It required the knowledge and skill of a Scottish historical specialist to recall the earlier designation as Ruthven Castle and the connection between the names Ruthven and Gowrie, and yet a young lady who had never left her native Illinois was able to speak of Ruthven and Gowrie and the year 1600 and the two towers, all in one and the same breath. She was even able to speak of Glamis and Angus, not realizing the connection between the master of Glamis, which is in Angus County, and the Gowrie family. How could she know that Perth, which was mentioned in her very first letter to me, was the place where the earl of Gowrie was slain?

But Pamela W. had also written, "I leaped." Again the official Huntingtower Castle booklet was able to give me some clues as to the meaning of this cryptic remark:

> A daughter of the first Earl of Gowrie was courted by a young gentleman of inferior rank, whose intentions were not countenanced by the family. When a visitor at the castle, he was always lodged in a separate tower from the young lady. One night, however, before the doors where shut, she conveyed herself into her lover's apartment, but some prying duenna acquainted the Countess with it, who, cutting off, as she thought, all possibility of retreat, hastened to surprise them. The young lady's ears were quick. She heard the footsteps of the old Countess, ran to the top of the leads, and took the desperate leap of nine feet four inches, over a chasm of sixty feet, and luckily landing on the battlements of the other tower, crept into her own bed, where her astonished mother found her, and, of course, apologized for her unjust suspicion. The fair daughter did not choose to repeat the leap, but the next night eloped and was married. This extraordinary exploit has given the name of the "the maiden's leap" to the space between the two towers, which were originally separate.

After I had read the contents of the official booklet, there was a moment of silence when we all realized the importance of the information contained therein.

What remained to be found was further corroboration of the material—perhaps some knowledge concerning the further events of the Gowrie conspiracy itself, and the girl's name. All this had to be investigated further, but at least I knew then that either Pamela W. had authentic experiences reaching out into an earlier time or there had to be a logical explanation for her knowledge. I decided not to tell Miss W. anything whatsoever about my research but to arrange for an early meeting with her so that we could begin hypnotic regression. At this point I knew nothing whatsoever about Miss W., not even her age or status, and I could only hope that there would be no reason why she could not submit to the experiment I intended to undertake.

Also present at the delightful dinner at Muchalls were Mr. and Mrs. Alastair Knight. Mrs. Knight, whose first name is Alanna, is highly psychic. She is a writer of historical novels and offered to help me research this unusual case. In addition Elizabeth Byrd enlisted the voluntary aid of historian Carson Ritchie, but Mr. Ritchie made it plain to her that finding girls' names is a difficult matter. In those days girls' births were not registered unless they were royal.

Fortified by such a formidable team of helpers, I was confident I could crack the mystery of Pamela W.'s strange visions. The Knights decided to go to Gowrie Castle at the very first opportunity.

Two phrases in Pamela's original vision had not yet been fully explained or placed. There was, first of all, the expression "burn night." *Burn* is Scottish for brook. Far more interesting was the word *handsel*. The term seemed completely unfamiliar to me. Where was I to find an explanation for this strange word?

Through Elizabeth Byrd I had met authoress Margaret Widdemer some years before. Elizabeth asked for permission to consult Miss Widdemer, who is widely read and who had a fine research library. "From my Chambers' *Scottish Dictionary*," Miss Widdemer wrote, "I can give you an explanation for 'Handsel': an inaugural gift, a present, on Handsel Monday, a coin put in the pocket of a new coat or the like. Handsel means to inaugurate, to make a beginning, a gift." I was, of course, elated at this news that there was such a word as *handsel*. Miss Widdemer had an opinion of her own. "My first reaction to the word was earnest money, or something given as a sealing of a bargain, money or not. Possibly the red-haired girl you speak of was Handselled to the man she leaped to." So there was such a word after all.

More and more pieces of the jigsaw puzzle began to fall into place now, even though I had not yet met Pamela W. in person. Mr. and Mrs. Knight prepared for a visit to Gowrie Castle on my behalf. This came about in a most unusual way. On August 6 they found themselves on a routine trip connected with Mr. Knight's work as a geologist. They were looking for Scone Palace and having a hard time finding it, so they decided to go instead to visit a relative in Dundee. They decided to take a short cut but suddenly found themselves completely lost and, after a bewildering number of side roads, halted at a signpost reading HUNTINGTOWER CASTLE—TWO MILES. It was only much later that they realized that they had arrived at what had once been Gowrie Castle on the anniversary of the execution of the last two Gowrie lords.

Now, Alanna Knight does not take her psychic abilities too seriously, although I have seen her at work using her sixth sense to good advantage. She is apparently able to pierce the veil of time and to relive events in the distant past. As soon as they arrived at the castle, she experienced a strange sense of familiarity. The moment she set foot into Huntingtower Castle she was sure she had been in it before, except that she knew it when it was furnished. Her husband assured her that they had never been there. Suddenly Mrs. Knight knew her way inside.

"This was a bedroom. The bed was over there," she said, and pointed. As she went from room to room she found herself singing under her breath. Her son Christopher asked, "What is it that you are singing?" She couldn't tell him, but it was the same tune that had been running through her mind ever since I had mentioned I had written a song entitled "The Maid in the Meadow." Mrs. Knight had never heard my song nor had she seen any sheet music of it. All she knew was that I had written such a song and that there was some connection with Scotland. When they came across the custodian of the castle, she immediately asked her about Ruthven Field Meadow, as it is marked on the map. Following the custodian's directions, they meandered along some pretty lanes, which again seemed rather too familiar to her. Her feelings of déjà vu were rather vague, and yet, at the same time, they were definite.

When the Knights started to leave the area and Mrs. Knight's husband wondered how they would get out of there, having been lost once that afternoon, she immediately replied, "About twenty yards further on there is an old stone bridge on the right, which leads to the main road eventually," and there was. As they drove away she could not help but go over the events of the last hour in her mind.

Once inside the castle she had immediately gone up to the battlements, practically on hands and knees, as the steps were very steep. There she had perched on the edge of the battlements, about sixty feet above ground. Today the two original towers, which were separate at one time, are connected by a somewhat lower central portion. In the early seventeenth century, however, there was a chasm between the two portions of the castle measuring over nine feet wide. Anyone wishing to leap from the right-hand tower onto the lower, left-hand tower would still have to cover a distance of nine feet. But since the left-hand portion was one story below the right-hand portion, the leap would have been downward. Also, there is a ledge along both battlements, and as the buttresses protrude and overlap, it reduces the distance by a couple of feet. Thus it is not entirely impossible to make such a leap safely and without falling off the roof, but it is somewhat of a feat, just the same. Eventually Alanna Knight had left the battlement and returned to the inside of the castle.

In what she considered a bedroom she had had a very strong impression of a girl with reddish-gold hair, pale rather than dark, with freckles. She was what, in modern parlance, would be called a tomboy, Alanna reported—mischievous rather than passionately amorous. "The sort of girl who would do anything for a dare," Alanna felt, "and who would enjoy leading a man on, feeling rather superior to the poor creature. I think she was merry, laughed a lot, was strongly disapproved of by her family. I feel that the sixteenth century wasn't her time; she was a misplacement and would have been happier living now, who even then yearned for some equality with men, and watched them go out to fight with envy in her soul. I think also that her name was Margaret or Isabelle or both, but these names are particularly Scottish, so there is really nothing exciting about this feeling. I only hope that one day you'll know the answer."

I asked Alanna Knight about the song that kept going through her mind and that she felt had something to do with my ballad "The Maid of the Meadow." Not being a musician, she asked a friend, Ann Brand, to transcribe it for her. I looked at the musical composition with interest. There are four bars, and they resemble greatly four bars from my ballad, written in 1953 and unknown to Alanna Knight or her friend. To be sure, it wasn't the entire song; it was merely a portion of it, but the similarity was striking.

Alanna had one other bit of news to add: Dr. Ritchie had

found some reference to one of the Ruthven girls. In Robertson's *History of Scotland,* published in 1759, he had found a reference to the sister of the earl of Gowrie by the name of Mistress Beatrix. Of course, there might have been more than one sister, but the name is on record. In the meantime, Elizabeth Byrd had promised further inquiries in Edinburgh.

While all this feverish activity on my behalf was going on across the ocean, I went to Chicago to finally meet Pamela W. in person. She had agreed to come to the Knickerbocker Hotel, where I was then staying, and to submit to hypnotic regression. I had told her that I had found some interesting evidence relating to her dream/vision but declined to say anymore.

On October 17, 1969, Pamela W. came to my suite at the Knickerbocker Hotel. When she entered I was somewhat surprised, for she didn't look at all like the person I had somehow imagined her to be. Instead of a fey, somewhat romantic individual of indeterminate age, I found her to be a young girl of twenty or twenty-one, lively and practical, and not at all interested in the occult. I explained that I would interview her first and then attempt to put her into hypnotic regression. Since she was agreeable, we proceeded immediately.

In the following pages I am presenting the exact transcript of our interview and of what happened when Pamela W. became another person.

"Pamela," I began the conversation, "where were you born?"

"Chicago Heights."

"What does your father do?"

"My father is deceased. He worked in a factory which built locomotives, and my mother works in a hospital as a dietary worker."

"What is your background?"

"My father's family are from Germany, the Black Forest, and my mother's side of the family are English."

"Was she born here?"

"Yes."

"Is there anybody of Scottish ancestry among your family?"

"Not that I know of."

"Do you have any brothers and sisters?"

"I have half sisters and a half brother."

"What is your family's religion?"

"Well, my father's side of the family is Lutheran, and my mother's family is Baptist."

"And you yourself?"

"I consider myself a Mormon."

"You're twenty-one. Do you work?"

"I was doing work in a hospital. I was going to nursing school, and now I'm just taking care of a woman part time. She's ill, and once I get the money I want to go back into nursing."

"What is your schooling like? What did you do? You went to public school?"

"I went to school in Glenwood, right outside of Chicago Heights, and the rest of my schooling was all in Harvey, where I live now."

"Did you ever have any flashes or visions or feelings of having been in places that you hadn't really visited?"

"I've seen people that I'd swear that I'd seen somewhere before, and no possibility of it."

"Have you ever been to Europe?"

"No."

"Have you ever had any desire to go to Europe?"

"Oh, yes, I'd love to go to Europe. I want to see castles."

"When did you first notice this desire?"

"Oh, I'd say maybe three years ago, when I was eighteen."

"Do you know the first time you had this sudden desire to see castles?"

"I had a castle, all in my mind—a big, white castle with towers."

"How many towers?"

"Two or three, I think, and it was like up on a stone, a mountain or something."

"What kind of books do you read?"

"Well, I read a lot of mysteries."

"Do you read any history?"

"No, history doesn't really interest me too much. I read about Waterloo one time, but that's about the first one I read."

"What kind of music do you like?"

"Classical music and folk songs. I don't mean folk songs like you hear now. I mean of the European countries, the British Isles."

"Do you ever have a particular song running through your mind?"

"I hear bagpipes sometimes."

"When do you hear these bagpipes?"

"Usually at night when I'm getting ready to go to sleep."

"How long has that been going on?"

"I would say off and on now for maybe a year and a half, two years."

"Have you ever had a feeling of strangeness in your present surroundings?"

"Yes, I'd say so. I don't think I've ever belonged *around here.*"

"Can you be more specific as to when this feeling started?"

"I would say I've noticed it for the last couple of years, two or three years possibly, but I don't really feel like I know anybody here. It seems I know people that are in other places of the world, and I *don't.*"

"What places would you say they are at?"

"Well, I think I'm really drawn more to the British Isles than I am to Europe. There's just something about the British Isles that fascinates me."

"Have you ever had a feeling, perhaps when you were very tired, of looking in the mirror or walking, seeing yourself *different* from what you look like now, see any change in yourself, personality, character, or in face?"

"Yes, I know one time I can remember very, very clearly, because it startled me. The girl that I talked about in the dream I had, with the red hair—I looked in the mirror one day—I don't know if I pictured myself *as her* or if I saw here there, but it set me back."

"How long ago was that?"

"Oh, I'd say maybe nine months ago."

"Is that the only time you had this feeling?"

"I have had the feeling that I'm somebody besides who I am."

"How long have you had this feeling?"

"I'd have to go back two or three years."

"Anything, do you think, that started it off?"

"No, not that I can think of."

"Now, let us talk about the dreams."

"The dream happened the first time about two years ago.

I've had it quite a few times since then. I've seen a girl with red hair. She has a long, white gown on, and it has gold braiding on it, and she's kind of walking like she's dazed. When I have this dream I also see two towers there, and I hear her say, 'Handsel to me,' and then I hear her mention 'Glamis, Angus,' and she'll say 'Ruthven, Gowrie,' and one time she said, 'I leaped.' Sometimes she seems very peaceful, and sometimes she seems very angry."

"How old a girl would you say?"

"I'd say somewhere around twenty."

"Is she short or tall?"

"I would say short, somewhat petite."

"Pretty, ugly, anything special about her?"

"No, nothing really. She has beautiful red hair. That's the thing."

"Short or long?"

"Long hair, very thick."

"Does the dream vary at all or is it exactly the same each time?"

"I will say it is basically exactly the same every time, except there's times when she'll seem angry."

"How many times have you had the dream all together?"

"I'd say five or six times."

"When was the last time?"

"The last time, let's see, July I think."

"Of this year?"

"Yes."

"Was she angry then?"

"Very angry."

"Do these dreams last all night, or are they short dreams?"

"Very short. I mean, I'll just see her, and she'll say what she has to say, and then she's gone."

"How is that you remember this particular dream so vividly? Do you remember all your dreams as well?"

"Her I do, because I'm not really sure if you can classify it as a dream. I don't really think I'm asleep."

"Does it happen early in the night, middle of the night, or late at night?"

"I would say after eleven-thirty and before two to two-thirty."

"Outside of those dreams, did you have any feeling of a presence around you in any way? While awake, I mean?"

"I don't know if I can say specifically *her* or not, but I have had the feeling at times that *someone's* around me. I mean, when I'm home by myself."

"When you contacted me, do you think that someone made you do it?"

"I felt I just *had* to write you, for no reason."

"Did it make any sense to you personally?"

"The only thing I ever really thought about was the 'Handsel to me.' I thought the 'to me' must mean something. Maybe 'Handsel' means come to me, but I wouldn't know why she'd want me coming to her."

"Have you any particular tastes in clothes, accessories, music, habits, phrases—anything you find is alien to your own personality, especially since you were eighteen, let us say?"

"I love to cook anything which is from the English Isles. I have three English cookbooks. As for clothes, the old-style dress really appeals to me."

"Do you have any boyfriends who are of English or Scottish background? I don't mean American English, but I mean true native."

"No, none whatsoever."

"Have you ever done any reading about Britain to any extent—history, background, geography?"

"I read one time about the Tower of London, and I've read about the royal family, but really nothing else."

"What is your own view of the meaning of the phenomena that have occurred in your life? What do you suppose it means?"

"I don't really know, unless someone's trying to tell me something. I feel that I know her. I don't know *how* I know her or *why* I know her, but I feel *I know her.*"

"When the first dream occurred, the very first time, was it out of the blue? There was nothing that would indicate any reason for it?"

"The first time I really didn't pay much attention to it. I noticed it, and I knew it was there, but I thought, 'Well, one of these wild things,' but then it kept coming back, and every time it would come back I'd feel closer to her."

"Are you ready to be hypnotically regressed now?"

"Yes, I am."

A few moments later, Pamela was in deep hypnosis, fully relaxed and obeying my commands. "You are going to go back a hundred years, two hundred years, three hundred years. Go back until you see the redheaded girl."

After a moment she spoke. "Ruthven," she said quietly.

"Do you live there?" I began my questioning.

"I live there."

"Who is your father?"

"He's not there."

"Is there anyone else there?"

"My mother."

"What is her name? What is your mother's name?"

"I don't know. We can't talk about it."

"Why not?"

"Because they're conspiring against us, and we're not supposed to talk about them."

"What year are we in?"

"Sixteen hundred."

"Sixteen hundred what?"

"Just sixteen hundred."

"What country do you live in?"

"In Scotland."

"Why are you worried?"

"We're going to have to leave."

"Why do you have to leave?"

"They'll kill us if we don't leave."

"Who will kill you?"

"I don't know. Father just said, 'the men.' "

"What are you going to do?"

"I don't know. Mother's packing."

"Where are you going to go?"

"To Glamis."

"Why there?"

"The royal family is there."

"Will they help you?"

"I don't know."

"Describe your home."

"Stones."

"What is it called?"

"Breasten."

"What does the building look like?"

"Two towers, garden."

"Have you been up in the towers?"

"I used to play up there."

"How did you play?"

"I had little china cups."

"How old were you then?"

"Four, five."

"How old are you now?"

"Twenty-two."

"Are you single or married?"

"Single."

"Do you know any man you would like to marry?"

"Yes."

"What is his name?"

"I can't tell his name."

"Why not?"

"I'm not supposed to see him."

"Why not?"

"The family says no."

"What is his first name?"

"Mother said I'll be punished if I tell."

"And what will you do? Have you seen him lately?"

"Yes."

"Where?"

"By Loch Catherine."

"Is that far away?"

"Not too far."

"Has he ever been in the castle?"

"Yes."

"Where? In what part of it?"

"In the main hallway."

"Never upstairs?"

"Only once, but he's not allowed in the castle."

"Was he upstairs in the tower at any time?"

"Only once, when Mother wasn't supposed to know he was there."

"What did you do?"

"We talked."

"And will you marry him?"

"I can't."

"Why not?"

"The family won't allow it. They want me to marry some-one else."

"Who?"

"I don't know him."

"Why do they want you to marry this other person?"

"The family is very wealthy."

"And your friend isn't?"

"Yes, but not to their wealth."

"Why is it that you have come to speak through this instru-ment? What is your connection with her? Are you her or are you speaking *through* her?"

"I am *her*."

"Where have you been in between? Have you been anyone else?"

"No, I was caught in the wind."

"How did you die?"

"I jumped from the tower."

"Did you die in jumping?"

"Yes, I died after."

"Where did you jump to?"

"I was trying to jump to the other one."

"Didn't you make it?"

"No."

"Where did you fall?"

"In front of the door."

"Was that the first time that you ever jumped from one tower to the other?"

"No."

"You've done it before?"

"Yes."

"And it worked?"

"Yes."

"And this time it didn't, and you died? How old were you then?"

"Twenty-two."

"Was it an accident, or did you want to jump?"

"I wanted to jump."

"Were you unhappy?"

"Yes."

"When you were down there dead, what happened to you next? What did you see next?"

"Nothing."

"What was your next memory after you had fallen? What is the next thing that you remember?"

"I was in wind."

"Did you see yourself as you were?"

"Yes."

"Where did you go?"

"Nowhere."

"Did you see anyone?"

"No."

"Did you stay outside, or did you return to the castle?"

"I went to the castle once."

"Did anyone see you?"

"No."

"And what happened after that? Where did you live?"

"I was caught in the wind again."

"And what was the next thing you remember after that?"

"I saw people."

"What sort of people?"

"Funny people walking around."

"Were they also dead?"

"No."

"Where were you?"

"I was in a city."

"Were you in another body?"

"No."

"You were still as you were?"

"Yes."

"What was the city?"

"I don't know."

"Were the people dressed in the same way as the people you knew in your time?"

"No."

"Were you the same way as you were in your time?"

"Yes, I could see my gown."

"These funny people—did they notice you?"

"No, they walked by me."

"What was the next thing you remember after that?"

"I wanted someone to take me back."

"Back where?"

"To Ruthven."

"Did you find anyone?"

"Yes—Pamela."

"How did she take you back?"

"She'll take me back."

"How did you get *into* Pamela? Did you select her yourself?"

"Yes, she looked like she'd go back."

"Who told you about Pamela? How did you find her?"

"I found her when I went into the building."

"Which building?"

"In her building."

"But what makes you so sure that she can?"

"She'll feel sorry and take me back."

"Are you within her? Are you in her body?"

"Yes, I've got to go back with her."

"Who sent you to her?"

"No one."

"Then how did you know where to find her?"

"I don't know."

"Did you talk to anyone and ask for help?"

"No one could hear me. They walked right by."

"There was no one, no person who said, 'You must go back to earth,' or anything like that?"

"No."

"Do you remember being reborn as a baby?"

"No."

"What was the thing you remember after you saw Pamela?"

"She looks like someone."

"Like who? Does she look like you?"

"No."

"Then what does she look like to you?"

"She looks like the clan McGibbon."

"Which one of the clan McGibbon?"

"She looks like Catherine."

"Catherine of the clan McGibbon? Who was Catherine to you?"

"I didn't know her too well. I met her only in Angus."

"Why did you go to Angus?"

"We had to go to Glamis."

"And did you pass through Angus?"

"No, Glamis is in Angus."

"What was she doing in Glamis?"

"She lives there."

"What does she do there?"

"A maid."

"Whose maid was she?"

"At the castle of the royal family."

"And Pamela reminds you of her?"

"Yes."

"But what is it that binds you to Pamela? Is it your own destiny?"

"Yes, I must go back."

"And do what?"

"I've got to look for something."

"What do you have to look for?"

"My ring."

"Who gave you the ring?"

"I can't talk about it."

"What does it look like?"

"It's round, an opal."

"Is there anything inscribed in it?"

"No."

"Why is it so important to get this ring?"

"*He* gave it to me."

"Who did?"

"I'd be punished if I tell."

"You will not be punished . . . on my honor. Give me his name so I can help you."

"I can't find him again. I only want my ring."

"Call out for him, and he will come to you."

"I'll be punished if I tell."

"And when you find the ring, what will you do then?"

"I'll go away."

"Where will you go to?"

"Loch Catherine. I was happy there."

"With whom?"

"*He* would take me there. We would talk about going away."

"Where would you go to, if you could?"

"Away from Perth."

"And where to?"

"He'd like to go to London."

"What sort of work does he do?"

"He wants to be an architect."

"Has he studied?"

"Only a little, but without permission."

"He's not a nobleman?"

"He's a nobleman, but his father does not want him to do that."

"Why is it that you came to Pamela when she was about eighteen and not before?"

"She's old enough to go away now."

"Will you help her go there? Why did you seek *me* out?"

"Maybe you would make her go."

"Is that what you want me to do?"

"I want to go back."

"Suppose I promise to help you, will you then tell me who the young man was?"

"Can I go back?"

"I will try to find a way for her to go back, yes. I have already made contact over there, and I know you are telling the truth."

"Will she take me back?"

"I will do my best for her to take you back within a year's time."

"I've waited too long."

"How long have you waited?"

"For hundreds of years."

"Then you can wait another year. But a lot of time has gone on. Perhaps the ring isn't there anymore. Then what?"

"I'll look till I find it."

"Are you happy being in Pamela's person now? Are you reconciled to being her? Do you like being her?"

"Only to go back."

"I am still curious why it is, and how it is, that you found her over here. Do you know in what country you are? Do you?"

"No."

"Where do you think you are? Do you know the name of the country in which you are? It is not Scotland."

"I'm not in the Isles?"

"No. Do you know how much time has gone on since you lived? Do you know how much?"

"Hundreds of years."

"Do you want to tell me the name of the young man?"

"I can't have him again. You won't bring him back."

"Tell me more about this conspiracy that frightened you so. Who was involved?"

"Father just said they were against him."

"Who?"

"I only know him as Gowrie."

"What rank did he have?"

"I don't know. When they came, I had to go to the tower."

"And when they called for you, what name did they use?"

"I want him back!"

"I will help you. You can tell me your name now, your true name."

"I have to look in the Bible."

"Go and look at the Bible and tell me what is written in it."

"No, I have to go see him."

"You will see him, if he *wants* you to see him."

"No, I want Peter."

"Peter shall be yours. I have promised it. Now, your name."

"I want Peter."

"Peter, come to her. If you have been reborn, let her know where you are, so that she may come to you again. You have to say, 'I,' and say your name, 'want you.' Then he will come to you."

"We can't tell any people."

"You and I are the only ones to know."

"No; when we left the castle, Mother said, 'No.' "

"Speak your name."

"No, I'll be hit."

"What did the servants call you?"

"They always called me by my proper name of Ruthven."

"But what did they say when they meant you were there?"

"They called me 'Lady.' "

"Lady what? What is your Christian name?"

"I can't."

"You know it?"

"Yes."

"What is the initial? The first letter of your name?"

"I'll be punished."

"You will not be punished to speak your own name."

"I can't tell you."

"You would like to find the ring. Is there anything else you want?"

"No."

"Then will you be at peace? If you find the ring, or when you find there is no more ring, will you be at peace then?"

"Yes, if I may go to the Loch."

"Alone?"

"Yes."

"Be patient, and I will see whether it can be done. Have you any other requests?"

"No."

"If I ask you a question, will you answer it truthfully? Do you promise to answer it truthfully?"

"Yes."

"Are you *Beatrix*?"

"I can't tell you."

"You must say yes or no."

"But I'll be punished."

"You will not be punished, because you are not *telling* me. You are simply saying yes or no. If you say yes and it is the truth you will not have said it; and if you say no and it is the truth you will have perjured yourself and lied and invited damnation. So you had better tell the truth. For the third and last time, I ask you, *are you Lady Beatrix*?"

"Yes."

"I will now release you, and I will see to it that as soon as it is possible you shall see your favorite place again."

"Yes."

"Then go in peace with my blessing."

After Pamela woke up, remembering absolutely nothing of her hypnotic regression, I asked her how she happened to get the name Pamela in the first place.

"My mother couldn't decide on a name, and she wanted a name no one in the family had, and she read a society page and there was a girl by the name of Pamela being married."

"I'm going to name a few women's names. Tell me if any of them rings a bell in some way or means anything special, all right? Dorothy or Dorothea."

"My grandmother is named Dorothy."

"You like that name?"

"It's all right."

"How about Barbara?"

"No."

"How about Beatrix?"

"That's pretty. *I like that.*"

"You like that better than the others?"

"Yes, as long as people didn't call me Bea. I don't care for that."

The material obtained from Pamela while she was in hypnotic regression was very interesting indeed. Now I knew what the *handsel* was: the ring that meant so much to her because of the one who had given it to her. When I realized that she wasn't going to give me her name, it was best to try to see what reaction I might get from her by mentioning several names. Although I do not consider the evidence thus obtained in the same light as spontaneous admission of facts or names, it is nevertheless of interest in the context of this entire investigation that she did react to the name Beatrix significantly differently from the reaction to the other names mentioned by me in the same tone of voice.

After awhile, Pamela sat up and joined me for a cup of coffee. Only then did I open the latest letter from Elizabeth Byrd, which had reached me the day before in New York. In it was enclosed a communication from the Lord Lyon of Scotland; that is to say, the nobleman in charge of registering claims and coats of arms of noble families.

> The daughter after which the maiden's leap at Huntingtower was named was Dorothea, who married before June 8, 1609, John Wemyss, of Pittencrieff. Dorothea, however, though the thirteenth child, was not apparently the youngest daughter, and information on Barbara, the fourteenth child and youngest of that family, can be found on pages 266 and 267 of Volume Four of the Scots Peerage, referred to above.

Thus read the report from the Lord Lyon of Scotland. Of course the list of Gowrie daughters is by no means complete. A further thought entered my mind. True, Pamela in her other identity as

Lady Gowrie had spoken of leaping, but was she the one for whom the Maiden's Leap was famous? Could she not have been another person, leaning and falling where another had leaped and landed safely? When I reexamined the testimony, it appears to me that the Lady Gowrie who spoke to me in Chicago, and who fell to her death from the battlements of Gowrie Castle, was not in the habit of practicing the leap to reach her love, but then again the true evidence may be confused. Nigel Tranter, in his book *The Fortified House in Scotland*, speaks only of the battlements and the buildings themselves, so the legend of the Maiden's Leap was not as far-spread as we might think.

Before I parted company with Pamela W., I asked that she observe anything that might happen to her after our hypnosis session. In particular I then asked that she record any dreams/visions that she might have in the future; for it is possible that a memory can be stirred up as a consequence of hypnotic regression.

Four days after our meeting, I received a letter from Pamela. Now, I had briefly told her that her Scottish memories had been confirmed by experts and that she apparently had lived once before as one of the Ladies Gowrie. Thus anything duplicating that which she already knew would be of no evidential value, of course.

> I don't know if this will mean anything or not, but I felt compelled to write you. It's almost 2:30 A.M., but I have just awoken from a dream which seems very real to me. In my dream I found myself on a horse in a place I don't know, but still I feel I know it. I started riding, and after about forty miles or so I stopped and tied my horse to a tree. I started walking in what seemed to be a valley, and it was very wooded. I also saw mountains around me. As I was walking, there were thorns, or something sharp scratching my leg. I started to approach a river, and then I began running. After that I found myself in bed again, and the thing that startled me most is that I felt the most terrible burning sensation on my legs. Then I was taken back by the most awful crying and moaning sounds, which I thought would awaken the entire neighborhood.

> Two words have impressed themselves strongly

onto my mind. One is either "dab" or "daba." I don't know where it came from, but it's been bothering me. The other word is "Beitris," which I saw clearly on the ceiling of my room last night, with the lights turned off. I don't know if all this will mean anything or not, but I had to write you.

Since the words did not have any meaning for me either, I asked Elizabeth Byrd to check them out in Jamison's *English-Scottish Dictionary*. *Daddown* means to fall forcibly and with noise. Did the term have reference to her fatal fall from the battlements of Gowrie Castle? But there is also *dablet* which means an imp, a little devil. Didn't Alanna Knight describe the girl she saw in her visions as something of that sort?

In early November Pamela had another dream/vision. The same image impressed itself upon her mind twice in a row, and she was a little worried about the message it contained.

"You will die by *Newa Vleen*," the girl said in the dreams. Pamela wondered *who* was to die—the redhead or herself—and what, if anything, did Newa Vleen signify?

On April 30, 1972, I received a letter from Mrs. A. McDougall, who lives in Perth, Scotland, shedding some intriguing light on the authenticity of Pamela's statements:

The girl in question was the daughter of the fourth Lord Ruthven who was married to Lord Methven's daughter whose family name was Stewart and she was Lady Dorothea Stewart. He was given the title of the Earl of Gowrie after he and Lord Lindsay had escorted Queen Mary to Loch Leven and extorted a commission from her which empowered them to overthrow the government in her name.

The young daughter who made the now famous leap, eloped with her lover Squire James Wemyss of Pittencrieff, which is almost adjacent to Loch Katrine, in the Trossachs.

The word Newavleen is quite possibly of Jacobite origin which is now called Gaelic. I have looked up this word in my book, and this is a suggestion I have come up with as there is no place of the name in Scotland: Nieve, which would be pronounced Newav

in a Scot's accent and it means fist. Linn, a gorge
through which a torrent of water falls, is pronounced
leen. So there is your word newavleen.

The other statement you made about *Quote* (Better
bairns greet than bearded men) was a remark made by
the Master of Glammis to King James VI in that well
known piece of Scottish history known as the raid of
Ruthven.

Gowrie and others of the Barons having formed
the generous design of freeing James VI when a youth,
from his worthless favourites, inveigled him into this
castle (Ruthven Castle), on his return from a hunting
match in Athol. When about to depart, he was stopped
by his nobles, who presented him with a memorial of
their grievances. He endeavored to free himself from
their restraint, and burst into tears; upon which the
Master of Glammis observed, that it was better children weep than bearded men. The nobles carried him
off; but he escaped, and again gave himself up to the
Earl of Arran; and though he passed an act of oblivion
in their favor, pronounced the conspirators guilty of
high treason; and after a mock trial, perfidiously put
Gowrie to death at Stirling.

On March 21, 1970, Pamela reported an unexpected "resur-
gence" of impressions about the Scottish girl.

The girl is having one of her "spells" again. I wanted
to tell you of some names; of which I am not sure if she
said or if I imagined them.

The names are: Lord Patrick, Earl William, and
Earl Hom. Also, would Saint John's stone and black
pike mean anything to you? She also says of being
something of honor to a queen.

Bearing in mind that I had told Pamela nothing whatever
about her previous incarnation except that it had to do with
Scotland, I was fascinated by this material. I contacted my good
friends in Aberdeen for documentation.

Under dateline of April 14, 1970, the historian Carson
Ritchie informed Elizabeth Byrd as follows:

Earl William may be William Earl of Douglas, murdered by King James. Earl Hom must be Alexander Hume or Home, first Earl of Home, 1566–1619. Lord Patrick, the third Lord Gowrie, father of the Earl Gowrie. St. John's Stone is St. Johnstone, old name for Perth.

Alanna Knight and her husband checked the material out also and discovered that the ancient name for the city of Perth was St. Johns' Toun and that it was two miles from Huntingtower!

From an archaeologist friend, Dr. Margaret Steward, residing in Perth, the Knights discovered that "black pike" may be a corruption for *Black Park*, a small estate with an old mansion house, four miles north of Huntingtower.

Not to belabor my point, but how could a twenty-year-old Illinois hospital worker with only a high school education have such intimate and detailed knowledge of a very small and obscure area in Scotland . . . unless she had been there . . . *sometime.*

Chapter Twenty-One

The Many Lives of a Connecticut Lady

RUTH MACG. CONTACTED ME for the first time on May 10, 1967. She had read two of my books and was fascinated by her own ability to foretell future events, which she has been able to do through most of her adult life. She felt that she wanted to communicate them to me and perhaps obtain some information as to how she could develop her own mediumship in the process. I asked her to return a report to me in which she would state briefly all that she considered of an ESP nature throughout her life.

Ruth MacG. lives in a former inn on one of Connecticut's busier highways. Separated from her husband and later divorced, Ruth lives the life of a Connecticut gypsy, not the least bit worried about tomorrow or financial problems, knowing somehow that everything will be all right in the end.

One sentence in her letter made me take notice and gave me a vague feeling that this visit might be something more than a routine checkup on someone who has had psychic experiences in the past. Wondering if I had ever done any studies in the field of reincarnation, such as Edgar Cayce had done, she reported, "I have a strange memory of England in the last century which has obsessed me since childhood, and although my ancestors were

English, Irish, and Danish, and I was born here, as were my parents, I find that when I'm very tired I always use the English spelling as in honor, with honour and theatre. I don't do this when I'm aware of what I'm writing, but only when extremely fatigued."

How could I resist such an interesting sentence? That and the name of her place, the Old Chestnut Inn, were enough to make our meeting come about as soon as I could arrange a trip to her area. I offered to regress her hypnotically on the occasion of my visit, and she accepted gladly.

"You mentioned some form of reincarnation memories," I began when everyone had settled down. "Can you tell me when this first started?"

"I have always remembered my early years," Ruth began, "and so it wasn't much of a surprise that I could see places at an early age that other children could not. When I was four years old I had the very distinct impression that I knew a fourteenth-century garden somewhere in France. There wasn't much else, just the picture of the garden. Then, when I was six years old, I had the impression that I had lived in seventeenth-century Holland. It was a feeling of having lived at Leyden as a Puritan expatriate in poor health and disgusted with the robust Dutch revellings in the inn where I lived. I remember an early death. When I was seven I had a very strange longing to dance around a Greek temple in the moonlight, but for a seven-year-old this seemed to be rather a passionate longing. I have always had a longing for Greek things ever since, and the feeling for the white temple has persisted in me strongly since that time. Around the same time, I developed a strong feeling for England, and I gradually turned into an Anglophile, which I still am.

"My whole life became oriented toward England—that is to say, the England of the last century—so much so that I was convinced that it still existed somewhere."

"Can you give me any details of these past lives?" I inquired.

"It was always as a woman," Ruth replied. "Once I drowned. I know what it is like to feel the suffocating water close over one's face and to slip down into the darkness. I also know what it is like to lie in an open coffin and to listen to comments, or to try to raise your arm to tell onlookers that you are conscious, only to find the arm like iron, utterly immovable.

The awareness of these experiences, the drowning and death, came to me in a vivid dream when I was nine.

"Now, I must admit to having a phenomenal memory, which goes back to one year of life. My aunt and my mother often used to say, 'But you can't remember that. You were only eighteen months old.' Yet I would describe a kimono my aunt wore or the lighting fixtures in an apartment, and both turned out to be correct.

"I also have a vivid imagination, which is one reason I try to hold myself in check. There is also another strange thing: I can on occasion reach feats of accomplishment that do not have any relationship to my ordinary capabilities, almost as if I did not do these things. Once I came home from a movie, and although I play very badly, if at all, I was able to play a concerto by Max Steiner on the piano as if I knew it."

"Another time I painted a seascape because I had to see the sea. I had never before painted in oil. I am not a painter. I have danced a Hindu fold dance, made Danish pastry, and recently acted with an amateur drama group and have been accused of professional status in all these endeavors. No wonder I feel like an impostor."

After a moment of silence I continued questioning her. "Have you at any time had a definite impression of being in a place where you could identify people or the names of towns or anything like that, perhaps?"

"I have very strong feelings about the year 1857 in India. I feel that that was a tremendously traumatic year for me. I have a feeling that my life ended in 1857. When I was just a child, I picked up a ten-cent piece dated 1857. As I looked at the date on the coin, I felt terribly depressed, and my body was seized with trembling. Somehow the date meant something to me."

"You mentioned memories of having lived in England, India, and Holland. Have you ever been to these places?"

"No, unfortunately not. I was born in New York City; both my parents were born in New York City, and except for a brief visit to Canada, I have never left this country."

"Have you ever had any recurrent dreams?"

"Yes, when I was a small child I often dreamt of a scene in which I saw some flat land and two women who were with me. The dream always ended in sheer panic. In the midst of the flat land there were some dark, cylindrical objects which seemed to frighten me. When I was in Canada and stood on flat land with tall buildings in the distance, there was a vague feeling of recognition, as if the tall objects were some forms of buildings, but gradually I realized that what I was seeing were windmills in the Dutch landscape, which of course is very flat.

"Gradually I became aware of the fact that there was a terrible sense of pressure and hurrying and trying to escape, and it tied up with another dream I had had all through my childhood, of running down steps—flights after flights of steps— with someone in pursuit. I used to wake up in terror, absolutely unable to breathe, so real was the experience. I had the distinct impression that I was running for my life. Somehow the two dreams interconnected."

"Did you see the person who was pursuing you?"

"No, I only knew there were people. I could hear the footsteps. I seemed to feel that they were some kind of guards or soldiers, but I couldn't see them. I saw swords. The atmosphere was that of the middle sixteen hundreds. Glimpses of boots on the stairs; high boots and a cloak, but not really the person. I felt it was in Holland."

"How long did this last?"

"I'd say for about ten years, and then it gradually faded away. It didn't occur any longer. The dreams were almost identical all those years. It never came back, but in the 1940s I had a terrible sense of terror again when I saw a Dutch plate with a windmill on it. Somehow it reawakened forgotten memories in me."

"Did you see yourself in these visions and dreams?" I asked.

"Yes."

"How did you look?"

"Very much the same as I look now, except that my hair was darker and I think I had brown eyes; I'm not sure. The face was very similar, the nose a bit sharper, pointed upward, and slender. I have also seen myself in another incarnation as an Englishwoman, one who died at age twenty-seven, I believe."

"Do you ever get any names?"

"No, I'm sorry. I didn't get any names, just a strong sense of identity."

"Do you ever get any feelings about locations, places?" I asked.

"I get Lucknow, in India. I have a feeling about that, but

not as an Indian, rather as an Anglican living in India. I've always had a very strong pull toward India, mixed feelings of fascination and loathing at the same time."

"You mentioned the year 1857 and India before. Is there any connection between that and the memory of India and Lucknow, which you have just mentioned?" I asked.

"It could be. There is a feeling of terror and yet a great love of Indian music, and then there is a great fear of a dark-skinned man. I don't know what it is."

"Consciously speaking, and logically, does the year 1857 mean anything to you?"

"Well, the only thing I can think of is my grandmother. She was born in 1857, but that hardly seems important."

"Have you ever had dreams where you seem to be falling from great heights?"

"Yes, something to do with the stairs. When I was being pursued, I would touch the top of a long flight of marble steps, touch it with my foot and fly and touch the bottom step with my foot, as if I were taking giant strides. I had a terrible sensation of pain in the pit of my stomach, much as one feels when the elevator misses the floor slightly and pulls up."

"Was there any continuance of the picture?"

"I just kept on going. It was as if, if I stopped, something terrible would happen to me, but I never knew quite what it was. I never stopped running."

"How did you get out after you fell down the stairs? How did you see yourself get out?"

"I didn't really fall, I just sort of touched. It was miraculous the way I took those stairs."

"How were you dressed?"

"I had a cloak and long skirt. That's all I can see—lots of petticoats and long skirts."

"What period would you say they belonged to?"

"I'd say the early 1600s, perhaps 1630 or 1640."

"During your meetings with mediums or psychics in connections with your interest in ESP, did you ever discuss your visions and dreams?"

"No, I really have never discussed it with them. Many psychics have told me that I too was psychic, but I didn't feel like discussing this, as I was afraid of being laughed at. I didn't want people to think I was too imaginative."

"Have you ever been hypnotized?"

"No."

"Do you think you would make a good subject?"

"I think so, because I have a very cooperative nature."

I then proceeded to suggest to her that she should relax completely and told her that I would take her back ten years at a time.

When she was ten years old (by suggestion, that is), I asked her where she lived.

"In Manhattan, 3852 Nagel Avenue."

"What is your father's name?"

"Thomas Francis Raymond."

"What is your mother's name?"

"Charlotte MacGuire."

"Where do you go to school?"

"P.S. 52."

"What is your favorite teacher's name?"

"Miss MacLoughlin."

"What does she teach you?"

"Poetry; she proclaims poetry."

"What is your homeroom teacher's name?"

"*She* was. She taught me everything. She wore black chiffon to school with beads. She said, 'I wish children would be neater. I get a very clear picture of the kind of home they come from, and I know if I went to Ruth MacG.'s home everything would be lovely. Everything would be very neat and perfect, because that is the impression that she gives,' and I was very much chagrined because the other children laughed."

I then regressed her to age seven and asked her again where she lived.

"2339 Davidson Avenue in the Bronx."

"Where do you go to school?"

"St. Nicholas of Tolentine Parochial School."

"What is your favorite teacher's name?"

"She was a nun, Sister Bonaventura."

I proceeded to take her back further, year by year. Then I crossed the threshold of birth and suggested that she go back to minus five, minus ten, minus twenty years.

"What do you see now? Look around."

"It's all vapors, big thick clouds and vapors, and it's cold, very cold."

I suggested she go back even further and told her to go back to one hundred years before her birth. "Where are you now?"

"I'm in England—Sussex,"

"Where in Sussex?"

"I don't know yet—wait, there is a house and a lawn and my sister."

"What is your sister's name?"

"Ann."

"What is your name?"

"Martha."

"What is your father's name?"

"George."

"What is the family name, his entire name?"

"Andrews."

"What does he do?"

"A lawyer."

"Where does he live? What town?"

"Buck . . . Buck . . . no, Stokeley. Something to do with Stokeley and Buckminster. I don't know, He's not here all the time. He goes away."

"Where is the house?"

"It's in the country, but he had to go to the city sometimes."

"What town is the house in?"

"Two names—Stokeley on Bow . . . no."

"What county is it in?"

"Stokeley on Bow in Sussex . . . something like that."

Later I checked up on these places. It was most unlikely for Ruth MacG. to have any intimate knowledge of villages and obscure little towns in England, having never gone there nor having studied English geography to any extent. There is no Stokeley in England. However, I found a Stockesley in Yorkshire. There is also a Stockesby, and as for Buckminster, it does exist. Buckminster is on the border between Leicestershire and Lincolnshire, and as I looked at a detailed map of the area, I discovered that very close to Buckminster there are two other villages that might conceivably be the "Stokeley" the entranced Ruth MacG. was talking about. There is a Stonesby west of Buckminster, and there is a Stokerochford north of Buckminster. Both of these villages are very close to Buckminster. As for the word *Bow*, there is a village named Bow in Cornwall, but I doubt that there is any connection between Cornwall and Yorkshire in this instance. There is no Stokeley on Bow in Sussex. In fact, none of the places here mentioned are in Sussex, which is much farther south. Why the entranced subject confused the counties, I do not know, but I find it rather remarkable that she came up with the name Buckminster, a village or small town of which I have never heard and which I found only by consulting the detailed map of British counties I have in my possession. Meanwhile, I continued my questioning.

"What year are we in now?"

"1809."

"What is your mother's name?"

"My mother isn't here. She is dead."

I insisted on her mother's name.

"Mabel."

"What was she before she married your father?"

"Mabel Breen."

"When did she die?"

"She died when I was two years old, in 1800 I think."

"Where did you go to school?"

"I didn't."

"Where did you go to church?"

"The parish church . . . Saint something. I didn't like the minister."

"What was his name, and what was the name of the church?"

"He had two names, Holly Benton, and he spit when he preached."

"Do you remember the name of the church? "Yes, St. Hildegard."

"Where was it located?"

"In the village. We walked, and I had such a pretty hat."

"Where was your house?"

"Just outside the village. Oh, it was a pretty little house. It had dormer windows. It was of stone . . . no, brick, and big, wide windows and a green lawn, and such lovely roses in the garden, and they took very good care of the garden of Mrs. Benton. . . . Mrs. Benton was the housekeeper."

"Did you live there or did you leave town?" I asked.

"I lived there until I got married."

"Whom did you marry?"

"An officer in the service."

"What was his name?"

"Ronald Whiting."

"What branch of the service was he in?"

"Her Majesty's Troops Dragoons. I hated it."

"Do you remember what number the regiment was?"

"Number 67, I think."

"Who was the colonel of the regiment? Do you remember the commanding officer's name?"

"Oh, him. I didn't like him at all."

"But what was his name?"

"Edgeworth."

"Do you remember any other officers in the regiment?"

"No, I wasn't very well, and I went sometimes to the regimental affairs, but I didn't like them very much. I hated the military."

"After you were married, where did you go to live?"

"I always dreaded being sent away . . . sent to places so far away."

"What do you mean, 'so far away'? Where were you sent?"

"We went to India."

"Where in India?"

"Calcutta and then another place, where there was an uprising."

"Where was the uprising? Was it a town, a fort?"

"Not a big city like Calcutta. I think it was a town—Mysore, if there is such a place."

When I nodded that there was indeed such a place, she continued.

"My husband was very angry because I didn't like that kind of living . . . always on the move. I wanted to go back to England. It was so hot. Sometimes it was so dirty, and the natives distressed me while they fascinated me, and I couldn't cope with the whole problem in India. I wanted to do something about it, and I couldn't. I just fumed and fretted. I felt it was all wrong. I couldn't see why we had to be there, and then he would go away. He would always go away, leaving me with the servants. There were plenty of servants. There was nothing for me to do, of course."

"Was that in Mysore?"

"Both in Calcutta and Mysore and then this other place."

She seemed to have trouble remembering the other place, so I asked, "What year are we now?"

"Eighteen fifty-two we went there. We had to stay there for five years before we could be sent anywhere else, and there was this terrible day when he wasn't there. He had gone away."

"Where had he gone to?"

"Oh, he had to go away. They had to go away. They thought trouble was coming."

"Who was making trouble? Who were the people that were making the trouble?"

"The natives were very angry. They didn't want us there."

"Were these the native Indians?"

"Yes."

"Were they civilians?"

"Oh, they were civilians, and there were some army Sikhs, and they came in one day like a dam breaking . . . came in, the bodies screaming, shouting, pillaging, raping. I ran and hid. The children, they got it, it was terrible . . . all the bloodshed and the wickedness, and there was no place to run . . . nowhere. I was so soiled . . . so deeply crushed. They spared nobody. They were frenzied, wild, with bloodshot eyes, angry, rioting."

"What year was that in?"

"We went to India in 1852, and we stayed there five years."

"It was 1857, then?"

"Yes."

"And what happened after that? Did you leave India?"

"Well, yes, we did. I had to leave, but it was the end of everything for me. Well, I wasn't killed. It would have been better if I had been."

"What about your husband?"

"He wasn't there. He had been sent on this other foolish chase. They thought trouble was coming."

"Where from?"

"The other end. The other end, two miles away, and then they came and nothing was sacred, absolutely nothing . . . the children killed and wounded, stomped upon."

"Where was that?"

"In Lucknow. Yes, in Lucknow, at the officers' quarters. It was terrible, and this Indian came. He was very tall, very menacing, very dark. I thought he was going to strangle me, but he raped me. Isn't that awful? I never knew why there had to be an empire. Just that little green island would have been enough. Why did we have to go out there in the first place?"

"Where was your husband at the time?"

"He had been sent with the troops to the other end, where they had suspected there would be trouble, and while they were gone, the men came, wild, a flood of human hatred, and, oh, there was no appeal. There was nothing that could reach them. This large menacing man, with a large aquiline nose, pinned me to the wall. He had a stare, and I hoped that he was going to kiss me, but he didn't. He was disgusting, fascinating, but it was awful, because some of us didn't die. We have to live with that memory."

"You went back to England then?"

"I never got there."

"What happened to you?"

"I fell."

"Where did you fall?"

"On the ship. I don't know whether I fell or whether I was pushed. I was so unhappy."

"Where did the ship go to?"

"It was going back to England. My husband was furious."

"Why was he furious?"

"He was very unreasonable. I think that he wished that I had been killed instead of raped. He said I was . . . well, having been touched by a native, was unclean. He wouldn't even talk to me."

"And when you fell on the ship, what happened then to you?"

"I drowned. I could feel the water closing over my face, and I didn't care, and it was frightening. For a moment I struggled, and then a strange feeling of happiness came over me. I had tried to breathe, but I couldn't, and so I gave up the struggle."

"What was the next thing that happened to you then?"

"I fainted, I just breathed in the water, and I don't remember anything. Yes, I remember being dead. They must have got my body. I remember being in a coffin. They must have retrieved it, because it was in a coffin, and they were making the kind of remarks that people do."

"Did you see yourself in the coffin?"

"Yes. I must have been on shipboard. I saw the coffin and

the people passing by, and I wanted to tell them, 'I hear what you are saying. I hear, and I tried to move my arm. I tried, and it was like lead. I couldn't move. I couldn't wiggle. I couldn't even move my nose . . . couldn't even indicate that I was there and I was listening."

"And after that?"

"Nothing after that . . . nothing."

Later I researched this amazing account of her presence in another lifetime during the Indian rebellion. To begin with, Ruth MacG. is not a student of Indian history. If she had any general knowledge of British imperial policies in India during the nineteenth century, it would not include specifics as to where battles and sieges took place. But I questioned Ruth thoroughly, and I am convinced that she did not even have that much knowledge about British India during the time of Queen Victoria, nor did she indeed show any interest in this period except for what happened to her in another life.

If Ronald Whiting was a member of the 67th Dragoons, he could have been in British India at the critical moment. The rebellion took place in 1857. The Sikhs did indeed play a role in it, although at various times they supported the British colonial effort and not always that of the rebels.

A little later I asked the entranced Ruth to go back into her Indian past and to answer a few questions.

"What is a *sepoy*?"

"Without a moment's hesitation, she answered, "A sepoy . . . it's a kind of a native."

"What does he do? What does a sepoy do professionally?"

"He's with the troops, isn't he?"

I very much doubt Ruth MacG. would have had the knowledge to describe correctly the meaning of the word *sepoy*. The fact that she did not use this term does not mean that she did not know it. I deliberately tried it on her to see what her reaction would be.

She spoke of Lucknow and the terrible things that happened there. It is a historical fact that the compound at Lucknow was under siege by the rebel troops and that thousands were actually killed during that period both at Lucknow and at Delhi. Delhi had been in the hands of the rebels but was finally besieged and taken back by the British colonial troops, at which time a great bloodbath took place. Lucknow was then free, and the women and children and the remnants of the garrison left. It is also true that many if not most of the women were shipped home to England after their two years of terror during the rebellion in India.

Since Ruth had spoken of other incarnations when we discussed her memories in the conscious state, I decided to take her back even further. I commanded her to go back beyond India and to go further back in time.

"It is now three hundred years before your present birth. What do you see?" I asked.

"Smoke in the room. A fireplace. I am in a room in a cottage, and the fireplace is smoking. It burns my throat, and they can't open the window. It's cold, and they won't open the door."

"Do you see yourself?"

"Yes."

"How old do you look?"

"About twelve."

"Do you know your name?"

"It's a biblical name . . . Magdalene . . . Magdalene Darling."

"In what town are you?"

"Now we are in Holland. We are not in England, but we speak English, and the other people don't."

"What is the year?"

"The year is 1613."

"And what is the town?"

"Leyden."

"Why are you here?"

"Everything gets sort of stupid. My father was there but he wasn't around very much, and my aunt and my mother are both there, and we have to wait and, there is something about the new world, in passage."

"On what ship is the passage?"

"We don't know. We are waiting, and we have rooms at the inn—this inn in the town."

"Who is sending the ships?"

"Well, you see, we are not very well thought of in England, I am sorry to say. We are very respectable people really. Perhaps too respectable.

"What faith are you?"

"Oh, we are Puritans."

"Do you remember the name of the company who sends the ships . . . the name of the owner of the ships?"

"Well, I didn't pay very much attention to things like that. I wasn't well, you see. I had this cough. My mother and my aunt—they were there. They hated it, and they kept saying that I had to have good courage, strong faith, or, we'd come to the new world . . . everything would be different. We wouldn't have to be persecuted and all that, but it seemed so hopeless. We were there so long."

"What town did your people come from in England?"

"My father comes from the North."

"What town does he come from?"

"North Riding on the Moors."

"Where in the North Riding? What village?"

"Horton."

"What is your father's name?"

"John Darling."

"And your mother's name?"

"My mother was Johanna."

"And what was her maiden name before her marriage?"

"Bliss."

"Where did she come from? What town in England?"

"She too came from the North . . . Durham. It's near New-castle somewhere."

Again my later research established the validity of Ruth's statement. Horton is indeed in Yorkshire, although on present-day maps it is in the West Riding rather than in the North Riding, but it is in the northern part of the West Riding, as this particular area is even now called. Durham is indeed directly south of Newcastle and also not very far from Horton. Only someone very familiar with English geography would have such knowledge. I have been in the area, and I do not recall these places. The name Darling, incidentally, is quite common in Yorkshire.

In 1612 the Dutch founded New Amsterdam, which is now New York City. Actually the Puritans who had come to Holland because of persecutions at home in England emigrated a few years later than the date of 1613 given by Ruth in trance. Most of the emigrés left between 1629 and 1637, but it is entirely possible that some left on an earlier date. There is no doubt that

English Puritans did spend time in Holland, which was much more favorably inclined toward their religion. Leyden is the nearest large city toward the coast opposite England. Many Puritans did, indeed, find refuge in seventeenth-century Leyden.

I continued to question Ruth. "Now you are going with them to the New World?"

"Yes, my aunt, my mother's sister, we are supposed to go to the Plymouth Colony, but are we ever going to get there? There is never any room on the ships. We have to wait and wait, and disaster after disaster, and mother said I'd end up speaking Dutch, which she didn't particularly want. She said they were . . . oh, she used a word that expressed contempt . . . *blubbers*. She said they were bear blubbers; but you see, it was at the inn, and these men were quite coarse. Mother was not, of course."

"Do you remember the name of the inn in Leyden?"

"Three Turks, I think."

"And the year is still 1613?"

"Yes, and it's damp and cold, but the fire is always smoking, and then of course it's always brighter and warmer downstairs, but we don't want to go down there because those roistering Dutchmen . . . well, my mother doesn't want me to be exposed to them."

"Did you take the ship across?"

"No, I never got there. I died in Leyden."

"How old were you then?"

"Thirteen."

"And your parents returned to England?"

"I don't know what happened to them, really. I had this cough, and it was miserable, and I was in bed. I couldn't leave the room, and they kept saying, 'Courage, child. You'll get well,' but I . . ."

"How long did you stay in Holland?"

"Three years."

"Did you always live in the inn?"

"Well, we lived with a family at first, but it was rather crowded, and my father said we were best off at the inn."

"What sort of place did the family have?"

"It was a farm out in the country, and I liked that much better because there were apple trees and the cows and windmills, and it was fun to watch them going around."

"Did you like the windmills?"

"Yes, I liked them in the daytime. I loved to watch them, but at night they sort of frightened me because they looked so like giants with seven arms going around and around, waiting to devour. The children were nice, and the Dutch people were nice on the farm, but when we had to go into town, it was different."

"What was the name of the farm in the little village you lived in? Do you remember that?"

"Greck, or something."

"Was it near Leyden?"

"Leyden was the nearest big city to it."

"What province was that in?"

"It began with a U . . . U . . ."

"Was it Utrecht?"

"Yes, that was it—Utrecht, but we didn't pay much attention to where we were then. We were glad to get out of England, and there were lots of things to do—ice skating in the winter, an iceboat, and I loved that, but then when we went to the city it was horrid and not very clean, and then I died in the inn, in the room at the inn."

The hour was growing late. I detected signs of weariness in Ruth and decided to bring her back into the present.

In February 1968 she communicated with me again. She vividly described a marketplace in Calcutta and then added some details to her frightful experience of going back to England by ship. Apparently she had become pregnant as a result of the experience that she had gone through during the siege of Lucknow. In addition she had formed an attachment to an Indian officer aboard ship, who had first protected her from the others and then forced his attentions upon her in private. Despite the strong impression, in her own mind she still doubted the validity of these prenatal experiences and made it a point to warn me that she could not prove any of it.

We communicated and corresponded off and on and met a couple of times for dinner. These occasions were always delightful and festive, but we did not discuss the serious business of reincarnation at such times. Evidently the visions remained in her subconscious mind, and in some instances became deeper, for in July 1969 she jotted down some of the most important ones for me.

The vision of a marketplace in Calcutta was even more vivid now. The colonel's wife is named Dora, and she is in the market to look at brassware, pottery, fabric, and food. Dora wears a green and white plaid dress with a flounced skirt, while Ruth wears a pale, straight muslin. Both women wear bonnets and carry sunshades. A woman squats near a low table on which are arranged some sweets made from apricots. She is nursing an infant whose head is covered with flies. Dora takes a handkerchief from her bag and gives it to the woman, indicating that she is to wave off the flies with it. The woman smiles her thanks and places the handkerchief on the baby's head. The two women move on.

A second vision concerns a stone church in England with a square tower covered with ivy. Ruth sees herself standing on the steps with her new husband. He is in uniform, while she is wearing a bridal gown and veil and is very nervous. There are friends and villagers at the bottom of the path throwing petals at them. Ruth is embarrassed by this. She wishes they were on the steamer that is to take them to Calcutta. She closes her eyes and knows that she will have to walk through the crowd to get to the carriage, and she dreads it.

The third vision sees her in the compound in Lucknow. All the men have gone except for a few who are doing guard duty. The drums have been going for hours, and some of the women are beside themselves with fear but are trying not to show it. Mrs. Jennings' ayah is about to give birth. Dora is bustling about, preparing for the event. She has commandeered linens from all sources and has unguents and jars in readiness. Someone is burning incense. The ayah's moment has come. Ruth is standing by with a basin of water. She cannot stand the sights and smells, and everything turns dark green and she faints dead away.

The final vision sees her aboard ship, going home to England, but it is not a happy time. She sees herself in the bunk, with the ship pitching and tossing. She is very ill. Dora thinks it is merely seasickness. She is trying to feed Ruth gruel and tea. However, Ruth is sick for another reason. She is pregnant by the sepoy who ravished her. She is defiled. Her husband said so. There is nothing for her to do but turn her face to the wall and die. He said so. When everyone is sleeping she will go out on deck. She will lean over, who will care? There is nothing but disgrace, and she would be done with this life.

Now, these fours visions are, in fact, only repetitions and embellishments of the material Ruth had spoken of consciously in part and more elaborately under hypnosis, but there are some details not found in the earlier versions. It is, of course, entirely possible that Ruth embroidered her stories, either consciously or unconsciously, with details that would make them better stories, but I do not think so. She had nothing to gain from this. It is rather an unsavory experience that she was recording, and a less truthful person than Ruth might in fact suppress it or certain of the details. Apparently, in telling me all her reincarnation memories Ruth also relieved herself of the pressures that came with them. She, I think, accepted these experiences as a legitimate part of her character and acknowledges the need for her earlier sufferings.

Chapter Twenty-Two
The Reincarnation of an Atlanta Belle

JUNE V. WAS BORN IN A SMALL TOWN in Pennsylvania, the daughter of an average couple who live in retirement in Florida. When she was only a teenager June married Sam V., a man of Italian extraction. She herself was of Dutch-German background. Eventually they moved into a small town in western Pennsylvania, where they bought a house and where Sam followed a career in the glass industry. His work was neither extraordinary nor dull, and June's family was no different from her neighbors'.

With four children her life was always busy, and even when the two older children left home there was plenty to do around the house. The elder son was in the service, and one daughter was married. Only the two younger children still lived at home with June and Sam. They lived a pleasant if somewhat uneventful life, far from the mainstream of adventure, far from any big city. To reach Pittsburgh, the nearest big city, requires many hours of driving.

June has been to Long Island and knows some parts of New York State in addition to her own Pennsylvania, but it wasn't until 1959, when she was twenty-nine years old, that she went on her first major trip. In June of that year she undertook

260

her first visit south, to Florida, where her parents then lived.

The first week of her stay in Silver Springs passed uneventfully. It had been raining, and June was somewhat concerned about the lack of good weather. One evening she found herself sitting in the kitchen mending some clothes, when her older daughter, who was then living with June's parents, came up to her and said, "Mamma, before you go home I want you to come and see the haunted house."

June started to laugh, for the very notion of a haunted house was totally alien to her. She just didn't believe in such things, but her daughter insisted.

"No, really, Mamma. They say it's haunted by the lady who used to live there."

June is a practical-minded person, and she was about to dismiss the remark of her fifteen-year-old daughter when her mother spoke up, suggesting that she go over to the site next morning right after breakfast. June, wanting to end the conversation, agreed halfheartedly to go and have a look at this haunted house. With that the subject was dropped, and the conversation turned to family matters.

Around eleven-thirty June went to bed and quickly dropped off to sleep. Suddenly she found herself in a two-seated wagon with a fringed top. Two men sat in front talking and a large colored woman was at her side, grumbling to herself, seemingly quite concerned for June's welfare. The strange thing was the June saw *herself* wearing a long, full, ruffled white dress. Her hair was long, auburn in color. In her hands she held a parasol, which she was moving around with nervous gestures. She wanted to hurry, to go faster, and she felt excitement racing through her body as she pleaded with the driver to go faster.

They drove now through a small town and over a dirt road, past wooden frame and brick homes, shops, and a church—all of them with metal hitching posts, most of black iron with a horse's head or an angel on top and a metal ring to tie the horses to. Next she saw a little red railroad station and narrow-gauge track, and a pretty fountain with three cherubs blowing little horns, with the water streaming out of them. The streets were lined with palms and large shade trees dripping with moss. A warm, pleasant breeze blew, ruffling her skirt and hair, which was hanging long about her shoulders. Now the carriage reached the end of town and went down a dirt road to her left.

On one side she noticed tall, golden wheat swaying in the soft breeze. On the other side of the road there was tall corn. The young man driving the two-horse carriage turned and shouted to her, "There it is. You can see it from here."

"Where, where? Oh, yes, I can see it. Please hurry. Hurry or I shall get out and run to it by myself."

The man laughed in a teasing way and hurried the horses on a bit faster to the curve at the end of the lane.

A large, white, two-story house stood there, with a circular drive and a large shade tree in front of the porch, which extended across the front of the house. Flowers grew about the yard, and the lawn was a green carpet spread out as if just for her. The carriage had barely stopped when she stepped down and went up onto the porch and through the front door into a large hallway. She heard herself screaming with delight as she raced from one room to the next.

"Oh, it's beautiful and I love it, and it's mine, all mine," she heard herself say. She noticed a stairway going up to the right. At the foot of the staircase was a room toward the left. Then, coming through the front door, to the right she noticed a library. A painted mural of a hunting scene was on the left-hand wall, above a red velvet love seat decorated in the Victorian manner. Bookshelves, reaching from floor to ceiling against the wall, were separated by a lovely wood and brick fireplace. The walls were all white throughout the house.

She found herself walking through the house looking at all the rooms, noticing that there were five bedrooms upstairs and noticing that each of them had a fireplace and that they were furnished beautifully. An overwhelming feeling of having come home pervaded her, and she was very happy and filled to the brim with contentment.

In the dream she saw herself, yet not looking like herself but somehow feeling identical with the person going through the house. The girl she saw looked to be about eighteen or nineteen years old, possibly a few years older, and not at all like the person June was at the time of her dream. Still, she could not understand how she could be both her present self and also the girl in the dream.

She awoke early with a strange, eerie, almost sickening feeling. She couldn't understand this, for it had been a lovely dream. Why would it make her feel so bad? The more she tried to shake off the vivid memory of the dream and the strange, unsettled feeling that came with it, the worse she began to feel.

The rain had stopped now, and it was a warm, humid morning. As soon as breakfast and the dishes were finished, June's father reminded her that she had promised to go and have a look at the haunted house. Still under the unsettling influence of her dream, June reluctantly agreed. Her daughter Lolly and her son Mich came along for the ride. Evidently her father noticed that she wasn't quite herself. "What's the matter with you this morning, June?" he inquired. She only shook her head. "It's nothing. I just had a bad dream. I'll be all right." Her father nodded and let the matter rest.

After awhile the scene seemed strangely familiar. With mounting excitement she noticed that she knew the way, yet she also knew that she had never been here before in her life. Soon the car entered a totally deserted "ghost town" called Red Mill. The town was exactly the same as she had seen it in the dream the night before, but now the houses and shops were all crumbling; even the fountain in the middle of town was in shambles. June knew every part of the place. She knew where her father would have to turn off to get into the lane leading to the house of her dream, and before she knew it that was exactly what he was doing. It was all very frightening and confusing, yet the excitement was as strong as it had been in her dream.

Her father stopped the car at the entrance to an overgrown lane. The wheat and corn fields of her dream were gone now, and only weeds, tall grass and underbrush grew. The house was black with age and falling down. The porch was all but gone. Suddenly she found herself racing as fast she could toward the house, with the children in close pursuit. Her father had declined to come along, as he had some business to take care of in town. He would be back for them later. Her daughter had been to the house many times before without experiencing anything special. To her it was just an old house, perhaps with eerie overtones, and fun to play in, but there were no actual psychic overtones, nor was there anything out of the ordinary surrounding the old, broken-down house.

The house was quite empty now, except for some grain that was being stored in the living room by a rental farmer, but June did not see the house as it was now. Rather did she experience it, somehow, as it had been when she had known it in another lifetime. She felt a surge of happy contentment, as if she had been away for a long, long time and had finally returned home.

Room by room June and her two children went through the house now. She remembered how the lace curtains moved gently over the dining room windows, but of course that was impossible. There were no lace curtains anymore. Everything was gone except the faded-out hunting scene painted on the library wall. It was the same scene she had seen in her dream the night before.

"There used to be a desk over there," June heard herself mumble. "And the settee went over there."

"Mamma, how do you know?" her daughter said, somewhat frightened by her mother's strange knowledge of a house she had never seen in her life before.

June did not answer. She wondered about it herself.

On the way over, Lolly had told her mother about a terrible murder that had taken place in this very house. This was the first time that June had heard about Mrs. Simms. Apparently her daughter had picked up some of the local stories concerning the abandoned house. A Mrs. Elizabeth Simms had once lived in it and had been murdered, but the cause of her death and the name of her murderer had never been discovered.

Now June stood in the house that she knew so well and yet couldn't really know. She followed her children up the stairs and heard her daughter say, "Mamma, this is the room that Mrs. Simms was murdered in." Despite the grim words, June felt peaceful in that room. After awhile she descended the stairs and returned to the library.

Outside, a thundershower was coming down, and they decided to wait until it stopped. By this time June's father would have returned and was probably waiting outside at the end of the lane. While they were waiting Lolly suddenly said, "I wonder what the last thing was she did before she went upstairs and was murdered that night."

No sooner had her daughter said this than June felt unseen hands clutch her waist from behind, and she seemed to have no control over her body at all or even over what she was saying. Somehow she was moved first to the fireplace.

"She stood here for a moment, looking at the pictures on the mantel," she heard herself say in a very strange voice. Next she was literally moved across the room, through the doorway, and up the stairs. "She held the candle with one hand and held up her skirt hem with the other. She was very tired and worried about something."

June could hear her daughter say pleadingly, "Mamma, what's the matter? You look funny, Mamma. You're so white. You're frightening me, Mamma. Don't do that. What's the matter?" But June couldn't really hear her. She couldn't speak. When she reached the second step from the top she heard loud footsteps hurrying down the hall, coming close to her. Suddenly she panicked and turned. She could not move down the stairs. Something was pushing her back, wanting her to go on up. Desperately June grabbed onto the railing and, hand over hand, pulled herself to the bottom of the staircase. Her new blouse was ripped up the back. She felt sick to her stomach and stood on the front porch, or what was still left of the porch, for awhile, breathing deeply and with difficulty the fresh, cool air. Her panic was gone now, and she could vividly remember the impression of human hands on her back. No doubt about it, someone in the house, unseen though that person might have been, wanted her to go up the stairs.

June and her children started to leave, but she kept hearing someone calling to her from the house, "Come back. Please come back. Don't go, please." Desperately she fought a battle within herself not to turn and run back to the house and up those stairs. Finally she turned to look back, and when she did she saw a young girl in a long, white dress, with long, brown hair, standing at the window. The girl in the window looked a lot like her.

In the car on their way back to Silver Springs, the children asked why she had behaved in such a strange manner. "You frightened us, Mamma," her daughter said. June nodded grimly. She was frightened herself. Neither of her children had heard the voice nor seen the apparition at the window, but they had seen her behavior on the stairs and noticed the tearing of her blouse.

That evening she mentioned her experience to her parents. "Well, these things do happen," her father had said, and with this remark the matter was dropped.

As the days went on, June became more and more convinced that the apparition at the window had been merely her exaggerated imagination. For some reason, she thought, she had become agitated, and in the nervous state she was in, due to the strange experience on the stairs, she might have imagined seeing a woman where there was in reality no one.

During the rest of her stay in Silver Springs, she had no further unusual dreams. When she returned home to Pennsylvania a month later, however, her husband noticed a great change in her. It was almost as if she had become another person. Where her temperament before her trip to Florida had been rather timid and complacent, she now seemed to be much more demanding and sophisticated in her interests. There was a lively enthusiasm, a desire to fight for what she believed in, that had not existed before.

Ever since her strange experience at the crumbling house, she had a strong desire to return, and she knew that she would have to go back there someday. From time to time she noticed a southern accent in her speech. The whole incident left her no peace, and eventually she wrote to her father and asked for his help to find out once and for all what it all meant. Her father suggested that she get in touch with an old gentleman who had been the postmaster when Red Mill was still a going town. He might be a good source of information about the Simms family and that which transpired about a hundred years ago.

After several letters, June finally received an answer. Yes, there had been a Simms family, with seven children, and there was a lot of heartache in that family. There was, first of all, Laura Lee, who had run off and disappeared, and then there was Robert, who was a crippled because he had been run over by a horse and wagon.

When the place at Red Mill was still a thriving plantation, it was one of the best in the area. Apparently Mr. and Mrs. Simms had married young. They had come from an aristocratic family in Atlanta, Georgia. They arrived in Florida around 1860, just when Florida was beginning to develop.

Allen, the oldest boy, joined the Union forces when the Civil War broke out, despite his father's protests, and was immediately disowned. He was killed in Atlanta, Georgia, trying to protect his grandparents from being killed when the Union troops moved onto their plantation. The plantation itself was burned, looted, and destroyed.

Another son served in the Confederate Army, at the dispatcher's headquarters. After Robert died in an accident in the swamps, the mother was left alone, for Robert the elder had died of a stroke due to the sudden death of Allen, his favorite son.

When the war was over, Mrs. Simms decided to open a small store, not so much for financial gain as to keep herself busy. It was a grocery and supply store. At the time June had visited the house for the first and only time, she had found some yellow ledgers and notebooks in the house. They pertained mainly to the running of the grocery store. She had picked them up and kept them in her possession. There were also some letters, and it appeared from them that there was another son, James.

Mrs. Simms was eighty-nine at the time of her death. Apparently she was brushing her hair in the bedroom when she was shot in the back with a shotgun and killed instantly. The story goes, according to the former postmaster, that James had become a traitor to the Southern cause toward the end of the war. Having gambled heavily, he was in great need of funds. For that reason, he worked with Union spies, selling them Southern secrets, but the Confederate espionage apparatus got wind of it, and he escaped by the skin of his teeth. James then became a fugitive, always careful of Confederate agents. Even after the war, James was afraid for his life. No one knows whether James's mother was killed for some sort of revenge or by mistake, but the killer was never found. Apparently the tragedy happened in 1896. The ledger, which June had discovered in the house, gave entries all the way up to 1913, so it is probable that the son still lived at that date.

When June's father heard that the place had been torn down, that there was nothing left to remind her of the once-proud plantation, he relayed the news to her. Despite this, June's longing for the place was as strong as ever. In her mind's eye she would see it as it was, and she could hardly resist the desire to return to "her old home."

In addition to the house, she saw another scene time and again, a creek with lots of stones and water ripples around it, and on one side a big tree with Spanish moss hanging down from it, touching the water. The scene was peaceful and quiet, but she had never been to such a place, nor had she ever seen a similar picture.

As if her strange experiences, her change of personality, and her overwhelming desire to return to a place she hardly knew weren't enough to upset June, there was something else.

Gradually she had become aware of another experience somewhere in the dim, dark past of her existence. This was a memory of a girl with soft brown hair who looked a lot like her. This girl arrived home with three other women, two older ones and one her own age. They were traveling in a buggy of sorts, drawn by two horses. The driver wore a black suit, and something told June that this happened about 1693.

As the scene unrolled, she saw them stop in front of a long brick building and felt instinctively that this was not in America but in Germany. She noticed that the girl pulled back the curtain and stepped down from the buggy and that she was followed into the house by the others. The girl was about twenty years old, of slender build, and wearing a long, dark hooded coat wrapped tightly about her.

June felt that they had returned home from visiting a Dutch relative. The relative lived in a wood-shingled house of two stories, with a waterwheel connected with it. There was a quiet, red-faced, heavily built man sitting in front of the mill, and June seemed to hear some conversation in a language she thought was Dutch. Then June suddenly felt that it was she entering the kitchen of the house. A large, heavily built woman who was fussing in the kitchen welcomed her. That night she slept in a large, straw-filled "swinging" bed on the second floor. There were three people to a bed because it was warmer that way, and the beds were very wide.

Since June is of German-Dutch descent, she assumed that this scene had something to do with her ancestry. She did understand some Dutch and German, although she could not speak either. Still, the memory was more than just a fading scene from the past. It was something that was also very strong, though not as compelling as the identification with the unhappy woman in the Florida plantation house.

Her memories of what appears to be previous lifetimes were not like some of the ordinary memories of things she did in her past. Somehow they were much more vivid, and they disturbed June. At one point she decided to discuss the matter with her priest. The good father listened patiently and seriously, and when June asked him whether he thought there was something wrong with her, he shook his head. "No," he said. "There is nothing wrong with you, my dear, except perhaps that you are too sensitive for your own good." And with that, he dismissed her. But June was not satisfied with such bland advice. She went to a clinic in Ridgeway, Pennsylvania, and subjected herself to every conceivable psychiatric test. Dr. John D., the resident psychiatrist, eventually sent her home with the remark that she was probably mentally healthier than he was and that there was nothing wrong with her at all.

Since June had always rejected the possibility of the supernatural, it disturbed her to have dreamed of the Simms home before she had ever laid eyes upon it. The memory of the girl in the carriage in Germany had actually been with her for a long time before the visit to Florida. But she had never paid it any heed. Now, however, in the light of the Florida adventure it took on new dimensions.

All these matters were on her mind when she turned on her television set one fine morning and watched me discuss psychic phenomena with Marie Torre on Pittsburgh television. All of a sudden she knew whom she could ask about her strange memories. When she contacted me I immediately wrote back, asking her to come to meet me the next time I was in Pittsburgh.

Unfortunately, however, June was not allowed to travel much. One valve of her heart is completely blocked and she must avoid strain. Her town is over one hundred miles from Pittsburgh. Regretfully June declined to meet me and instead issued an invitation to come and meet her at her home. Then some doubts arose in my mind. If she had such a heart defect, could I safely hypnotize her? I asked her to check the entire matter with her physician before I went any further. Then, too, I wanted June to ask her husband whether he had any objections to my starting to work with her, since it might entail a considerable amount of time and research.

If her reincarnation memories proved to be evidential I felt that we might have to continue for a considerable length of time with hypnosis, and I wanted to make sure I would not be interrupted halfway to my goal.

On March 20, 1968, I received a most cordial letter from June. Both her personal physician and the doctor at the clinic had encouraged her to proceed with the experiment. I was told only to avoid fatiguing her, and this I readily agreed to. Her husband, Sam, also put nothing in our way, so I made arrangements for June to meet me in Pittsburgh on the first of May.

Despite my offer to have her flown in from her little town in western Pennsylvania, she came by bus and was none the worse for it.

Even our first meeting in person was rather strange. My plane had been delayed, and I had begun to worry that Mrs. V. might find waiting uncomfortable. Mentally, perhaps, I may have sent out some thoughts that reached her mind. After all, she had had ESP all through her life. When I reached the hotel at which she was staying I picked up the house phone and asked for her room. At that precise moment she stepped up from behind me. She had been in her room and had suddenly gotten an intuition to go down to the lobby to greet me. Thus we met, and returned immediately upstairs to begin our first hypnosis session as soon as possible.

After I had put her under, I suggested that she was getting younger. Physically her face slackened, and when I suggested that she was just six years old you could almost see the little girl. Then she became a baby before my eyes, and finally I sent her back across the threshold of birth and suggested that the time now was fifty years before her birth as June. Another personality now seemed to possess her body.

I asked quietly, "What is your name?"

"Mary Elizabeth."

"Where do you live?"

"I live in Georgia."

"What is your mother's name?"

"Catherine."

"What is your father's name?"

"Frank."

"Where do you live in Georgia?"

"On our plantation."

"What is it called? What town is it in?"

"Atlanta—Atlanta, Georgia."

"And what's your family's name?"

"Tibbits."

"Do you have any brothers and sisters?"

"I have a brother."

"What's his name?"

"Melvin."

"How old is he?"

"Twenty-three."

"How old are you?"

"I'm eighteen."

"Where were you born?"

"Right here."

"In Atlanta?"

"Uh-huh, in that little room up there at the top of the stairs."

"Where's the house? What street is the house on? The plantation, where is it? In Atlanta?"

"We have one of the largest plantations here in Atlanta, Georgia, that you'd ever want to see."

"Where did you go to school?"

"We had private tutors come in—taught my brother and me, in the library."

"What church did you go to?"

"White Baptist Church."

"Where is it located?"

"Down the lane."

"What's your grandfather's name?"

"He's dead."

"What was his name?"

"Gordon."

"Does your father serve in the army?"

"No, Pop's too old."

"Does he have a brother in the army?"

"No, they keep talking all the time about the army and carpetbaggers and high taxes."

"What year is this now?"

"It's 18 . . . 18 . . . I don't know."

"What's the president's name?"

"Jackson."

"Tell me a little bit about yourself. What do you do all day?"

"Go to teas."

"Do you have any friends?"

"Robert."

"Robert what?"

"Simms."

"How old is he?"

"Twenty-two."

"What does he do? Where does he live?"

"His family lives the next planation over."

"How far away?"

"Across the creek. Over the lane."

"Are you going to marry him?"

"Oh, yes, if I could only get him to tell me he wants to marry me. I know he wants to marry me. I don't know . . . he doesn't want to get married yet."

"Why, is he too young?"

"No, something about new land."

"New land where?"

"Florida, I guess they call it."

"He wants to go there?"

"Yes. I don't know why he wants to leave Georgia. This is the most beautiful state in the whole world. He makes me so mad. We could be so happy."

"Would you go with him?"

"Yes, I'd go anywhere with him, if he'd just ask me to marry him."

"What do your parents think about him?"

"Our families have been friends for a long, long, long time—way before we were ever born."

"Elizabeth, you are now twenty-eight years old. It's ten years later. What is your name now, Elizabeth?"

"I'm Elizabeth Simms."

"Where do you live?"

"Red Mill, Florida."

"What is your husband's name?"

"Robert Simms."

"Do you like it in Red Mill?"

"Yes, it's my home."

"Do you have any children?"

"Yes."

"How many?"

"Five. The baby's just small. She's a little doll. I called her Mary Jane."

"You are now ten, twenty, thirty years . . . you are becoming older now. The children are grown. The children have left the house. You are now a very old lady, Elizabeth. Do you see yourself in the house?"

"Yes."

"You are alone in the house now. What's happening in the house?"

"I'm sad."

"What are you doing?"

"Looking at the pictures on the mantel."

"How old are you now?"

"Eighty-nine years old."

"And you're all by yourself?"

"No, poor Daisy."

"Who is with you?"

"Daisy, the colored maid. Ninety . . . she's gone to bed."

"Then what happens?"

"I'm not well."

"Something happens."

"I'm so tired."

"One day you stand in front of the mirror and someone hurts you. Who is it? Do you remember? Now we can talk about it. It's all over. No one can hurt you again."

"My baby."

"Your baby? What is he doing? Which one of your babies?"

"James."

"What is he doing?"

"Rifle."

"What does he do?"

"Catch his button . . ."

"And what happens then?"

"Ohh!"

"You're all right. You can't be hurt anymore. Do you remember what happens then?"

"Everyone, everyone's gone."

"What do you do? Where do you stay?"

"Here. This is my home."

"Is there a difference now? Do you look different?"

"Yes."

"Now, after he shoots, what happens?"

"I don't care."

"You don't care for what?"

"Don't punish him. It was an accident."

"You mean, he didn't mean to?"

"No, his jacket . . . the button . . ."

"But why was he pointing it at you?"

"We'd been having trouble with prowlers. My niece and the maid had been seeing . . . seeing dark shadows of a man prowling around the house, and he tried to get in and they had a shotgun in the hall, by the hall window, leaning up against the wall by my room."

"What did he do?"

"James had come home unexpectedly, come upstairs, and I was brushing my hair. I always took great pride in my hair. It was still pretty."

"I'm sure it was."

"James picked up the rifle. He was wondering what it was doing there, and he tucked it under his arm. I saw him in the mirror, over my shoulder. As he greeted me, the trigger caught in the button of his jacket pocket."

"And it hurt you."

"Yes, it hurt me."

"And then what happened? What did you do then? Did you see yourself after that?"

"Yes."

"How did you look?"

"Crumpled on the floor."

"But you were not really on the floor, were you . . . you yourself?"

"I stood looking at myself."

"Then where did you go?"

"Wandered."

"Did you meet anyone you knew?"

"No, I was all alone."

"In the house?"

"In the house."

"How long did you stay that way?"

"For a long time."

"What was the next thing that happened to you after that?"

"A young girl came to the house one day, with two young children. She was so much like I was when I was that age. A sweet little girl."

"So what did you do?"

"She seemed to like my house, my home."

"Did you know her?"

"No."

"Did you communicate with her before she came to the house?"

"I showed her my house."

"How did you know where to find her?"

"*I don't know*. I showed her my house, and when she

came . . . when she came it was like living again. She made me happy."

"Are you her? Is she you? Or are you two different people?"

"I don't know."

"When you were in the house, floating around for awhile, did you at any time disappear from it or not remember anything?"

"Yes, there was a time when I seemed to rest. There was nothing."

"And then what?"

"Just darkness, and then I showed this young girl my home."

"In between, did anybody talk to you?"

"No."

"Nobody came to talk to you before that young girl came?"

"No. In the house, people came. They wanted to look about the house . . . curious."

"But not to talk to you?"

"This little girl was different."

"Do you remember being a child again? After the darkness, the period when everything was dark and you rested, after that, do you remember being a child?"

"Yes, yes."

"How was it? How did you become a child from the darkness? How did you go from the dark period of rest to become a child again?"

"Baby."

"You remember a baby?"

"A baby was playing on a porch with a clothesline and some clothespins."

"What was the first thing you remember when you woke up as a baby?"

"A woman came out and picked me up and carried me indoors."

"And the years went by, and then you grew up, and then one day you told this girl about your old home, is that it?"

"Yes."

"Why did you suddenly think of your home? What made it happen?"

"She was so much like I was. Not her temperament. She was so, so pure and good, I guess you could say."

"So you decided you would want to remember."

"I wanted her to live in my house. It was our house together."

"Did you know that the house has since been torn down to make way for another house? Time has gone on. Are you aware of that?"

"No, they can't take my home away."

"You still own it?"

"Yes."

"And this girl who is now you, are you her? Are you going to live in her mind with her, as her?"

"I must. She gives me purpose."

"Did you know someone who was a postmaster when you lived in Red Mill?"

"There was a young man who wanted to be postmaster for a long time."

"What was his name?"

"Jeremy McDonald."

"Do you remember any of the people in Red Mill who were in the army?"

"There were many, many of our boys."

"Any officers that you can recall by name?"

"My son was an officer."

"Which one?"

"One fought for the Union forces against his father's wishes."

"What regiment was he in?"

"Cavalry, Persing . . . Persing of Cavalry."

"Anyone in the Southern armies?"

"My son."

"Which one?"

"Allen."

"What regiment? What rank?"

"He was lieutenant, Confederate forces. He was Lee's dispatcher. He was a fine loyal officer, wounded three times."

"He was a lieutenant, cavalry or infantry?"

"Cavalry."

I decided to bring June out of her hypnotic state. After all, it was our first session together, and I did not wish to overtire her. There would be time for another session the following morning.

When June awoke she remembered absolutely nothing. She

felt as if she just had a nice long nap. I immediately questioned her about any knowledge she might possess, either consciously or unconsciously, about the Simms family, but it appeared that she knew nothing more than what she had already told me. "The only thing I know is what the old postmaster told me," June explained. She could not *now* recall the postmaster's name. She did not know what name Mrs. Simms was known by prior to her marriage.

I don't think June lied to me. She answered my questions immediately and without reflecting, in a straightforward manner. There was no particular reward in her coming to Pittsburgh to see me, nor would there be any publicity for a long time to come. June had nothing to expect in a material way from our working together, and I do not believe that her makeup was such that she would have enjoyed telling tall tales. When she denied any knowledge of the Simms family beyond what the old postmaster had told her, I took her at face value. I honestly had no reason to feel otherwise.

I questioned her then somewhat more closely about her own background. Married at fifteen and the mother of four children, she had lived in only three places: in western Pennsylvania; in East Hempstead, Long Island; and again in western Pennsylvania. At no time had she taken any interest in the South or in southern history. None of her grandparents or other members of her or her husband's family are from the South, nor have they anything to do with the state of Georgia. She has never been to Atlanta. Yet June has always shown a great interest in the history of the War Between the States. She doesn't know why the Civil War period attracts her so much, but it all started when she was about eighteen years old. She read some books dealing with the period, without ever studying it formally. Her education ended at the high school level. But she took night classes in such diverse subjects as interior decorating, psychology, history, and writing.

It was getting late, and I suggested that June get some rest.

The following morning we met again. This time she went under even more easily than the night before, which is not surprising since the second or third session in hypnosis does go easier than the initial effort. I quickly took her back to her own birth and then fifty years before it. Once again we established that her name was Elizabeth. Then I reminded her that we had talked before and that we would continue our conversation about Georgia now.

"Tell me, Elizabeth, what street do you live on in Atlanta?"

"We don't live on a street."

"Do you live in the country?"

"Yes."

"What's the name of your place?"

"On a large plantation."

"What is it called?"

"Hill Place."

"Who are your neighbors?"

"Our neighbors are quite far away—across the creek."

"What's the nearest place to you?"

"The Simms plantation."

"How far are you from Atlanta?"

"Oh, that all depends on, if it's a hot day it seems longer."

"How do you go to Atlanta? By what conveyance?"

"Papa always says, 'Jacob, bring around the buggy.' "

"What sort of church do you go to on Sunday?"

"The Baptist church."

"Has it got a name?"

"Just the Baptist church."

"It doesn't have a special name?"

"No."

"What's the minister's name?"

"Reverend Harold Clemens."

"Do you know the mayor?"

"Yes, I like to tease him."

"What's his name?"

"I call him Tubby."

"Why do you call him Tubby?"

"Because he's so round."

"Well, that's good enough reason; but what do the people call him? What's his real name?"

"Judge Boland."

"What is his first name?"

"I don't think I know."

"Boland, huh? Has he been mayor very long?"

"Yes, for a long, long time."

"What party does he belong to?"

"Women of the South, sir, do not indulge in politics."

"You do know who's president of the United States."

"Of course."

"Who is? Who is president now? Every schoolchild must know that, and you're an educated young lady. Surely you know who is now president. You've read about him. What kind of a man is the president?"

"A great man."

"What does he look like?"

"He's tall and handsome. A distinguished young man."

"Where does he come from, North or South?"

"From the South, sir."

"Is he a military man or a civilian man?"

"He was a military man of great distinction."

"What's the color of his hair?"

"A light blond color."

"What's your papa's favorite newspaper?"

"Georgia . . ."

"The Georgia what?"

"*Tribune.*"

"Talk to me about some of your fine friends in Atlanta. The people that come to your father's house—who are they? I know that you're interested in Mr. Simms, but you must have other friends, and your father must have some friends. Has he any friends who are in the Senate or in the House?"

"There are men who are much confused about our government and the way our country is being handled. They join my father in the drawing room twice a week."

"What are they talking about?"

"I don't know."

"What do you think they ought to do about the government?"

"I don't know. Something drastic must be done."

"Do you know any of the names of these people that come to see your father?"

"Generally, before they arrive, the womenfolk are allowed to retire."

"Do you know who the senator is from your state, in Congress?"

"Yes."

"What is his name?"

"I'd rather not say."

"Why? Don't you like him?"

"Not particularly. Last year he asked my father for my hand in marriage. I will not marry a man I do not love!"

"When you went to Atlanta, did you do any shopping, buying goods and things and finery?"

"We went to Atlanta, Mamma and I and my cousin."

"What is the cousin's name?"

"Alice Jenkins. She lives in Virginia."

"Where in Virginia?"

"Norfolk."

"Do they have a house there?"

"Yes."

"What did her father do?"

"He was a bookkeeper."

"For whom?"

"Munitions firm."

"What is their name?"

"Jenkins."

"Is he an owner of it?"

"No, in the family some way, I guess."

"So your cousin and your mother and you went shopping in Atlanta. Where did you go? Where did you do the shopping? What place, what store? Tell me about it."

"In a big department store. That last time we went, Mamma scolded me."

"Why did she scold you?"

"You know the cute little stools where you sit down to relax? I whirled around them, and Mamma said it wasn't dignified at all."

"What's the name of the store? Do you remember?"

"Harry Millin's . . . on Main Street."

"Did you see any other stores?"

"Confectionery store."

"Do you remember the name of the place?"

"Mr. Willike's. He was always nice to me. He used to save two little pieces just for me."

"Did you have anyone living in Atlanta, any friends or relatives?"

"Mamma had many friends."

"Do you remember any of them? Did you ever visit any of them?"

"Yes, sir."

"Like who?"

"Mrs. McDennis."

"What's her first name, or her husband's first name?"

"I'm not sure. I was always instructed to call people by their last name."

"Mrs. McDennis. What does her husband do?"

"Foreman."

"In what?"

"On a plantation."

"Any girlfriends?"

"Some of them are like cats. You ought to hear the way they talk about the new colt that Papa just gave me."

"Where did he get it?"

"It was born to Mr. Silver Black."

"Who is Mr. Silver Black?"

"He's a horse."

"Did your father have an attorney, a lawyer, to take care of his business?"

"Yes, sir."

"Do you remember what his name was?"

"Gaylord Linholm."

"And your father was Franklin Tibbits. You're eighteen now, right?"

"Yes, sir."

"What year were you born?"

"Eighteen two."

"You were born in 1802?"

"Yes, sir."

"What is your birthday? When do you celebrate your birthday?"

"August second. My mother says that's why I have such a violent temper, because I was born in August when it was so hot."

"How long has the plantation been in the family now?"

"My great-grandfather built it."

"What was his name?"

"Harrison."

"Harrison Tibbits?"

"Yes."

"What was your great-grandmother's name?"

"Marie."

"Marie, and then their son would be your grandfather?"

"Yes, sir."

"What was his name?"

"I think my grandfather's name was Franklin."

"Your father is Frank, and your mother is . . . ?"

"Catherine."

"With a *C* or a *K*?"

"With a *C*. Father likes to tease her. He calls her Katie. It makes Mamma mad, but she doesn't stay mad at Papa."

"You were baptized in the same church that you always go to now in Atlanta?"

"Oh, yes, sir. It has been a great tradition in our family."

"Now, today, think of today now. People are talking. Do you think there'll be a war? What do you hear?"

"There is great unrest. Everyone is a little afraid to say things openly. Men are angry. They demand that something be done soon."

"Done about what?"

"Our taxes. The government is trying to force, they say because of the slaves, they have raised . . . they have raised all the taxes, put a heavy levy on everything. The plantation businessmen are up in arms about it. They are trying to drain our blood from us."

"Have you ever been to a place called Red Mill?"

"No, sir."

"Never heard of it?"

"No, sir."

"Now, you know this boy, Simms, real well?"

"Yes, sir."

"Do you like him?"

"I love him, sir."

"And he loves you?"

"Yes, sir. He declared his love."

"How do your parents feel about him?"

"They are most pleased, sir."

"Do you think the two of you are going to get married?"

"Oh, yes."

"How soon?"

"I want to get married now."

"Mmm, but you're only eighteen."

"It makes no difference. Robert wants to wait until he has a home to take me to."

"When will that be, do you think?"

"I don't know. Soon, I hope."

"And have you met Mr. Simms?"

"Oh, yes, sir."

"What is Mr. Simms's first name?"

"John."

"John? You mean Robert's father is named John Simms?"

"Yes, sir."

"Mr. Simms has just one son—Robert?"

"Yes, sir."

"Are there any other children?"

"A daughter, Evelyn."

"How old is she?"

"Twelve."

"And Robert is twenty?"

"Twenty-two."

"Have you met any other people at the Simms's house from town?"

"At teas."

"Like what?"

"The women from the women's group at the church."

"Did you ever meet any officers?"

"One very handsome young man."

"What's his name?"

"Lieutenant Colonel Michael Wrinceson."

"That's an unusual name, isn't it?"

"Yes, it is."

"What's he in charge of?"

"He works in an office."

"In Atlanta?"

"Georgia."

"Cavalry or infantry?"

"Cavalry, sir."

"You've met him?"

"He came to the house one time. Papa was most pleased to see him, and they both hurried into the library."

"Have you ever met any doctors?"

"No, sir."

"Well, when somebody is sick, who do you call?"

"Daisy always takes care of us if we're sick."

"Have you ever seen any boats or ships?"

"We went for a ride on the Mississippi on a big paddle boat."

"What was it called?"

"The *Lilly Belle*."

"Where did you go on her?"

"Up the river."

"To what town?"

"We went to Louisiana."

"What did you do in New Orleans?"

"We went to a big ball there."

"Who gave the ball?"

"Mr. and Mrs. Thornton."

"Do you speak French?"

"A little."

"Did you meet anyone in New Orleans other than the Thornton's?"

"Handsome officers."

"Like who?"

"Paul . . . I remember their faces and their first names."

"Did you meet the governor?"

"Yes."

"What was his name?"

"I don't know. I suppose I forgot it because I didn't like him. He was a fussy old man, not one bit of fun."

"But you know the governor of Georgia. Surely you know him, in Atlanta. Have you ever seen him?"

"Yes, sir."

"What's his name?"

"I'd rather not say."

"Why, do you have anything against him?"

"No, sir. He comes to those meetings. We are not allowed to discuss who comes."

"You can talk to me."

"Papa says not to trust anybody. There are spies everywhere."

"I'm on your side."

"They have imprisoned quite a few of our men."

"Who has?"

"The government."

"Why would they do that?"

"They were trying to overthrow the government. The meetings are secret."

"Who would want to overthrow the government? Who is the leader who would want to do that? Is there someone in Washington who says that?"

"Mr. Seward. He's in the Cabinet."

"Your father doesn't like Mr. Seward?"

"No, sir."

"Are there any other cousins on your father's side?"

"There is a disturbance in the family."

"What happened?"

"The brothers . . . the plantation was left to my father. They don't correspond any more."

"Where did they go off to?"

"I don't know. They're not spoken about in our family."

"I see. Do you remember any other relatives in Atlanta, or in Georgia?"

"Aunt Genevieve Jenkins."

"Where does she live?"

"In Georgia, in the main part of town."

"And what does her husband do?"

"She's a widow, sir."

"What did he do before he passed on?"

"He was a boat captain, sir. He was lost in a storm at sea before Alice was born."

"When was Alice born? Is she younger than you or older than you?"

"A year older."

"So she was born in 1801 if you were born in 1802, and he was lost before she was born?"

"Yes, sir."

"How is the Norfolk Jenkins related to Alice Jenkins?"

"Cousins somehow."

It was time to bring June out of her hypnotic state. When she awoke, she felt fine and was ready to go home to her little town in western Pennsylvania. A few days later, I heard from her again. There was nothing special to report, really, except a certain unrest she kept feeling and a continuing, strong emphasis on a personality change that had begun after her return from Florida and that somehow was becoming more pronounced as time went on. Moreover June found herself saying and doing things that were completely out of character with her usual identity. Even her parents noticed this on the occasions when they were together.

Principally, June—that is to say, the old June—was somewhat timid and not likely to say anything without first thinking it over very carefully. The new personality was the exact opposite—tactful but sometimes painfully truthful, and if one didn't like what she had to say, that was just too bad. Many a family fight erupted because of pronounced opinions on this or that expressed by the "new" June personality.

Gradually, however, Sam has gotten used to the changes in his wife, for he truly loves her. There are things that he doesn't understand, nor does he wish to understand them any further. He accepts them and has learned to live with them.

Whereas the old June was simply dedicated to her domestic chores, the new personality suddenly developed an interest in the arts—music, amateur theatrics, all these things became a part of her new interests, and despite the fact that June lives in a small town, far away from the mainstream of cultural activities, she is trying to read whatever she can get her hands on to keep up with the sophisticated world outside. To her husband, this is all right, even though he himself does not have such ambitions.

As time went on, the personality of the alleged Mrs. Simms, and of the "old" June began to merge into one new personality in which, however, the elusive spirit of the plantation owner's widow was dominant, or became more and more dominant as time went on. To be sure, June neither encouraged nor sought this change but, to the contrary, found it upsetting. In order to allay her fears I briefly explained that I suspected a factual reincarnation memory and, without telling her of any verifications, presented the matter merely as a possible hypothesis. I also assured her that there was no danger involved and that if she wished to suppress the personality of Mrs. Simms in her character, she could do so by merely asking me to suggest this in one of our next sessions with hypnosis.

This June did not choose to do. Somehow she felt that it was her destiny to live with her prenatal memory and to make the best of it. Then, too, it intrigued her: in a life as placid and ordinary as hers any form of excitement was welcome. With all her tragedies the life of Mrs. Simms seemed a better thing to contemplate than the secure existence of June, the housewife in western Pennsylvania. If she could have the best of both worlds, so much the better.

I asked June to do no more checking into the subject of hypnosis or reincarnation and to avoid any books on the subject. I promised her to look into all the material at the earliest possible time and, when it was all finished, to tell her who she was, who she had been, and what the future of both personalities might be. This seemed to satisfy June, and from that time on I told her nothing beyond casual conversation on the subject in general. As soon as possible I would come and visit her in her little town in western Pennsylvania to continue my search for additional evidence dealing with the two lives June had apparently led in previous times.

I heard from her again in early June. What had puzzled me all along was the possibility of June's experiences being attributable only to ESP, perhaps through recognition, as in the case of her dream prior to seeing the ghost town of Red Mill. I wanted to make sure that extrasensory perception could not answer all the questions.

One night early in June she had retired and somehow could not sleep. The clock struck two as she felt a strange loosening of the bonds between her body and spirit, and she had the feeling that she was floating apart from her body. Looking down upon the bed, she saw herself lying on it. The filmy part of herself then faded away, and all at once she found herself standing in her parents' trailer.

Her parents lived in a trailer in Brookville, Florida, a considerable distance from western Pennsylvania. June had never been to this particular trailer. She stood there for a moment in what appeared to be a living room, and as she passed her father's room she could actually hear him snoring. She then stepped inside to her mother's bed, bent down, and kissed her on the forehead, at the same time touching her mother's soft, wrinkled hand. At this precise moment, her mother opened her eyes, looked up, and said, "Junie, what are you doing here?" With that, June just faded away again and found herself back in her own house.

The next morning she passed it all off as a dream, thinking that perhaps her unconscious was trying to tell her she should write to her mother. Three days later she received a letter from her mother. In the letter, her mother described a dream she had had in which she saw June standing by her bed the night before and then June suddenly faded away. This had frightened her because she knew about June's heart condition. "And it was so real," she added.

June's mother uses a particular bath powder with a certain aroma. That morning, June's daughter Cynthia came into her room and immediately remarked that her mother smelled particularly good this morning. Had her father bought her some new bath powder for Mother's Day? But June had not used any bath powder or perfume that night at all.

Her mother, on the other hand, had gotten up after June had faded away from her bedside and made herself a cup of coffee in the kitchen. When she looked at the clock it was exactly 2:20 A.M.

I was not too surprised to hear of June's astral projection experience. Oftentimes, psychic people tend to have stronger prenatal memories than ordinary people. This doesn't mean that the ESP is necessary to have prenatal memories but that the two faculties frequently go hand in hand. I suspect it has to do with the greater degree of sensitivity encountered in psychic people.

It was time to visit June and her family in her little town in western Pennsylvania, and I began to make all the arrangements. It meant changing planes in Pittsburgh and then being picked up at the little airport by June and her husband, but they were most eager to do so and invited my wife, Catherine, and me to spend the night at their home, since it would be impossible to return before the following day.

On July 30, 1968, we arrived after a somewhat bumpy flight from Pittsburgh. The little airport was exactly as I had imagined it, just large enough to accommodate small planes, and the country around it was rolling hillsides, wide open and inviting in its own peaceful way.

Sam and June drove us to their town, which was about a half-hour distant. Their white house sat back from the road somewhat, surrounded by tall, shady maple trees. In back of the house there was a hillside lot rising up to the edge of the woods. The two-story house, twenty years old, had a pleasant downstairs parlor and kitchen and several bedrooms upstairs. We were given the best room in the house and found it comfortable and quiet.

Later, when we made the rounds of the little town, we realized that this was far removed from the mainstream of city activity such as we had come from; nevertheless this was a busy little town, wrapped up in its own problems. Perhaps these problems were enlarged by the people who created or solved them, but to them, matters involving a charity affair or the latest scandal were about the only things that created excitement, and excitement is what the American countryside lacks most.

June had very carefully concealed her own case of excitement from her neighbors, for she did not want them nosing in when her guests from New York arrived. Thus it was unnecessary for me to have warned her not to talk to local newspapermen, for she had guarded our secret well. About the only thing June had ever done with her Florida experience was write a fictional account of the Simms murder case such as she knew it, based entirely on the skimpy story told her by the old postmaster in Florida. I read her notes for that story and found they contained nothing we had not already discussed. There was nothing about reincarnation in the story, of course, or about Atlanta or Georgia, only an extended account of the Simms family and particularly of how Mrs. Simms died by hands unknown.

June has for years tried to write professionally, and she has even used the services of a New York literary agent, but she has sold very little, unfortunately. It is amazing that someone who writes as colorfully as she does and who has a flair for poetry nevertheless is unable to spell even the simplest words. This, however, does not deter her from continuing with a would-be literary career, even though she realizes that the chances for publication of her stories are slim. Truly creative in her own way, she finds the greatest joy in writing them and does not worry too much about whether they will eventually be accepted.

I had asked June to contact her father in Florida, requesting him to authenticate the existence of Red Mill if possible. I felt that this type of information would not harm whatever we might obtain through hypnosis, since we had already discussed it consciously.

June's father, a total skeptic concerning matters of this nature, had done a pretty thorough job, and the results were somewhat distressing to June. It appeared that the old Simms place was located in the village of Anthony, in Marion County, Florida, two miles north of Oak, on Old Route U.S. 301, about seven miles north of Ocala. This village was founded prior to the Civil War and named after Susan B. Anthony, the family supporter of woman suffrage.

The area is in north-central Florida and is perhaps best known for the tourist attraction of Silver Springs. The chamber of commerce in Ocala had no records of a village called Red Mill. As far as they were concerned, there never was a ghost town by that name. June would have believed that her experience was nothing more than a vision or a dream had it not been for the fact that her father had taken her and her children there. She remembers distinctly seeing a faded sign reading "RED MILL" hanging on the still standing little red railroad station, but there's little doubt in June's mind that Anthony and Red Mill are one and the same place.

Depressed by the discrepancies in what she remembers as fact and what her father was able to obtain, she decided to leave the corroboration of her experiences entirely to me. She really didn't care whether it was all her imagination or reality. All she wanted to know was what it meant to her and her future and her family, and as long as it would not hurt anyone, she was perfectly content to accept my verdict, whatever it might be.

Shortly after we had arrived and settled down comfortably at June and Sam's home, I asked Sam for his own impression concerning the changes that had come over June after her return from Florida. He acknowledged that there had been a major change in her personality. For one thing, her sudden interest in the local community theater was out of character. She wasn't the kind of person who wanted to be an actress, but all of a sudden she wanted to participate in the stage plays put on by the little theater.

"Before her visit to Florida, she wasn't interested in anything, as a matter of fact. After she got back, she was interested in politics, something she never cared for before, and in archeology and other things that hadn't interested her at all."

Sam works as a laboratory technician at the local glass factory. He himself has had some psychic experiences and is not hostile to the idea of ESP itself. His father had psychic experiences before him, so perhaps there is a tradition in the family about that sort of thing. Sam had been born in the little town, and his father had come there as a child. His outside interests include forestry and the preservation of animal life in the surrounding area, which includes a large state park. Sam is not particularly concerned with such things as reincarnation memories, and he really hasn't thought about the results of Mrs. Simms's influencing the character of his wife. He takes it all in stride.

It had gotten late, and we decided to go to bed. The following morning, right after breakfast, I decided to have my first hypnosis session with June. The children were sent to play outside, Sam was at work, and my wife, Catherine, was still upstairs asleep. Except for an occasional bird chirping outside, it was very quiet. Quickly June was under hypnosis, slipping back to her previous existence as Elizabeth Simms. This time June seemed particularly agitated by something. I asked if there was anything wrong.

"I'm afraid."

"Why are you afraid?"

"There is so much fighting."

"Who is fighting?"

"Robert and Michael, my son and my husband. Always arguing."

"What are they arguing about?"

"The plantation. Robert wants Michael to settle down, take over his responsibilities, and he won't. He hates the plantation. He loves his horses. He raises thoroughbreds."

"Tell me about the plantation. What is it called?"

"We don't have a name for it."

"How far is it from Atlanta?"

"Quite a ways."

"How many miles? How long does it take to go there?"

"A day and a half."

"Do you remember your father's plantation in Atlanta? What was that called?"

"Hill Place."

"How far was it from Atlanta?"

"Oh, about two hours' drive by buggy."

"Do you think that there will be a war?"

"Yes, sir."

"Between whom?"

"The states."

"Why do you think there will be a war?"

"It has to come eventually."

"You're thirty-five years old. You are living on the planta-tion. You are Elizabeth Sims. You are married. Tell me, is there a war on now?"

"Yes, sir."

"What kind of a war is it?"

"Between the North and the South."

"And how old are you?"

"I'm thirty-six."

"The war has been on for how long?"

"A year."

"Who is the governor of this state?"

"A southern woman does not discuss politics, sir."

"Whom would you like to see governor?"

"Our main interest, sir, is who shall become our president."

"Well, who should be?"

"Thomas Jefferson . . . there's someone coming."

"Who is coming?"

"Cavalry men . . . they have to go into the glades. A pris-oner escaped . . . a very important prisoner . . . a Yankee."

"Then what year are we in now?"

"Eighteen sixty-one."

"You are eighteen years old. You are Mary Elizabeth Tib-bits. What does the town look like? How much of a town is it?"

"There's not much of it. It's just a small town."

"How many people?"

"About a thousand, I'd say."

"What do they call the place?"

"Atlanta, sir. It's not a very big place."

After I had brought June out of her hypnotic state, I began to question her concerning any knowledge she might have of life in nineteenth-century Georgia. I threw the name Tibbits at her. It made no impression. She thought she had heard it somewhere before but really didn't know for sure. I tried Hill Place. No reaction. I said, "Jenkins, Liholm, Boland." All I received in reply was a firm no. June's face showed absolutely no sign of recognition. Now I tried Seward. This seemed to ring a bell. "The only Seward that I would know anything about would be in history, something to do with politics." she said. How far, did she think, did Atlanta go back? "I haven't the slightest idea when it was settled," she replied firmly.

"After you came back from that Florida trip, did you discover any change in you?" I asked.

"It was just as if I had been asleep for a long, long time and I woke up, and I have a lot of living to catch up with."

Where she had been a conformist prior to her trip to Florida, June had turned into a freethinker after her return. In the years since then, she had never gone back, however. That one and only visit to the house had lasted about an hour and a half. During her stay in the house, she had found time to scan some of the yellowed papers in an old trunk in the house. Unfortunately she had not taken anything along with her except for a few of the ledgers, which she had showed me during our first visit in Pittsburgh.

"Was there any difference in the way you would cook or in the way you would do certain chores?" I asked.

"Yes, as far as sewing is concerned, and then there was this urge to sort of feather my nest better, and I took a course in interior decorating, and things like that, but I seemed to know automatically how to make drapes, slipcovers, even my own clothing, which I didn't do before."

Even though June's great-grandfather had been a sharpshooter with the Union forces, she had always had a sense of sympathy for the South. This existed even before her visit to Florida. She somehow felt bad that the South had lost.

Another strange thing concerned June's liking of clocks. After her return from Florida she had become increasingly conscious of time and had installed clocks in every room of her house.

It was time for lunch now, so we ended the session. That afternoon after June had rested somewhat, I put her again under hypnosis.

"You are Mary Elizabeth Simms. You are fifty years old. You live on a plantation. You are Mrs. Simms. So you know the instrument through whom you are speaking? Why did you come and seek her out?"

"So everyone would know."

"What?"

"That my home was a family home and a happy one."

"Is there anything that you want done to make you happier?"

"No, not right now."

"Are you planning to stay with her?"

"Yes."

"What was the town in which you lived in 1820 when you were eighteen years old? What was the name of the place? Was it Atlanta?"

"People called it that, yes, sir."

"In 1820?"

"Yes, sir."

"That's very strange, because the records do not show this. Are you sure it was Atlanta?"

"The other plantation owners called it Atlanta because of a legend. They hoped that the day would come when it would become the Golden City that once sank to the bottom of the sea."

"At the time, when you were eighteen years old, there wasn't any city yet, was here?"

"No, sir."

"What was it then, farmland?"

"Yes, sir."

"How many people lived around there?"

"There are quite a few plantations."

"Were there any Indians around?"

"No, sir."

"Where had the Indians gone?"

"They had been driven back into the marsh."

"Were they civilized or were they wild?"

"There are no civilized Indians, sir."

"You remember the name of the county in which all this was situated? The part of the territory?"

"County Claire."

"What was the main village, or main town, in that county?"

"There was a place where we could go to do our shopping, about two miles away."

"What was it called?"

"Well, it was called Atlanta."

"Were there any other towns farther away that you can remember?"

"You could travel for miles and see just plantation land."

"How did people get there?"

"They came by carriage from Georgia . . . by paddle-wheel boats."

"On what river?"

"Generally down the Mississippi and then over across land."

"Wasn't there any railroad?"

"Not yet."

"When the railroad came, where did it end?"

"It went from Atlanta down through North Carolina, down through Virginia, all the same line."

"Now, Atlanta, was that the end of the railroad, or did it go further?"

"A little farther, down to the tip of Virginia."

"In Georgia, what was the name of that place where the railroad ended? What did they call it?"

"A small town, Billings."

"And how far was that from Atlanta?"

"Not too far."

"Do you remember, sometime during your long life in that part of the world, any names of governors or of the mayors? Any of them?"

"There was a Calhoun."

"What was his rank?"

"Senator, I think."

"How about any of the people around the city of Atlanta, mayors, governors?"

"Well, there was Tubby."

"What was Tubby's name, real name, I mean, in the books, in history?"

"I'm so tired."

"Was he the first mayor of Atlanta or where they any others before him?"

"I believe Tubby was the second or third."

"How old were you at the time?"

"Eighteen or nineteen."

"You are living in Atlanta. It is 1849. How old are you now?"

"I'm thirty-nine."

"Tell me, who was the mayor in 1849?"

"Why are these things so important?"

I noticed an unwillingness to answer my questions, so I decided it was time to bring June out of hypnosis. She awoke apparently fully refreshed and again with no conscious memory as to what had transpired during the half hour or so that she had been under hypnosis.

On January 31, 1969, June again "visited" with her earlier incarnation in Georgia. This time she recalled the name of a politician visiting her father's home: Quincy Cabot. There seemed to have been some connection between this man and a foreign government, June felt.

I instructed her to watch out not only for dream impressions but also for anything that might come to her at odd moments while awake. To facilitate this, June put aside a few minutes a day for regular meditation sessions when she could be alone and relaxed.

One might argue that June, who liked to write poetry, was making these scenes up from her own mind, guided perhaps by her unconscious. Be this as it may, they were certainly correct for the time and situations given, and while not evidential in themselves, are interesting in evaluating the entire case.

"When the shutters were closed during the day's heat," June wrote down her impressions, "the darkened rooms were damp and cool with the smell of tree moss. A dull, flat smell it was. The afternoon nap in the cool, darkened rooms was a delight. The heat outside was so dry that even your nostrils felt dry, and the air hung heavy over the fields, and the men would glance up at the heat of the sun, beneath their wide-brimmed hats, astride their mounts in the field, and take scarves that hung around their necks and wipe the sweat from their necks and faces, and curse the heat. The air in the large room seemed to hang motionless all about us, and the house was quiet. The quiet footsteps of Daisy and Jacob in the hallway outside the large white room were the only thing that could be heard as we dropped gently off to sleep. Our heads rested against large, soft pillows. Papa called it 'the ladies' pantaloon time,' shushed by Mamma. By this time we gratefully stripped to our pantaloons and undervests. It gave me a sense of freedom, and I wished I didn't ever have to wear those long, old dresses, again. Mamma fussed and fumed and said I was no better than the animals God had placed on earth and that they had to wear clothes He had given them, and theirs was of fur. One time I announced that some day I was going to wear pantaloons riding at midnight, and Papa dropped his dish of mashed potatoes and Mamma choked on her cup of tea. Daisy just growled at me and

shook her head, but I don't care. I just want to be free and ride—
the wild wind about me."

I instructed June to continue watching for any impressions
or visions she might have naturally but not to try to force any of
this material from her subconscious.

Beth, as June now seemed to call her more and more instead of Elizabeth, was particularly reluctant to yield any more
names or actual information concerning the visitors at her
father's place. There seemed to be a sense of endangering people
by naming them. Now, one might argue that was simply a
subterfuge, and that June consciously or unconsciously was
simply playing a game in order to avoid having to give concrete
information. I don't think so, because the character of Beth
Simms does indeed fit in with the fear of compromising political names by naming them to me, a stranger.

Far more interesting was the change that was now taking
place in June's whole personality. Thirty-nine years old at this
time, she felt far younger. There was a sense of jubilation
within her in being alive that she had never had before. She felt
almost reckless and searched for something crazy to do. This
was totally in contradiction to her "old" character. She felt like
writing poetry, and she wrote some pretty good poetry. It was
May, and spring was all around the house. Western Pennsylvania can be very beautiful around that time of year, and June
loved those days to the fullest.

Impressions came to her all the time now, at irregular
intervals. Some of them merely duplicated visions that she had
had in September, October, and November 1968, but now and
again there was something new. The name Joseph Mayo, for
instance. She saw him as a short, fat man in a gray suit with a
wine-red vest, little hair, and small-rimmed glasses, together
with a tall, stately gentleman, who stood on the porch of their
large, white colonial house in the South, and they talked.

On another occasion she saw herself halfway up the
Simms's staircase, wearing a long, wine-red dress with a small
black swirl design all over it. It had long sleeves and white cuffs
with small buttons almost to the elbow. She was happy, humming to herself. She saw herself holding up the skirt of her dress
just to the proper height. It seemed that she was about thirty-
eight years old, with long hair that was wrapped about the top
of her head into a large, soft bun. Again she sees the small, fat

man called Joseph, only the name Tubby seems to be associated with him now. She hears someone refer to a waistcoat and doesn't understand what the word means.

Then there was the word *Gwinnett County* and a vision of lush green fields, tall trees, and a Creek Indian squatting down at a rippling creek that flowed on endlessly through the fields and woods, and the Indian drinking the cool, clear water. His horse bends its head to drink of the water too.

Another scene shows her a group of young girls in long, full dresses, sitting and drinking tea from little cups and laughing and talking. She hears them speaking with a southern accent, and she registers some of their names—Mae Thornton, Anna Blake, Evelyn Simms, Pauline Pendleton, Mary Bawds. Then there is a trip to a department store on Whitehall Street in Atlanta, Georgia, and she somehow knows she is forty-eight years old.

More names rise up from her suppressed subconscious. Friends of her father, smoking cigars and drinking brandy, are seen in a vision in a large library. There are arguments among them, and their voices are loud. She hears some of the names. There is Jefferson Davis, a tall man with shaggy hair, Paul Bragg, Tom Pendleton, Harmon Gilmer, James Herald, Alfred Helm, Talbert Westcut, John Holt, and Jessica Jennings. John Holt seems close to the Tibbits family. He is from Norfolk, Virginia, as is Jessica Jennings. He is a mayor, and the year is 1820. She sees the image of a tall Confederate soldier, Captain Robert M. Simms, born May 18, 1823. He serves on Longstreet's staff.

A scene in Norfolk, Virginia, in a brick-faced colonial house at the corner of Willow Street and Church: President Monroe is being discussed by two men passing by in front of the building. They wear high felt hats, and the year is 1819.

Then again, she had something more to add to the circle of friends Mrs. Simms had known in Gwinnett County. There was an Agatha Tiffin who lived on a farm with her parents, Ethel and Paul; her father made wagon wheels. The year was 1833.

As I started to sift all this material to begin my research to find as much corroboration of June's impressions as possible, I decided it would be best to have one more hypnotic session with her. Even though a great deal of this knowledge was now in my own subconscious mind and one could argue the possibility of June's getting it from me, I felt that an additional session might also yield new names that were not known to me at the time. Thus I invited June to join me once again in Pittsburgh, and on June 23, 1969, she did just that. I quickly regressed her to the year 1820 and asked her to describe the place she lived in.

"Was there a city anywhere?"

"No, sir."

"What was the nearest village?"

"There weren't any villages. There was a trading post."

"What did you call the trading post?"

"It was just a trading post. Papa used to go there. He'd tell me a lot of stories when I was a little girl, about his trips."

"Now, if you wanted to buy something in a store, where would you go?"

"To the post or to Virginia."

"Where?"

"Virginia, Norfolk."

"Wasn't that far away?"

"Yes, sir, but my aunt lived there."

"But near the Hill Place, wasn't there anything nearer?"

"There was land as far as you could see, and crops, and green grass."

"What did they call the state?"

"Georgia."

"What was the capital of Georgia?"

"Why do you want to know?"

"Where did the governor of Georgia live?"

"I don't want to talk about it."

"Were there any Indians around?"

"Yes, sir, Creek and Cherokee."

"Were you friendly with any of them?"

"Yes, sir."

"What happened to them?"

"They were forced to leave."

"Who forced them?"

"I don't want to talk about things that aren't happy."

"Where did they go?"

"They were sent away."

"What happened to their land?"

"It was taken over."

"Now, when you were living at Hill Place in those days, did you ever write letters to anyone?"

"My cousin."

"What was her name?"

"Alice Anne Jenkins."

"Have you ever been to Norfolk?"

"Yes, sir."

"Did you like it?"

"Yes, sir."

"What did you like most about it?"

"All the fancy balls."

"Who gave those balls?"

"Friends of Papa, and Aunt Jessica."

"Do you remember the music they played?"

"Waltzes."

"How many musicians did they usually have?"

"Six."

"What sort of instruments did they play?"

"There was a harpsichord and a harp and a violin. . . ."

"Do you remember some of the songs they used to sing?"

"One."

"Can you tell me about it?"

"Yellow the Blues."

"How did it go?"

"Yellow the blues, my girl, my girl. Yellow the blues I love thee true. . . ."

"Was there a regiment stationed in Norfolk in those days? Don't tell me what they said to you. Just tell me a couple of the names, all right?"

"There was a Lieutenant Arnold Himbrook."

"Was he in the infantry?"

"Cavalry, sir."

"Oh, and do you remember what regiment he served in?"

"No, a girl never cares about the regiment, only the soldiers."

"Was it a state regiment or federal?"

"State, sir."

"You went there often?"

"Several times a year."

"What kind of a house was it?"

"It was like a whole block; like a house all on one block, but there were different houses all fastened together, and it was all brick, with a big, white, heavy door and a big brass knocker."

"Did you ever have any silver coins?"

"I have a penny."

"What did it look like, that penny?"

"Eighteen fifty, a new penny."

"What's on it?"

"It's large, and it's brass."

"What's on the front?"

"I don't know. There's an eagle on the back."

"Is there something on the front?"

"I can't turn it over."

"Is the eagle just sitting there, or does he have anything with him?"

"He has something in his talons."

"Tell me, Norfolk is on the water, isn't it?"

"Yes, sir."

"Did you see any ships?"

"Yes, sir."

"Do you remember any of them?"

"The *Billy White*."

"Was that a civilian ship or a navy ship?"

"A civilian ship, hauled cotton across the ocean."

"Weren't there any warships in Norfolk?"

"I don't remember them, only the loading of the big bales, four-masters."

"How old were you the first time you went to Atlanta?"

"I'm not sure."

"Were you still a little girl?"

"No."

"You weren't married yet, were you?"

"I think so. It's like looking for something."

"Well, you know Atlanta is a big city, isn't it?"

"Not when I was there."

"What did it look like?"

"There was a train."

"A train?"

"A train in 1848 or 1850."

"And did the train not go any farther?"

"No, northeast of Atlanta, I believe."

"What did they call that place? I mean, where the train ended."

"A *junction* of some sort."

"Was it then called Atlanta?"

"When the train went through, yes."

"Before?"

"No, not for awhile."

"Did it have another name?"

"Yes, but I can't . . ."

"Who was Uncle Tubby?"

"Joseph Mayo."

"What did he do?"

"He was the mayor."

"The mayor of what?"

"Of Mayo County."

"What year was that?"

"I don't know."

"Was this before Atlanta?"

"Uncle Tubby was the first mayor of Atlanta."

"Did you call your uncle 'Tubby'?"

"Yes, sir."

"What profession did he have before he became mayor?"

"He was a planter of tobacco, and he talked politics with the gentlemen."

"Now, when you went to Florida, how old were you then?"

"I was nineteen."

"And what was Florida called in those days?"

"It was territory that was to become Florida."

"Did you go down there by horse or by coach?"

"We went down by boat, paddle riverboat."

"On what river? Or on the sea? How did you go down there? Was it on the sea or the river?"

"I don't remember. I know we docked. It was a river where we docked at in Anthony."

"What was it?"

"Anthony."

"What was the name of the boat?"

"*Sue Clarity.*"

"When you were living in the Hill Place, did your father ever have any friends in?"

"Yes, sir."

"Did you meet any of them?"

"Henry Payne."

"What did he do?"

"A lot of the men were plantation owners all over the South."

"Anyone else?"

"Alfred Helm."

"Did any of them ever have any rank?"

"Jefferson Davis came to the house."

"Why did he come?"

"The gentlemen used to gather for meetings and take turns talking over politics."

"Did Mr. Davis ever talk money with anybody, and finances?"

"Yes."

"Did he have anyone in particular who could help him?"

"Papa's overseer used to help quite a bit."

Beth seemed to tire of the conversation now, and I noticed that it was time to bring June out of her hypnotic state, but since I did not know how soon we could meet again I discussed Beth's presence in June's body with her. To my amazement, Beth realized very well that she was living vicariously through another person. Even though that other person, in Beth's thinking, was also herself, she wanted to take over. I explained that it was necessary for June to remain herself to the outside world but that Beth could merge her own character, her own desires and unfulfilled hopes and wishes, with the personality of June. Perhaps a stronger, better personality would then emerge for June. But this wasn't what Beth had in mind at all. She wanted to continue her own life, untrammeled by anyone else's. I made it plain that this could not be, explained patiently that I did indeed have the power to send her away from June's unconscious mind forever. In the end we compromised, and Beth promised to help June strengthen her own character without, however, destroying June's own personality.

After June returned to herself, we discussed briefly whether there was anything she remembered, but as in all the previous sessions, she remembered absolutely nothing of what she had mentioned under hypnosis. The only thing new she could contribute was a strange feeling of suddenly having forgotten her knowledge of English, which had occurred to her a few times in the recent past. For a brief moment she had had the feeling that she was speaking a foreign language, although she could not really express herself in it. English had sounded strange to her ears at that point. Worried about her hearing, she had consulted an ear specialist, only to find that she was in perfectly good health as far as her hearing was concerned.

After June returned home to western Pennsylvania, a great sadness overtook her. This was not the first time that June had felt depressed. Over the years, she had sometimes contemplated suicide, for no particular reason, and on one occasion she had taken a few more sleeping pills than necessary, but whenever thoughts of death had come to her, something or someone within her had changed her mind and cheered her up. Now June knew that it was Beth, who didn't wish to lose her instrument of expression.

By the fall of 1969, the deep depression left her, and a more mature presence of Beth filled June's being. It was as if the two personalities had finally come to terms.

In trying to prove or disprove the accuracy of June's statements, I assumed that any intimate knowledge of early nineteenth-century Atlanta would be unusual for someone of June's background. If in the process of trying to prove the material to be accurate I should find erroneous statements as well, I felt that this would not necessarily militate against the authenticity of the case.

I have learned over the years that those on the other side of life frequently find it impossible to remember details of their previous lives, especially when these details are not of an emotional kind. If, however, the percentage of hits were to be considerable, the case itself would, to me, assume the ring of truth, even if there were also misses and omissions. I would, in fact, be very suspicious of any psychic communication that proved to be 100 percent accurate. No human being, whether in the flesh or in the world of spirit, is that reliable and exact. Here, then, is the evidence insofar as I was able to verify it.

Hill Place, the name of the plantation somewhere in Georgia, must have belonged to the Hill family at one time, hence the name. The name Hill was prominent in Georgia in the first half of the nineteenth century and in fact is still prominent in that state. One may only think of Senator Benjamin Hill, but there are many other Hills listed in directories of this area. A William Hill was a member of the Inferior Court in 1923, according to *Atlanta and Environs*, by the celebrated Georgia historian Franklin M. Garrett, published in 1954.

I was unable to locate the exact spot where Hill Place existed, but if, as June claimed, it took a two-hour buggy ride from what is now Atlanta, then it could have been much farther inland than I had at first assumed. There is also mention of a paddleboat on the river, and if this is the Mississippi River, it would be even farther west. I am fairly convinced that many of the data given under hypnosis are correct but that the sequence may have been different from that given. It may very well be that there existed confusion in the mind of Elizabeth Simms, speaking through June, if indeed she was, causing various names to be attached to different personalities from those to whom they should have been, or transposing the dates. Out of this chaotic condition I tried to get some order.

There is prominent mention of a Judge Boland. In the earlier sessions he was designed as a mayor of Atlanta. He is also identified as the man whom Elizabeth called "Tubby," but in the later sessions, Tubby is referred to as Joseph Mayo, who was also a mayor. Here, then, are the facts.

The second mayor of Atlanta proper was Dr. Benjamin F. Bomar, according to the Atlanta Public Library librarian Isabel Erlich. This was in the late 1840s and early 1850s. But there were three generations of well-known physicians bearing the name Boland in Atlanta during the nineteenth century, according to Franklin M. Garrett, research director of the Atlanta Historical Society. On the other hand, there was a Judge Bellinger, who died in 1853. He was a legislator, a justice of the Inferior Court, and active in politics between 1820 and 1853, according to *Atlanta and Environs* volume 1, page 361. But it was customary in those days to call any dignified individual, especially if he was of personal prominence, with the honorific name of "Judge." As a matter of fact, to this very day there are a lot of honorary colonels in Kentucky and other southern states. Could it be that Mr. Boland was not really a judge but only given this name as a matter of courtesy, or did the confused mind of Elizabeth Simms confer the title, rightfully belonging to Judge Bellinger, to one of the Boland family?

There was certainly confusion about dates. When the alleged Mrs. Simms speaks of the year 1820 in Atlanta, she must be mistaken, for the city as such came into being only in 1837. The land on which Atlanta now stands was owned and occupied by the Creek Indians until 1821, and there was no white settlement until then. The town of Atlanta was first called Terminus, because the new railroad, connecting the western part of the South and the Atlantic coast, terminated at this spot, in what was then DeKalb County. Later it was briefly known as Marthasville and eventually became Atlanta, so named after the well-known legend of Atlantis. But it is, of course, possible, speaking in retrospect, that the entity might have confused the dates. I have always found it true that those who have gone onto the other side cannot cope with figures, dates, and other details of time because there is apparently no such thing as time over there.

The description of Indians being driven from their lands is entirely correct. These were mainly Creek and Cherokee Indians. There is a hypnosis reference to a Claire County. The pronunciation isn't too clear, and it may well be that she meant to say Clarke County. This is the more likely, as I have found several members of the Hill family residing in that area in 1827. In the list of land lottery grants made to veterans of the revolutionary War, published in Atlanta in 1955, there are also a Clay County and a Clayton County in Georgia. Both of these are not too far from present-day Atlanta.

In discussing the coming of the railroad, the entity referred to the date of 1824 and also mentioned two towns—Dancy and Billings, North Carolina. Neither of these two places was I able to locate, but the records are not very reliable, since small places often changed names in the course of time. There is, however, mention of a Senator Calhoun. While Miss Erlich did not think that the famed Senator Calhoun was ever active in Atlanta, I found to the contrary that he was instrumental in bringing the railroad to Atlanta, or what was then called Terminus. Although the final stages of this railroad were only completed after the senator died in 1850, he was indeed connected with the fortunes and well-being of the area in and around Atlanta. Reference to this is made in *Atlanta and Environs* by the aforementioned Franklin M. Garrett.

Since Elizabeth was thirty-six years old in 1861, she could not have been born in 1802, as she had claimed in the very first session we had, but must have been born in 1825. When she spoke of her life as an eighteen-year-old in Atlanta, which would make this 1843, she mentioned that it wasn't much of a town, that it was small, and that there were about a thousand people there at that time. This is entirely correct.

In another session she also mentions the Cherokee Indians as being active in the area, which is something the average person wouldn't know. Elizabeth gave Tibbits as her maiden name. I have been unable, to date, to locate a Franklin Tibbits, but the United States Census of Georgia for 1820 does list a Thomas Tibbits on page 147.

She referred to a Baptist church as being the one she went to to pray, and the same church she was baptized in. It is true that the First Baptist Church was the most prominent church in Atlanta during the early days of that settlement. In a portion of the tape fraught with difficulties, I find upon replaying that she also mentions a Father Tillis as her teacher. The United States Census of Georgia for 1820 does list a Joseph Tillus on page 148. She mentioned President Jackson as having been in their house. The fact is that Andrew Jackson did come to Atlanta in connection with the redistribution of land formerly of the Cherokee Nation. This was in 1835, according to Mr. Garrett.

When speaking of the stores and establishments of the city of Atlanta, the entity referred to Harry Millin's Store on Main Street. According to the bulletin of the Atlanta Historical Society, there were an Andrew, James, and Thomas Millican listed in 1833 in DeKalb County.

As for the Simms family, with whom she later became involved, they are listed in various records. This is not surprising, since we know as a matter of fact that Elizabeth Simms did live in the house in Florida until her death. What is important to prove, however, is whether June is the reincarnated Elizabeth Simms. That the original existed, is a matter of record. There are Simmses listed for Clarke County, Georgia, between 1820 and 1827. There is a Robert Simms also in the list of land lottery grants made to veterans of the Revolutionary War on page 63, and the United States Census of Georgia for 1820 gives a Robert, Benjamin, and James Simms on page 134.

Although I was unable to connect a Reverend Harold Clemens with the Baptist Church, as claimed by the subject under hypnosis, there is a Henry Clements listed in the 1820 Census on page 29. Whether this is the same man I do not know.

Mr. Seward was indeed a prominent Washington politician, but I must discount knowledge of this name, since it is a prominent name that might have been familiar to June from reading books or simply from her school days.

On June 13, 1969, June sent me a typed list of all the names that clung to her memory in connection with her previous incarnations. I had not discussed any details of my findings with her, of course, and the list actually comprises both her dreams/visions and conscious flashes of reincarnation memories. All the names that occurred during our hypnotic sessions are contained in this list, but here are also a few others.

The name Harmon Gilmer appears. Gilmer is the name of an early governor of Georgia—during the time when Elizabeth might have lived in Atlanta. Among friends of her father's when she lived in Georgia, June mentioned also a certain Talbert Westcut. The Atlanta Historical Society Bulletin for 1931 lists a Tillman Westbrook as living in DeKalb County in 1833. June referred to the Jenkins family as being related to her own. There were many prominent Jenkinses in the register of land lottery grants made to veterans of the Revolutionary War, and they are also listed for 1827, the period under discussion.

The entity referred to a Whitehall Street in Atlanta that she knew. It is a fact that Whitehall Street was and is one of the main streets of Atlanta.

Dr. Benjamin F. Bomar had a store dealing in general merchandise on Whitehall Street in 1849. He was mayor of Atlanta at the same period of his life and also one of the founding fathers of the Baptist church. These three factors together seem to indicate that perhaps June might have been referring to Dr. Bomar, rather than to Boland, when speaking of her Uncle Tubby, since a mayor can easily be called Judge as a matter of courtesy also. Bomar fits far more neatly into the facts, as brought out under hypnosis, than any other names close to what June had said, but it is entirely possible that she was confusing several persons with each other.

By far one of the most interesting bits of information concerns her naming of Gwinnett County. Franklin Garrett was able to confirm that Gwinnett County was created in 1818 and existed indeed in Georgia at the time that Elizabeth Simms might have been a young girl. How could a Pennsylvania housewife have such intimate knowledge of a state she had never been to? What's more, in her June 13, 1969, roundup of impressions she says, "Father buys supplies from a trading post in Gwinnett County, Georgia territory, in 1818." Gwinnett was in existence in 1818 and is now part of metropolitan Atlanta, so it is entirely possible that she confuses in her mind that later name of

Atlanta, given to what was then only known as Gwinnett County, Georgia.

In evaluating the material obtained through hypnosis from June and correlating it with her wakeful visions, one must inevitably come to a conclusion that there are three possibilities for explaining her amazing memories of another lifetime: Either she has consciously or unconsciously obtained material from books she may have read and incorporated this material in her own unconscious mind, or it is a fantasy and the product of wishful thinking about a romantic South she never saw; or, finally, we are faced with paranormal material. After careful consideration, I must reject the first two hypotheses.

As for the paranormal aspects, there again we are faced with two possibilities. Conceivably she might have had a precognitive dream of her visit to the Florida house. Then, upon entering the dilapidated mansion, she might have served as the medium to a resident ghost who in turn was able to express herself through June and, in fact, possess her for a considerable length of time both in the waking condition and through dreams.

One final note to round out the picture: Some time later, June's niece acquired a place not far from the old Simms house in Anthony, Florida. With her parents, she visited the "ruins" of the Simms house only to find the place still standing, although in shambles. Thus the report of the house being totally gone was, to paraphrase Mark Twain, grossly exaggerated.

Not that it seems to matter, for Beth now makes her home in a small town in western Pennsylvania anyway.

Chapter Twenty-Three

The Strange Case of the Two Catharines

CATHARINE W-B. WAS BORN in Lancashire, England, a daughter of a naval commander and descendant of an old Northumbrian family on her mother's side. Many of her paternal ancestors were naval officers, including Admiral Blake, and her family is highly respected in England. Her ancestors also sat in Parliament, and some are noblemen. Her father was killed at sea in 1939 as a result of the Second World War.

Catharine led an interesting and unusual life while in England. On many occasions she had psychic experiences, ranging from the knowledge of future events to the ability to see ghosts and experience the uncanny in houses in which her family lived or where she was visiting; but her psychic experiences do not properly belong here, astounding though they may have been. She had visions of events in the past, experiences with displacements in time that too were truly amazing.

The family is Catholic, and Catharine comes from an area of England that is even today predominantly Catholic. Many of her friends were priests or abbots, and she considers herself a very good Catholic, even though she wonders why the church does not pay greater attention to the reality of psychic phenomena. She knows only too well that these things are happening and that they are by no means evil or to be feared.

She and her husband had been living in an old priory in 1959 when his father died and left them to cope with estate taxes. English inheritance taxes were staggering; thus the money left them by Mr. W-B.'s father was taxed to the tune of 92 percent. Under these circumstances they found it impossible to carry on life in England. They had to sell the house and farm, and in 1959 they came to the United States to start life all over at the ages of thirty-eight and forty-two.

When I met the W-Bs. in Hollywood in 1968 I found them to be friendly, unassuming people. Mr. W-B. was most interested in his new program of boat building, a career he had recently started, while Mrs. W-B. was particularly keen on doing a novel about a period that she found herself strangely involved in—sixteenth-century England.

As a result of our conversations I later went to England to follow up on some of the things that had happened to Catharine in her earlier years.

She has always found great comfort in her Roman Catholic religion, and when she moved to an old priory of the Knights Templars near Ross-on-Wye, she reopened the chapel with permission of the church and had priests from nearby Belmont Abbey say mass there now and again. As a consequence she received an authentic reliquary from Monsignor Montini, who later became pope. Although she had occasionally discussed the question of reincarnation with her monastic friends, it wasn't of particular interest to her one way or the other.

Later, in retrospect, certain incidents made sense to her, although at the time they had seemed to be completely out of context and truly strange.

When Catharine was only thirteen years old, the family had a governess by the name of Miss Gant. Catharine's mother liked her very much because Miss Gant was very learned. The children did not like her, because they found her to be a fanatic and given to holding forth on various subjects in history at the breakfast table.

On one such occasion the conversation turned to the life of Henry VIII. A book about this king had just been published, and Miss Gant remarked that he had just been a monster, worse than Caligula. At this, Catharine became suddenly very agitated and remarked that she was wrong. "Henry was a misunderstood man," she said quietly. Her mother insisted that she apologize to the governess, but ignoring her own mother. Catharine went on to speak of the life of Henry VIII as if she had known him intimately.

"The subject is closed," Miss Gant said rather snidely. "He was a very unpleasant man, and God punished him. He died of a very horrible disease." But Catharine's father backed her up at this point and let her have her say.

In quasi-medical terms young Catharine now described Henry VIII's fatal illness, denying that he had ever had syphilis, and in the process shocking her mother, and remarking that the king had died of obesity and a varicose ulcer in his leg that would not heal due to a high blood-sugar content.

Such knowledge on the part of a thirteen-year-old girl was amazing, but even Catharine thought no more of it at the time. There may have been other incidents bearing on the matter at hand, but Catharine does not recall them.

In 1957 she was very ill, recuperating at a private hospital in Bath, England. Due to a fall, she had had some surgery and was on the critical list when a close friend, the abbot Alphege Gleason, came to visit her at the hospital. He stepped up to her bed and said, "Poor Catharine, what are they doing to you?" Very sleepily the patient replied, "Here is good Master Coverdale come to comfort me."

Her visitor was taken aback. "Master Coverdale?" he said. "You are a learned young woman, but I should have thought I might have been taken for Cranmer, whom I'd always admired," he replied with a smile. By now Catharine was fully awake and asked, "Who on earth is Coverdale?" Many years later she discovered that Dr. Coverdale was a preacher friend and protégé of Katharine Parr, one of the queens of Henry VIII.

Mrs. W-B. had eight pregnancies but, due to a blood factor, has only three living children. On several occasions she would be in good spirits right up to the impending birth. At that point she would break into uncontrollable tears for no apparent reason. On one occasion she was asked by her physician, Dr. F., in Sussex, England, why she felt so depressed at this particular point when all seemed to be going so well. For no apparent reason Mrs. W-B. replied, "She was healthy too, but she died of puerperal fever." The doctor asked whom she was talking about, and Mrs. W-B. truthfully replied that she did not know nor did she have any idea why she had made the remark. The doctor then proceeded to tell her that this disease no longer presented any threat to mothers because it had been brought under control through modern methods, but that it was indeed a fatal disease centuries ago.

Years later, research established that Katharine Parr did indeed die of that disease.

After Mrs. W-B.'s son Giles was born, she became very ill and had what she called waking dreams, in the sense that they were far more realistic than ordinary dreams are. Suddenly she saw herself as a woman almost dead in a great canopied bed. The woman had long, red-gold hair. Then Mrs. W-B. would come out of this state and feel very depressed and sorry for the woman she had seen in her vision, but she always shrugged it off as a rather fanciful dream.

Ten years went by, and if there were incidents relating to the period of Henry VIII they escaped Mrs. W-B.'s attention in the course of her daily activities.

She had a good education, and her knowledge of history is equal to that of anyone with her background, but she has never had any particular interest in the period of Henry VIII other than what any Englishwoman might have. As for Katharine Parr, the name meant little to her except that she recalled it from her school days as the name of one of the wives of Henry VIII. Beyond that, there seemed to be no conscious connection.

In September 1968 she and her husband happened to be in Iowa. He had some business there, and she was working on and off as time permitted. She owned a pack of alphabet cards, and as she went about her work she kept finding these cards arranged to spell the word *Parr*. She had not done this, nor was anyone around who could have so arranged the cards. She recognized the name Parr and thought that perhaps it had something to do with an ancestor of her family's on her mother's side. For, a long time back, there had been some connection with the Parr family of Northumberland.

Since she had no one to discuss this with, she decided to try the method of divining by pendulum. She put her wedding ring on a thread, and to her amazement it worked. There was indeed someone present who wished to communicate with her, and being fully aware of her psychic past, she did not reject this notion out of hand. Instead she decided it would be more practical to have an alphabet to work with, so she got out her Ouija board, and despite her feelings that such a board represented mainly a person's unconscious mind she decided to give it a try.

"Who is there?" she asked.

"Immediately the board gave her an answer. "Seymour," it spelled.

"Are you my Uncle Seymour?" she asked, for she could think of no relative other than her uncle who might want to communicate with her.

"No," the communicator said sternly, "Tom Seymour."

It still didn't ring any bells in her mind. "Which Tom Seymour?" she asked.

There was a pause. Then the entity operating through the board replied, "The Lord Admiral."

This gave Catharine pause for thought, and then she decided to investigate this communicator more closely.

"When were you born?"

"Fifteen o three."

"Why do you want to get in touch with me?"

"Long have I waited," the board spelled out.

"What have you waited for?" Catharine asked.

The whole thing became more and more ludicrous to her. Her suspicious mind was ready to blame her subconscious self for all this nonsense, or so she thought. She knew enough about extrasensory perception to realize that there were also pitfalls that a sensible individual had to avoid. She wasn't about to fall into such a trap.

"For you, Kate." Now, no one has ever called Catharine W-B. Kate except her father, so she was rather dubious about the genuineness of the conversation.

Immediately she thought of what she had read that could have some bearing on all this. Years before, she had read *The Wives of Henry VIII*, but that had been in her school days. More to amuse herself than because she accepted the communication as genuine, she continued working the Ouija board.

The unknown communicator insisted that he was Tom Seymour, and that she, Catharine W-B., was Katharine Parr reincarnated. The notion struck Mrs. W-B. as preposterous. She knew, of course, that Katharine Parr was the last wife of Henry VIII, the only one who managed him well and who survived him, but she had never heard of Tom Seymour. It is well to state

here that all her research in this came after most of the information had come to her either through the Ouija board or in
dreams/visions.

Today, of course, she has a fairly good knowledge of the
period, having even decided to write a romantic novel about it,
but at the time of the initial communications in 1968, she knew
no more about Henry VIII and his queens than any well-edu-
cated Englishwoman would know.

The communicator who had identified himself as Tom
Seymour advised her among other things that she was buried at
Sudely. Now, Mrs. W-B. had always assumed that Queen Katharine Parr was buried in the royal burial vault at Windsor, but
upon checking this out she found Katharine Parr had indeed
been laid to rest at Sudely, an old castle at the border of Worces-
tershire and Herefordshire.

Later she was able to find references to Tom Seymour in
historical records. She learned that Tom Seymour and the widowed Queen Katharine had married after the death of King
Henry VIII. Their marriage lasted about eighteen months. Afterward, she died in childbirth. Tom survived her by about a
year, when he was executed as a result of political intrigue.

At the time of the first communications through the Ouija
board, Mrs. W-B. did not know this, nor did she know the name
of the child, the only child, "she" and Tom Seymour had had.
Tom referred to the child as Mary. Mrs. W-B. very much
doubted this, assuming that the child would have been called
Jane, since Jane Seymour was Tom's sister and a close friend of
Katharine Parr's; however, research proved the communicator
right. The child's name was Mary.

All during October 1968 she felt herself drawn to the Ouija
board and compelled to write down as quickly as she could
whatever was given her by that means. She didn't want to believe
the authenticity of that material, and yet she felt that, in view of
her earlier psychic experiences, she should at least have someone
look into this and authenticate the whole matter if possible, or
reject it if that were to be the case.

Thus in December 1968 she contacted me. When we met the
following spring we went over all the communications she had
had until that time. "What indication do you have that you are
Katharine Parr reincarnated?" I began.

"Well, this is what *he* thinks," Mrs. W-B. replied politely, "unless, of course, it is something from the subconscious mind."

"What are Tom Seymour's reasons to assume you are his long-lost Katharine?"

"Well, he keeps saying that he's tried to reach me for years, that he's been waiting and waiting, and I replied, 'Katharine Parr is dead. Why are you not together now?' "

"And how does he explain that?" I asked.

"They are on different planes, on different levels," she explained.

"But you were reborn because you were in a more advanced state."

The communications between Mrs. W-B. and Tom Seymour went on for about a month. There was still some doubt in Mrs. W-B.'s mind as to the authenticity of the whole thing. On one occasion the communicator referred to the date on which their child had been born. Tom had insisted that it was August 17. Mrs. W-B. went to the library and looked it up and found that the child had been born on August 28 and died eight days later. The next evening she reminded her communicator he had made a mistake in his calculation. "No," Tom Seymour replied through the board. "We had the Julian calendar; you have the Gregorian calendar." Quickly she checked this and found that he was right. The difference of eleven days was accounted for by the difference of the calendars.

"Before this communication came, did you ever have any slips in time when you felt you were someone else?" I asked Mrs. W-B.

"Not that I have felt I'm someone else but that I have known places that I have been to."

"For instance?"

"Pembroke Castle. When my uncle took me there, I said to him, 'Now we are going to such and such a room, which was where Henry the Seventh was born, who was Henry the Eighth's father.' "

"And how did your uncle react to this information?"

"Well, he was of course surprised, but you see, if I had indeed been Katharine Parr I would have known this because Henry the Seventh was her father-in-law."

"Is there anything else that reminds you of the fifteenth or sixteenth century?" I asked.

"Yes, many times I will catch myself saying something that sounds unfamiliar in today's use and yet that fits perfectly with the earlier period in English history."

"Any strange dreams?"

"Yes, but of course I would consider them just wishful thinking. Sometimes I would see myself wearing long, gorgeous dresses, and it seemed that I was someone else."

I suggested we try a regression experiment, but since Mrs. W.-B.'s husband was present and both were somewhat pressed for time I felt that this was not the best moment to try it. We said good-bye for the moment, and I promised myself to take the first possible opportunity to regress Mrs. W-B. back into the period in which she thought she might have lived. There wasn't sufficient time the following day to call her back and to try my hand at regressing her then. Also, they lived quite a distance away, and it would seem impossible to ask them to drive all the way to Hollywood again. But my time schedule was suddenly and unexpectedly rearranged. An appointment I had made for the following morning was canceled, and so I felt almost compelled to pick up the telephone and call Mrs. W-B. I explained that I had some free time after all, and would it be possible for her to come back again so that we could attempt our first regression session? She readily agreed, and within a matter of hours she arrived in Hollywood. I then proceeded in the usual way to put her into deep hypnosis. It did not take overly long, for Mrs. W-B., being mediumistic, was already attuned to this process.

I first took her back into her own childhood, making sure that the transition to another lifetime was gradual. She had come alone this time, perhaps because the presence of her husband might, in her own mind, impede her ability to relax completely, something very necessary for a successful regression.

When I had taken her back to her childhood she spoke in great detail of her home in England and the staff they had. I then proceeded to send her back even farther, and we were on our way to finding Katharine Parr.

"You're going backward into the past before your birth; way back, until you can find you're someone else. What do you see?"

"I see a home with stone. . . . It's Sudely."

"Whom does it belong to?"

"Belongs to Admiral Seymour. . . ."

"Do you see yourself?"

"Yes, I see myself."

"Who are you?"

"*He* calls me Kate. I'm terribly cold. I called the doctor, told him how cold it is. Dr. Tahilcus, he was so good."

"Are you ill?"

"Yes."

"What do you have?"

"A fever."

"Is anyone else with you?"

"Dr. Herk. He is the king's physician."

"Who else?"

"My sister, Anne, and Herbert, and Lucy Tibbett, my step-daughter. Lucy was a poor girl. She didn't like me when I married her father at first. Then she grew very fond of me. Lucy was most faithful. Lucy and Anne kept our marriage secret. I'm so cold, cold, cold."

"How old are you now?"

"Thirty-six."

"I want you to look back now, see what happens to you. You recover from this illness?"

"No, No."

"What happens to you?"

"I go away. I die. I die. I knew it would happen."

"Where do you die?"

"At Sudely."

"What happens to you immediately after you die?"

"Tom is upset, he goes, I'm buried."

"Where are you buried?"

"At Sudely."

"In what part?"

"In the chapel beneath the altar."

"What is on the stone?"

"HERE LIES . . . HERE LIES KATHARINE—THE QUEEN DOWAGER—BARONESS SEYMOUR SUDELY—Kate Parr—Katharine . . . Katharine the Queen. I never wanted that irony."

"Who is buried next to you?"

"No one, no one. He was gone. He was gone, and I loved him and I was angry with him. The protector told me he was seducing young Bess. I believed it for a time."

"Who was young Bess?"

"The king's daughter."

"Who seduced her?"

"The protector said that Tom did."

"What is his name?"

"Edward Seymour, Tom's brother. Edward Seymour hated Tom. He hated Tom's popularity. He hated the king's love for him. He was scheming. They even denied me my dowager rights. I had several manors, and I had dowries from my two husbands before—Lord Latimer, John Neville—good men."

"I want you to look at the chapel now. What is next to your tombstone?"

"Next to my stone . . . It's beneath the altar, a wall, and it fell. It fell on Cromwell's men. Cromwell's men desecrated my tomb."

"Is it still there?"

"It was rebuilt in later centuries."

"Can you see the windows of the chapel?"

"It was an oriel window, but it's changed. I left because Tom is not there. They took his body."

"Where did they put it?"

"They took his body back to Wiltshire. His family took it. Tom came from Wilkes Hall, in Wiltshire."

"Is he still there?"

"I don't know. I haven't found him since."

"Do you see him now?"

"I remember him. He had black hair, dark blue eyes; he was always tanned. He was at sea a lot. His brother was a cold fish."

"When you died, what did you do immediately afterward?"

"I remember looking at him. He was sad, and I was sorry that I had not trusted him."

"Did you see your body?"

"Oh, yes, just *as a shell.*"

"Where were you?"

"In my bedroom in Sudely. My spirit got up. My body was taken."

"What did you spirit look like?"

"How does a spirit look?"

"Do you wear clothes?"

"I suppose so. I suppose so, but they couldn't see me."

"Where did you go then?"

"I went to Hampton."

"Why?"

"That's where we had been so happy. I went to Hampton because Tom had liked it. He couldn't bear Sudely."

"Where is Hampton?"

"Hampton Court, and his house in Chelsea."

"Did anyone see you?"

"I don't know."

"What did you do there?"

"I looked around from room to room, but he'd gone. He went north to my home."

"What did you do then?"

"I went to Kendal."

"Where's that?"

"In Westmorland."

"What did you do there?"

"I looked around where I was born. And Tom *went* there. He went up there."

"Did you find him *there*?"

"I saw him, but *he* couldn't see *me*."

"Did you make any attempt to let him know you were there?"

"Oh, yes."

"What did you do?"

"Yes, I put my arms around him, and he shivered. He was sad, and he went to my cousin's. He went to Strickland."

"Where are they located?"

"On the borders near Westmorland."

"And you followed him there?"

"I followed. Then he went away. He had to go into hiding."

"Why?"

"His brother accused him of treason."

"What had he done?"

"Nothing. He had the affection of his nephew, the little king. He had never done anything. His brother accused him of trying to wed with Bess, which wasn't true. Bess was only fifteen. He just used to romp with her. He had no children, just one baby that I left."

"And his brother, Seymour, whose side was he on?"

"He was the lord protector, but the little king didn't like him. They kept him short of money, and Tom used to take a little money and give it [to him]. That's why the lord protector took the great seal to stamp the documents. He took it away from the king."

"Who did the lord protector favor for the crown?"

"Jane Seymour and his son. Not James Seymour. James Seymour was his brother . . . the king's brother. Jane, Jane, she was Jane."

"And what happened?"

"Jane Grey, Lady Jane, she was only a child. She was married to Guildford. He wanted to control the children."

"But how was the lord protector related to Jane Grey?"

"I think he was her uncle."

"Then Jane Grey had the right of succession?"

"Rather distantly, but she thought she was a niece of the late King Henry."

"And he favored her cause?"

"Yes, because he knew that little Edward would not live. He had the lung tisk."

"And he then helped Lady Jane to become Queen?"

"Yes, but it only lasted a few days. The poor child. They beheaded just a child."

"What happened to the protector?"

"He was beheaded too when Mary came. Mary had her good points. Mary had grown sour, but she was a good woman."

"Did she marry?"

"Yes, she was a sad woman. If she'd married younger and been in love younger, she would have been a happier woman, but the protector tried to kill Mary, and somebody counseled her to hide. Sawston, she hid at Sawston."

"What happened at Sawston?"

"They burned it."

"Yes, and what did she say after it was burned?"

"She said she would reward them and build them better. She was fond of them."

"Do you remember the name of the people that owned Sawston?"

"Huddleston."

"Were they Protestant or Catholic?"

"They were Catholic. The Huddlestons always were . . . I knew a Huddleston in another life."

"You knew a Huddleston?"

"He was a Benedictine priest."

"What was his first name?"

"Gilbert, and in religion it was Roger."

"Tell me this—after you left, after you couldn't find Tom, where did you go?"

"I wandered."

"Did you know you were dead?"

"Yes."

"Did it bother you?"

"I was sad to leave, sometimes content. I was happy in a sense but sad to leave, because somehow we couldn't find each other."

"Were you aware of the passage of time?"

"Not particularly. It seems I was aware of people coming, people changing. People came where I was."

"Where were you most of the time?"

"I don't know how to describe it. It was light. I think it was happiness, but it was not complete happiness."

"Was it a place?"

"It was not just one place. It was . . . it was space, but I could go on the earth."

"How did you do that?"

"I could just will myself. Just will, that's all."

"Now, this place you were in up above the earth, could you look down from it?"

"Yes."

"What did you see?"

"Just a great amount of people, people, places."

"And the place you were in off the earth, did you see people?"

"Oh, yes."

"Did you recognize any of them?"

"My grandmother, my grandmothers."

"Did you speak to them?"

"Yes, you don't speak."

"How did you hear them?"

"We think."

"And the thoughts were immediately understood?"

"Yes, and we could will things for people. We could help

sometimes but not always. Sometimes you would want to prevent something terrible from happening."

"And?"

"So we would try, but not always, you couldn't always. People don't understand."

"Is there some sort of law you had to obey?"

"I don't know. I don't know."

"Was there anyone who took charge? Any authority up there?"

"Yes, in a sense. You felt bound by something, by someone."

"Was it a person?"

"It was a rule."

"Who made the rule?"

"It came from someone higher."

"Did you meet that person?"

"Not really. We saw a great light."

"Above you?"

"Beyond."

"What was the light like?"

"It was clear, bright, bright light."

"Did you speak to the light?"

"Yes."

"How did it answer you?"

"It said to be patient, go on, try to help. I wanted . . . I wanted. I wasn't really unhappy, but I wasn't fully content."

"Did anyone tell you how long you had to stay in this place?"

"No, they said that I could go on farther or try to help."

"What did you choose?"

"I said I'd try to help, because time doesn't seem very long. Later, when I looked down, I knew the time *was* long."

"Who asked you whether you would want to go on farther? Who?"

"The voice from the light."

"You couldn't see a person?"

"No."

"How did the voice sound?"

"Wonderful."

"Male or female?"

"Male, male."

"Did you question who the voice was?"

"No."

"Did you know who it was?"

"I felt as though it was from God, although not him in person. I asked, had it asked something."

"What did it tell you?"

"I asked if I had done anything wrong, not to be there where the light was. What was wrong? And he said no, that it was not wrong, that I could choose, that I could choose if I stopped grieving, that I could go ahead, or that I could go back and help."

"If you went ahead where would you go?"

"To where the light was."

"Did he tell you where that was?"

"Not in words. I just knew that it was ultimate, ultimate peace. I came back and mothered all those children, Henry's children."

"You mothered them?"

"Henry's three children."

"Did any of them ever see you?"

"When?"

"When you were dead."

"Oh, no, but I think that's why I came back."

"When did you come back?"

"I think I had come back so much later. I took care of a lot of children. The war . . . we took care of a lot of children."

"Now, how many years after you had died did you come back?"

"In world years, a long time."

"But you say you took care of children. You mean on earth?"

"Yes, I took care of a lot of Polish children in this last war [World War II]."

"You didn't come back between the time you were up there and the time you're in now?"

"I don't remember. I searched for a long time. I searched for him."

"For Tom? Did you find him?"

"I saw him, but I could never get close."

"He was not up there?"

"Yes, but he wasn't with me, but he seemed to be looking."

"But after his death, did he not join you?"

"Not closely."

"Didn't you ask for him to join you?"

"Yes, I did, I did."

"Why didn't it work?"

"I don't know. He'd look at me; he'd look at me very sadly."

"What did he say?"

"He didn't . . . I don't know."

"Did you ask the light to let you find him?"

"No, I just waited."

"Now, when you came back in your present incarnation, do you remember how you were born? Just before you were born?"

"I remember my mother. She was a beautiful woman."

"When it was time to go down again, did someone tell you when the time had come?"

"I felt it was the time. I seemed to be shown."

"What steps did you take?"

"I didn't take any real steps."

"Was it immediately?"

"No . . . I saw them, but I knew my mother before."

"How did you enter the child's body?"

"I don't think I did by myself. *I was suddenly there.*"

"And what was the first thing you remember?"

"The first thing I remember, they put me to one side because they thought I wouldn't live. They thought I was premature."

"At that moment did you still remember your previous life?"

"No, it was so dark. There was noise, like I was going through a tunnel, terrible."

"Did you see anything?"

"It was dark and noisy."

"Did you see anything?"

"No, not until after."

"And then what did you see?"

"Then I was in room. They wrapped me up, but they said I wouldn't live, and I thought, Oh, I have to go back!"

"You remember that?"

"I remember that, and I thought, I must live. I must live. I had died before, and I was going to be happy. I was going to. I'd waited so long, eighteen, twenty years, and then it was so short."

"When you came back, you could actually understand what they were saying?"

"Yes."

"You understood every word?"

"I understood the words. I was premature, and it was rather difficult."

"And did this knowledge stay with you during the first few months, or did it disappear again?"

"It went after time. It went until the time when I was two. When I reached two until I was six, a great friend from the *other place* used to come and sit by me. Every night he'd come and sit by me."

"You mean, dead people?"

"Oh, it was wonderful. He came from where the light was."

"And why did he come?"

"He used to talk to me. He was someone very, very great."

"Did you remember his name?"

"We didn't call him by name because he was divine."

"Was he your master?"

"He was, yes, you would say 'master.' He sat by my bed, and then I lost him."

"What do you mean by 'master'?"

"He was what we understood as Christ."

"Is there such a person?"

"Oh, yes."

"Is he the same as the historical Jesus?"

"I think people embellish things, but he is *Christ.* He is the son of a great spirit."

"Is God a person or is God a principle?"

"Perhaps I'd call it a spirit. I never saw God, but I knew that one day I would. I would see behind the light."

"Now, after you come back, had you forgotten these things?"

"I forgot, but sometimes you dream and remember. He left when I got older. I realize I was the cause of his leaving. I was disobedient. It was a childish disobedience, but he told me that I would find him again, but I would have to go a long way."

"Did you ever find him again?"

"No, but I will."

"Did you ever find Tom again?"

"I know that I will, because Tom is trying to find me. Before, he didn't *try* to find me."

"What about Tom? Where is he now?"

"He's waiting to be with me. The time will come."

"Do you think he will pass over again?"

"I think so, this time."

"Why did he have to wait so long?"

"He had things to do."

"What sort of things?"

"He had to wait. He had to *obey* someone."

"What about you?"

"I was widowed at eighteen. I was wed at sixteen to Lord Borough."

"How old were you when you married Henry?"

"I was thirty-two when I married Lord Latimer. I was married in St. Paul, Yorkshire. Latimer was a good man but headstrong."

"Tell me about Henry. What was he like?"

"He was really not as fierce a man as they say."

"How many years were you married to him?"

"He sought my company several times when I was in mourning. He knew me from when Jane was his queen. Jane and I were friends. Jane asked me to take care of her little Edward. Jane died in childbirth fever."

"How did Henry ask you to marry him?"

"He just asked me. He said that he would wed with me. I knew inside that he was going to ask me, and I was hoping that he would ask me to be his mistress, not his wife. I didn't want either, really. I wanted Tom. We felt safer not being married to Henry. A mistress he could pension off. But he didn't have many mistresses, really. He was rather prim."

"How old was he then?"

"He was about fifty-two; he was very, very obese. He was very handsome, virile."

"Now, when you were married, did you celebrate your wedding?"

"Oh, yes."

"What were some of the songs that were sung at your wedding?"

"*Green Sleeves* is one, and a lute song."

"Do you remember the words?"

"I remember some of *Green Sleeves*, not much. Henry wrote music. He wrote one they do not credit him for."

"What was it?"

"*Western Wind.*"

"How does it go?"

"Western wind, when wilt thou blow? With the small rains . . . I caressed my lover in my arms and lie in my bed again.' Henry wrote that, but they missed it. They missed it, I know. Henry played the lute. He was very musical. He was a very clever man. He had a very hot, angry temper, but he was quickly over it. But Gardiner and Wriothesley took advantage of this when they wanted to get rid of someone; they would pick a moment when it was easy to get him angry. That was how he got rid of poor Kate Howard. She was foolish. She was not fit to be queen, but he loved her. It was just an old man's love for a girl, and she was vain and silly but she wasn't evil. But they took her away, and they wouldn't let her speak to him. She wanted to speak to him. She knew he would forgive her, put her aside. Henry told me that."

"What had she done?"

"She had committed adultery. She had loved someone else all her life, but she was flattered to marry the king, and you couldn't very well refuse the king's hand. But she should have told him. He begged her to tell him."

"And she didn't do it?"

"No, she was afraid. She was a foolish child."

"And was Henry upset by her death?"

"Yes, he prayed for her. He was angry. He went away. Gardiner and Wriothesley had hastened the execution. Cranmer and Austin. He didn't like the Howards, you see. The Howards were very powerful. He didn't like them, and Henry felt betrayed by them. He had two Howard queens."

"Which was the other one?"

"Anne Boleyn."

"Tell me, why did you pick *this* incarnation, *this* body, *this* person to speak through? Was there any reason, anything you wanted her to do for you?"

"I was vain. I believe I was considered a good woman, and I loved my husband and I loved Tom. But I had vanity, and I came back into a world which had frightening things. She has tried so many things."

"You mean the woman who has it hard?"

"She's a woman who loves beauty around. She loves beautiful surroundings. It happened at a time when she was young. When she was stupid. She craved for it. This would upset her vanity."

"This is your punishment?"

"Perhaps it is a punishment, but also I wanted to help those children."

I noticed that Mrs. W-B. showed signs of tiring, and as time had passed rather quickly I decided to bring her back into the present and her incarnation as Mrs. W-B. This done, she awoke without any recollection of what had transpired in the preceding hour. She felt well and soon was on her way home to rejoin her husband.

All the historical data given by her in the hypnotic state were correct. Some of these are perhaps available in history books, and other data, while available to the specialist in that particular period, are not readily accessible to the average person. Katharine Parr had been twice widowed before she had married Henry VIII. The names of Lord Burgh and Lord Latimer are historical, and her death in childbirth is also factual. After the death of Henry VIII, there was political intrigue in which Tom Seymour fell victim to the machinations of his own brother, the lord protector. The fact of Katharine Parr's being buried at Sudely and the account given of the flight of Mary Tudor to escape her political enemies are entirely correct. Mary did hide at Sawston Hall, near Cambridge, which was burned down by her enemies and later rebuilt in great splendor by the queen. Huddleston is indeed the name of the family owning Sawston, and the Huddlestons to this day are a prominent Catholic family. The reference to the entity knowing another Huddleston in this incarnation makes sense if one realizes that Mrs. W-B. was friendly with Father Roger Huddleston in her earlier years in England. Father Huddleston was a Benedictine priest.

But more than the factuality of historical data given, the descriptive passages of life between births and on the other side of life are fascinating and match similar accounts from other ources. It may be difficult for a nonreligious person to accept the visit of the Christ to the young Catharine W-B., and yet there are other accounts of such visitations. Surely the possibility that the master looks after his own is not entirely illogical or impossible, for even a nonreligious person will generally grant the historical Jesus his great status as a teacher and healer.

On June 4, 1969, the day after our last meeting, Mrs. W-B. had a meaningful dream, which she proceeded to report to me immediately. The following night she had another dream, also tying in with the regression experiment. Here are her reports.

DREAM 1

I sleep badly, and was awake until after 3:00 A.M., so this took place between 3:00 and 5:00 A.M. It was in color, and voices appeared to be normal or real. We were riding through woodland or heath country, am sure it was Richmond, the Surrey side of London. I was still Latimer's wife. Lucy Tyrwhitt, my stepdaughter by Lord Borough, rode with me. We were with the King's party; he was hawking. There were bearers and hawk boys, hounds, etc. Tom was there, home from France; he and Henry wore the Tudor colors of green and white. I felt very happy; in fact, happiness permeated the dream. It was a wonderful morning, early and misty, sun breaking through, the smell of crushed grass beneath hooves and gorse. I rode a gray; Tom rode beside me whenever he could, although Henry would keep bellowing for him. They were on terms of great friendship.

Henry rode an enormous horse, dark bay. He was very heavy but rode magnificently. We cantered up a grassy slope to a clearing, and Henry released his hawk. He removed her hood, undid the leash from jesses, and threw her. She darted up in circles, and we all watched. In a very few minutes, she had sighted her quarry, then pounced in to kill. Henry was delighted. He laughed and joked. They had laid wagers. Then, in turn, the others, Tom included, released their hawks. Henry called the hawk boy to him. The boy knelt on the grass, and Henry roared, "Don't kneel, damn you. We are all men out here." He chose a small merlin and gave her to me, showing me how to carry her on my wrist. He asked after Latimer's health. Very assiduously, I told him that he seemed better, though very tired, and that he was at home translating a Greek work. Then His Grace asked me to ride beside him, and he chatted and thanked me for riding out to Hatfield House to see the children, Prince Edward and young Bess. He was in high good spirits. He waved his cap, plumes waving, and called out, "We shall meet again, my lady at Greenwich." He led his party off at a mad gallop, leaving Tom to ride with me and Lucy and a page.

I felt very free from care. Tom took the small hawk from my wrist and gave it to the page, and he, Lucy, and I raced one another up the slope. I felt aware in the dream of a breeze, and joked with Lucy at not having to wear the awful boned corset the women wore then. Tom said that a horse felt good after days at sea, and he was going to Syon house. I felt guilty for being so happy when my husband was at home, ill.

DREAM 2

I was back in the past, at Hampton Court, in what had been Jane's apartments. Katharine Howard had been beheaded months before. In fact, I knew that the King had been alone since her death. I was aware of the year in my dream—1543—and I was a widow; Latimer had died. I felt alone. Tom was in France about the King's affairs, and I wished that he were here. The King had sent for me, and I was afraid that I knew why he had sent for me. There was a noise outside, and the doors were flung open. The King and two gentlemen-in-waiting came in. I curtsied to him, and His Grace took my arm and raised me, saying to his men, "Leave me gentlemen I pray you. I would speak privily with Lady Latimer."

They left, and Henry led me to a window seat. He kissed my hand and held me by the arm, then kissed my cheek and said, "How fair thou art, sweet lady, and kind as thou art comely. Today I was at Hatfield, and my motherless boy told me of your visits." He was in excellent spirits. His rages after Katharine Howard's death were all gone. I felt almost choking with fear, as I knew what was to come, and yet I pitied him. He was a crumbling lion and ruled a turbulent country as only a strong man could. He said, "You could give me much comfort and peace, Madam Kate, and, who knows, perhaps more heirs for England." In the dream I felt at a loss for words. He went on, saying, "My offer does not please you? I thought to do you honor and ask you to wed with me, for truly I have grown to love you very dearly." I told him bluntly, being a North Country woman, that I had not expected this, and, while honored, also felt a little afraid to accept, seeing the fate of two of his queens.

He was not angry, but told me to ". . . have no fear." I had "twice been wed and widowed" and was "known to be virtuous," and "no scandal could ever attach" to me; that I had "both intellect and gaiety." He asked me to let him know very quickly as time passed and he was aging, but felt for me as any stripling. "Be kind to me. Be kind to England." Now, what woman could resist a proposal like that? Even in a dream or centuries ago? Incidentally, he removed my widow's veil and tossed it on the floor. That was Henry. We walked down the long gallery, and in my dream I knew it was where Katharine Howard had run screaming to try and reach the King. Henry seemed to sense this and told me, "Forget what has gone before." We went into another room he called his closet, and he seemed very gay, almost boyish, and told me that I could refurnish the queen's apartments as I wished; the Exchequer was low, but so be it. I told him (North Country thrift) that I had loved Jane's apartments and hangings, and that I had brocades and hangings in storerooms at Snape if he would like me to use them. He told me I was the first woman who had not sought to ruin him. And that was the end of the dream, all very domestic and practical. I remember, his eyes were small and sunk in heavy jowls, but he still had remnants of his former handsomeness, though he limped. I was aware in the dream of being sad that Tom had not returned in time and that the only way I could refuse the royal offer without offense was to enter a convent, and that did not appeal to me. I also knew it would endanger Tom to refuse Henry and hope to marry Tom later; heads fell for far less.

Mrs. W-B. has, of course, read a few books on the period by now, especially Agnes Strickland's *The Queens of England*, and *Hackett's History of Henry VIII*, but she has not become a scholar on the subject. Perhaps she needn't, having primary access to information scholars have to dig for year after year.

Is Mrs. Catharine W-B. the reincarnated queen of England Katharine Parr, last and happiest of the wives of Henry VIII? She does not claim to be, but I think that the evidence points in that direction. The manner in which the first bits of personal data were received indicates that they came from a source that knew well what the lives of Tom Seymour and Katharine Parr were like. I am satisfied that coincidence, unconscious knowledge, and other ordinary factors do not play a dominant role in this case.

Chapter Twenty-Four
What Happens Between Incarnations?

WHILE IT IS FASCINATING TO DELVE INTO THE question of previous lives or to ferret out traces of memories with significance to the present one, such as the payment of karmic debts, it is perhaps equally fascinating to investigate the state in between lives, the transitional period when one life on the physical plane has been terminated and another one has not yet begun.

In the case of Pamela W. of Illinois, who lived in Scotland in the early sixteen hundreds, the subject spoke of the experiences immediately following her death by jumping from the tower of Huntingtower Castle. "What was your next memory after you had fallen? What is the next thing that you remember?" "I was in wind." "Did you see yourself as you were?" "Yes." "Where did you go?" "Nowhere." Following that, however, she traveled to the castle and to various places in the vicinity. As she floated through time, observing people dressed in what to her were strange clothes, she was interested only in getting back to Scotland and to the loved one she had left behind. Eventually she discovered Pamela W., who reminded her of a friend she knew in the sixteen hundreds. Somehow she was reborn in Pamela's body. No one, at least not to her knowledge, arranged this for her, nor was she told that she must go back to the physical plane.

In the case of Ruth MacG. the system seemed to work differently, however. According to her testimony in deep trance, she stayed "on the other side" for awhile, learning about her shortcomings in the life she had just left, and eventually progressed to a point where she could go back and try again. The old man who had been her teacher during that period told her that the time had come for her to go back even though she really didn't care to. "Well, I really didn't have any choice, you know. These things are all decided," the subject explained under hypnosis. "Just what happened?" I asked. "Well, he said, 'It's time now for you.' He said, 'What you do here you've learned; you practice, you meditate, you get the right idea, the right attitude, but you can't know if you are going to make it stick until you try it in the world, and you have to try it in the world before you know whether you've really got it in your bones.' " "And how did they make you go back?" "Oh, they said, 'You have to be a baby,' and I said, 'I don't want to be a baby. There's nothing dignified in being a baby.' "

The subject then described being put to sleep and remembered only taking some sort of dive, or rather a spin, and the next thing she remembered was crying in her present mother's arms.

N.W., a lady in Michigan, contacted me with an account of amazing clarity in which she remembered not only a previous life but also her previous death. The lady, a university graduate, was born into a family with a very religious background. During her formative years up to age eighteen, she was brought up on a doctrine of a strict, vengeful God and was frequently told by her minister that she was doomed to hell because of her worldly outlook. Later she married a young man who became a minister in the Nazarene Church. Despite this, she always felt a rebellious spirit within her against the upbringing she was given and, five years before contacting me, had begun studying other religions in order to learn more about the world she lived in. It was at the time when she had just come across the works of Edgar Cayce that the remarkable incident occurred that prompted her to contact me.

"One day I lay down on my bed and almost immediately went to sleep," she explained, "when I found myself in a long line of slaves. In my hands was a round dish. We were walking toward the place where each slave was being served his daily ration. As I walked I kept my head lowered. I heard someone behind me whisper 'Don't do it! He will punish you. Don't do it.' I seemed to know better than to raise my head or speak aloud to answer, but I whispered, 'I must. I just can't do what he demands of me.' The next thing I knew I was running down a tiled corridor, past two guards in what I think was Muslim dress, through a curtain, where I saw two men sitting on cushions, deep in discussion. The guards were already advancing toward me. I tried to beg for attention and didn't succeed in being heard in the commotion. The master, the man I recognized as my master, had jumped to his feet and was berating me for interrupting him and his guest."

It should be noted that such clarity of detail is most unusual with ordinary dreams and nearly always points toward genuine reincarnation memories as the source. Mrs. W. continued her report to me, just as she remembered it the following morning.

"Next, I knew I was at the end of this corridor, and I had been severely beaten and was lying there suffering terribly. I heard a noise and saw my master and his friend coming out of the room. He ordered the guards to bring me to him. They came to me, grasped my arms above the elbow, and dragged me toward him. I heard myself say, 'Please, I beg of you; you're hurting me. They dragged me to him and dropped me to the floor at his feet. I saw he had a long, slender knife in his hand. I had never seen one like it before, and I wondered what it was. I heard him talking to the other man, but I didn't hear what he said. He then pulled me to a kneeling position, talking as he did, bent my head over, put his left arm firmly around my head while he knelt at my left side on one knee. I could feel him shaving my head at the base of the skull. I wondered what he was doing. I tried to speak. He said, 'Be quiet.' He didn't seem to be angry. Suddenly he plunged the knife into me and severed my head from my body. I screamed as he plunged the knife in, and suddenly stopped. I wondered why it didn't hurt anymore and why I had stopped screaming. Then I said to myself, 'Of course it doesn't hurt anymore. I am dead.' But I could still see what was going on. He had taken the inside out of my head, the part that my present knowledge tells me was my brain, and was showing it to his guest and explaining something to him about my brain."

At that moment Mrs. W. awoke, and as she did she heard herself say, "And that is why I always have migraine headaches when I'm under pressure or distressed. Now I needn't have them anymore." As a matter of fact, during the year following this remarkable dream, she has had only two headaches, and both were caused by other illnesses. All through her teenage and adult years until that dream, she had suffered from one to three migraine headaches a month and was under medication for them. There is another thing that seems to tie in with the flashback dream. Mrs. W. has a long birthmark at the base of her skull that turns an angry red whenever she has a headache. She is firmly convinced that the dream represents a true experience in a past life. Her husband unfortunately does not share her views. As a minister he objects to the notion of reincarnation, even suggesting that his wife might be misled by an evil spirit!

It is interesting to note that the subject had no difficulty observing the moments immediately following death. Similar descriptions have been given by others, even those who died violently. In *The Search for Bridey Murphy*, by Morey Bernstein, both the principal subject and a deceased priest report their continued and largely unchanged existence immediately following physical death. In both cases they are able to observe what goes on around them, including the funeral arrangements. Similarly the release of the etheric body from the physical counterpart seems in no way to impede the sensory ability of the personality, proving of course that the seat of consciousness is in the etheric body and not in the physical shell.

Alma B. from a small town in Texas and in her late forties, was born in a small backwoods village in West Virginia. Asked to describe the environment in which she grew up, she described it as "rutted roads, narrow lanes that were tree lined like in an ancient country." When she was old enough to understand such things, her mother told her that she had been born with a veil over her face, meaning with psychic leanings. As a matter of fact, Alma has at times been able to foretell the death of individuals. But she's not truly psychic in the sense that she has significant and frequent experiences. However, as far back as she can remember, she has perceived a scene in her mind that made her wonder about reincarnation. In particular, Alma wondered whether we pick our parents or are ordered by someone over there.

"I remember being very tired, really out of breath, as if I had worked awfully hard on something. I was sitting on something soft, white, and hazy like a cloud and thinking, now that was not so very hard, but I'm glad it is over. Then a person stepped up to me and said, 'You are here.' I said, 'Yes, I just got here.' This other person said, 'Well there is someone else you have to be, you are going to another couple.' I was reluctant but this person said, 'Look down; there they are, walking out that lane together.' I looked, which seemed from a great distance down. I could see them plainly. I was higher than a building, like maybe just floating in the air. I can't define this. I wasn't in an airplane until 1961, so I'm sure it wasn't a daydream."

Mrs. B. wonders whether her death in one life hadn't come awfully close to rebirth into another. There was something else that seemed indicative to her of a previous life. She cannot swim in her present existence and has a distinct feeling of having drowned at one time; also, at times when she is just about half asleep, she has visions of being buried alive and can even hear the dirt being thrown down on the coffin she is in. This has troubled her for many years and has given her parents some anxious moments.

If Mrs. B.'s life had been cut short by drowning and/or being buried while not quite dead, her return to the physical world might indeed have come comparatively quickly. Being shown one's prospective parents is rare; I recall only a handful of such situations. But it would appear in this case that there was some sort of need to explain the rapid return of the soul and perhaps reassure her that she was going to some very nice people.

"I really do not believe I have ESP or that I am neurotic," Bernice M. of Georgia explained to me as she described some early incidents of a psychic nature. At age three Bernice saw an apparition floating toward her bedroom from another room in the house her parents then occupied. The figure wore the clothes of an earlier period but was plainly visible to her. When she was eight, her grandmother took her to visit some cousins in Pennsylvania. As she stepped into the parlor, she observed a man with white hair lying in a coffin. At the same time, she

notic   oom, she complained
bittei   ken to a house where
there   ssured her that there
was i   , however, her grand-
motł   visited used to be a
funei   ad psychometrically
picke   she was seventeen, an
uncl   lose relations passed
away   ne to her in a vision,
expla   e conventional sense.
But d   volving extrasensory
perce   y seems undoubtedly
genu   case reported earlier.
        '   in a misty place and
not l   ed, "I was there with
three   of dress. I was wearing a   hair piled on top of
my h   nen and asked, 'How
long   Dh, you will see, you
will   ow   w much time passed,
but th   t o   ack now.' I said, 'But
I've d   ow, but it is time for
you to go back.' I don't remember my birth. I do remember
being about three or four months old and lying in my carriage
and looking up and seeing the sky and the trees and saying to
myself, *It is true; I am alive again.*'"

Just as in the previous case, Bernice M. also has a vague
memory of being dead once and lying in her coffin and, in her
case, screaming at people, "I'm not dead." But they did not hear
her. Since childhood she has always known that she lived before;
it seemed part of her, like breathing. When *The Search for
Bridey Murphy* appeared Bernice was about twelve years old.
She could not understand why so many people denied the truth
in the book. To *her* it seemed natural that everyone had lived
before.

It is rare, however, for a person to recollect large segments
of an earlier existence in the physical world, and it is even rarer
that they recollect their earlier lives from the beginning—that is
to say, from birth onward. Occasionally there are examples of
recollections in which people do actually recall their own birth.
In general, average people may remember as far back as their

early school years. I myself have exceptionally good recall, but I cannot remember anything before my third birthday. Although there is a dim memory of having been to kindergarten and having just turned three, this is not a continuous memory at all but merely a tiny flash in which I see myself in this existence. Now, this is not a reincarnation memory but represents a good memory, such as many people possess in the normal course of their lives.

Ordinarily people do not recall details of their own lives before such an early age. I am not aware of any cases in which people recall their own births—except, of course, the one I am about to relate. But I am sure there must be others of a similar nature in the annals of psychic research.

Mrs. Nancy A. of Alabama, thirty-nine years old, married to a professional musician, and a licensed practical nurse, has one son. Her interests are normal—music, the arts. She has an interest in reading books but there has never been any particularly strong interest in the occult or in psychic research. This is the more amazing as Mrs. A. has had, all her life, incidents of extrasensory perception, mediumship, and clairvoyance. She has taken these events in her stride without undue anxiety or extraordinary stress. Her ability to foresee the future and recall her impressions will be recorded elsewhere. Here I wish to concern myself solely with the amazing reincarnation memories she has had.

As a matter of fact, calling them reincarnation memories is technically incorrect, since in this case I believe we are not dealing with an earlier lifetime but with the beginning of this incarnation. Ever since she was a small child and able to speak, Mrs. A. has insisted to her mother that she can recall the moment of her birth into this world. She vividly described the day she was brought home from the hospital, a sixteen-day-old baby. I questioned Mrs. A. about the details of this extraordinary memory.

"My birth memories consist of an awareness of being blasted into a place where extremely bright lights and what seemed like the resounding echoes of human voices were imposed on my small person," she explained. "I vaguely seem to remember a detached observance of this affair, including blurred visions of figures clothed with masks and caps. The day I was brought home I remember riding snuggled in the arms of a woman with light brown hair and a prominent nose, arriving at a house where my Aunt Jeff and sixteen-month-old brother were coming out the front door onto the front porch, I supposed to greet my mother and me. I did remember it was the first time I had seen trees, and was impressed by them. More clear than anything is my memory of observing my mother and, in the thought language of the newborn, wondering, Who is she? What am I? And who are those people standing on the porch? Since I was a young child I have always had the feeling of total detachment from myself and others, as if I were on the outside looking in."

Now, one might argue that Mrs. A. manufactured these impressions of her own birth at a later date, either consciously or perhaps unconsciously, from her normal knowledge of what births are like, but this is not so in this case, for we do know that her remarks concerning her birth go back to a very early time in her life when, being a small child, she had no access to this kind of information. Also, her impressions and descriptions of her own birth are so vivid and so detailed that they seem to indicate an authentic personal experience.

The more we understand the period "in between" lives, the more we will understand how reincarnation works. It is clear already that every case is different and must be judged on its own merits. Yet there are undeniable parallels in the reports coming to us from widely scattered sources, sources that have no contact with each other, no way of comparing notes or of discussing their individual findings with each other or with a third party. In this respect, we should think somewhat more kindly of the fanciful notion found in many religions that there is a heaven populated by people sitting on clouds, who sometimes can look down on earth and see what goes on among mortals.

Chapter Twenty-Five
What Exactly *Is* Karma?

"KARMIC RELATIONSHIP" and "paying off old karma" are terms bandied about frequently among esoteric people (those who are interested in the occult, psychic research, and astrology). But the average person doesn't quite know what the term *karma* means. The word itself comes from India and signifies something like "accumulated destiny." Possibly there is a link between the Indian term *karma* and the Greek idea of *caritas*, derived from Karys, the goddess of charms and destiny. Words such as *caring, care, charity, charm, charisma,* the technique called *Charismatics* (an idea created by me) may be interlinked, if not in meaning, then in derivation.

But Karys was also the goddess of the occult, of certain aspects of the underworld, and as such ruled man's fate. Any discussion of reincarnation is impossible without reference to the karmic law—that law which governs the nature of each incarnation. The karmic law is the set of rules under which the system called reincarnation operates. It is not a law in the sense of human laws, with judges and lawyers arguing the merits of each case. Under the karmic law there are no appeals and no interpretations that may differ from interpreter to interpreter. The karmic law is more comparable to a law of nature, such as

342

the law of cause and effect, the law of attraction, and others found in the existing universe.

There are no exceptions from natural law; what seems at times a breach or circumvention of natural law is merely an aspect of it that we haven't fully understood. In time we will understand such strange workings of natural law to the point where they no longer are strange to us. I am speaking here particularly of some psychic phenomena that are seemingly in contravention to conventional physical law but are in fact merely extensions of it in areas where we do not possess sufficient knowledge.

The karmic law has several important aspects. It operates impersonally, regardless of who may be involved. Since it plays no favorites and is not emotionally tinged in any way, it cannot be manipulated to favor one or the other. The karmic law is not written in textbooks or contained in physical reference files. It exists beyond time and space in an orderly fashion. It has existed from I-don't-know-when, and it is referred to in many cultures at various times, independent from each other; yet no one has ever seen its scrolls. About the nearest thing to an orderly "filing system" are the so-called Akashic records. These records are said to contain the destiny and accumulated lives of everyone on earth—past, present, and future. The great seer Edgar Cayce referred to them in his trance readings, and lesser prophets have referred to the Akashic records whenever they have given so-called life readings.

While I doubt the ability of some modern psychics to consult these records at will and to extract information regarding former lives for individuals, I wonder whether the great Edgar Cayce may not indeed have been right in stating that these records do exist. There seems to be a need for some sort of central clearinghouse if human destiny is truly an orderly process. The karmic law would be very difficult to administer if some record were not kept of the individual's deeds in each incarnation. Thus, while I cannot say that I know where these records exist, I feel that they may well be a reality in the nonphysical world. Interestingly enough, Tibetan tradition speaks of a similar record in existence in a remote monastery in Tibet, where every person's life is recorded and where previous incarnations are also listed. If such a book exists on the physical plane, no trace of it has yet been found, but then there are many things that exist of which we know nothing *as yet.*

How do you acquire karma? If, as we assume, karma is the accumulated or acquired fate credit—either positive or negative as the case may be—then there has to be a point at which an individual has no karma at all. Unfortunately we arrive at the same unanswerable point where all religious philosophy must arrive sooner or later: the condition *before* the law took effect.

Every action people take, everything they think, say, do—whether on their own initiative or in response to another person's—is capable of being evaluated on merit. Some deeds or thoughts can be classified as good, others as bad, and others as indifferent. Common logic tells us this. However, from the karmic point of view it is not enough to judge a person's activities along conventional lines. Every action and reaction must also fit into the greater scheme of things. The karmic law asks whether the action undertaken by one individual helps or hurts another individual and conversely whether the activities of another individual create positive or negative factors in the receiver. First of all, karmic law concerns itself with impact on other individuals. Secondarily it deals with the impact of action or thought on other elements in nature, beginning with animals and extending right through to everything in creation whether animate or inanimate, if indeed there be such a distinction. (Recent research efforts seem to point to a needed reevaluation of our concepts of what constitutes animate in nature and what inanimate is.) In other words, a human's thoughts and actions are viewed not from the actor's point of view, or even from the point of view of the one who may be the receiver of that activity, but from a much higher reference point, as if the observer were way above the action, looking down upon it, removed from it personally but involved in it as a scorekeeper. Although there is some evidence that specially "trained" discarnates are assigned the task of evaluating human action and enforcing the karmic law, justice does not rely entirely on the actions of human beings, even of those who have gone into the next dimension. It appears that the law operates autonomously in that every single action or thought by an individual registers in the "central registration office," the storehouse of universal knowledge, the Akashic records (if you wish), the focal point of administration where everything is known simultaneously and eternally, both forward and backward in so-called time.

Karma is acquired continuously by everyone. No action is too insignificant, no thought too fleeting, nothing too small to weigh in evidence when the balance must be restored. That moment, of course, is rebirth, a moment when retribution or reward is in order. No one can avoid creating or acquiring karma. Karma itself is like magic; it is neither good nor bad, but whether it is good or bad in the long run depends entirely on the one creating it. This tantalizing thought presents itself as a partial explanation for the complexities of human personality: There are many opportunities laid out for a person at the moment of birth, encased in a denser outer layer called the physical body, and every action and reaction, every thought and feeling, are counted toward the next incarnation. They are in fact the equivalent of human personality. Or to put it more precisely, a person's personality is not a monolith but a loosely constructed combination of stimuli, thoughts, feelings, actions, reactions, attitudes, and interludes held together by the ego consciousness: the pilot of the human personality vehicle. On this basis everything happening to one small particle of the whole may have important repercussions for the rest of the structure. This is shown in nature by the fact that individuals can be greatly influenced by comparatively small and short-lived incidents in their lives. Even major deeds need not take more than a few seconds, yet may have lasting effects for the rest of that individual's life, in that particular incarnation. The amount of so-called time spent on certain actions or thoughts is quite immaterial in relationship to the impact.

Some comparatively slow developments, consuming much time, may still have only very limited meaning in terms of karmic value. It takes only a few seconds to murder another human being but the impact stays with perpetrators for the rest of their years. On the other hand, one may strive for many years to gain a certain advantage or goal; yet this effort will long weigh very slightly in the evaluation at the end of one's life. It is not even the honesty or sincerity with which one applies oneself to any given task. After all, human talents and abilities differ greatly. Then too we must consider that a life without previously acquired karma is merely a theoretic assumption.

For practical purposes and in order to understand the workings of reincarnation, we should begin with the earliest life on earth during which some previously acquired karma already exists. The question is, where does such karma come from? We have no evidential information concerning the number of incarnations possible for each human being. As I have already pointed out, the evidence for transmigration or the change from animal to human status is practically nonexistent in scientific terms. Yet something must have preexisted humanity's first incarnation as a human. I have no concrete solution to offer except the feeling that perhaps prior to a fully structured and individual personality, humanity may have drawn upon the forces of the environment to create karmic preconditions. From the *second* incarnation onward, the matter is much easier to grasp. Quite obviously, the actions and thoughts of the first lifetime in a physical body as a human being will determine what happens in the next incarnation. From then on it is a matter of action and reaction, determined by a rigid sense of values that differ greatly from the conventional human set of values.

Nobody can avoid acquiring karma, since without karma there is no life on earth. What man can avoid, however, is to acquire *bad* karma. Those who hold no beliefs in reincarnation will not see the need to do so, of course. It is their privilege to discover these truths at the proper time, when unfortunately they will be unable to correct things except by obeying and subjecting themselves to the very law they thought did not exist. But those who have learned that a system called reincarnation and karma exists and affects them can to some degree determine the shape of things to come in their next cycle on earth.

This does not mean that one need live a moral, strictly controlled life dedicated to humanitarianism and the denying of the self. It is nearly impossible for most human beings not to acquire some negative karma as well, even if there is a conscious effort to avoid it. We are, after all, emotional creatures and at times allow our lower instincts to run unbridled. On balance, however, knowing individuals can leave one lifetime with a vast surplus of positive karma and need not fear that the next incarnation will present them with too great a bill for the wrong they have done in this one. Avoiding bad karma requires, however, that individuals be conscious of their responsibility, not only to themselves as an instrument of divine expression but also toward all fellow human beings, fellow creatures, and the entire environment. The degree of responsibility toward the world in which one lives determines very largely the conditions in the next return. Unfortunately a large part of humanity is unable to grasp these very simple truths. The universe cannot function as a wholesome and harmonious creation if some elements in it persist in abusing it. It must therefore eliminate such elements by the natural means inherent in the karmic law.

Certain thoughts and actions are obviously negative in character, even if the individual involved is not cognizant of reincarnation evidence. To kill, to cheat, or to abuse another human being or an animal, to steal or destroy property—all of these actions are not only morally wrong in terms of our conventional society, they are equally wrong in terms of the universal law and karma.

But the obvious breaches of law are not the chief cause of so much karmic debt: it is in areas that are not easily recognized as being negative that most of the negative karma is acquired. Studied goodness, organized charity, actions designed to ease one's conscience rather than stemming from spontaneous feelings do not help one's positive karma at all. On the other hand, refraining from actions that would interfere with the harmony in nature or in a fellow human being can weigh very heavily in one's favor.

Those religions that speak of a Judgment Day are merely personalizing a continual appraisal going on under the karmic law. How do you avoid negative karma? Consider yourself a vehicle of divine expression in that you have been put on earth to perform a certain task or tasks. Do not assume that there is not a definite mission or purpose involved, for nothing in nature is accidental or wasted. By assuming that you have a job to do, determine what that job may be and, once you have found it, do it as well as you are able. In knowing what you are all about and implementing that knowledge to the best of your ability at all times, you are coming closest to fulfilling the spiritual purpose of your existence. Your own inner barometer will tell you when you are on the right track or when you are off it. There is a certain feeling of satisfaction in knowing one has done something well or that one has done the right thing. Those who do not have this ability as yet within themselves can develop it by learning to be calm and, at times, introspective. Sooner or later the ability to sense what is right or wrong does come to everyone. Action taken intuitively is more likely to be correct from that point of view than is logically dissected and weighed action influenced by the logical mind, environment, upbringing, and other external factors. *Feelings, of which intuition is a part, are a direct pipeline to the reservoir of truth.*

In this connection it is not wrong to seek personal advantage or success on any level, but it is wrong to seek it to the detriment of others. To look for fulfillment on *all* levels is not only right but the natural and instinctive expression of a fully developed human being. To seek such progress through the destruction of others, however, is wrong.

When the opportunity presents itself to advance without destroying someone in one's path, then *that* is the positive karmic thing to do. Critics might argue that it is almost impossible to succeed in the world without stepping on or over someone else. The answer depends on the circumstances and the ways: for instance, if a clever businesswoman, through her own resources, acquires the capital to buy out a competitor, that competitor will have to look elsewhere for professional fulfillment. Had he fully utilized his own resources, he would not have been bought out. The same businesswoman using immoral or illegal tactics to undermine her competitor while the competitor is doing everything within his abilities to advance himself would yield the same end result, of course. The competitor would be bought out by the stronger person, but the means used to attain this end would have created negative karma.

I am not suggesting that all of us must look out for our fellow humans in order to progress. Everyone must look out for himself or herself to begin with. Only when a person *consciously* or, by default, unconsciously causes harm or destruction to another being does negative karma come into effect. On the level of human life itself, through violence and fear, one might argue this point of view to the extreme: How does a soldier performing his patriotic duty to defend his country and kill an enemy compare to the murderer who kills a woman for her money? Does the motivation determine the evaluation of the outcome? In my opinion the taking of life, especially human life, is *always* negative karma. War and violence themselves are carriers of negative karma; consequently all actions taken as part of such activities can only lead to the acquisition of bad karma—whether the individual concerned does so for seemingly lofty motives or not. In the words of George Bernard Shaw, "There are no just wars."

Those who advocate a completely prearranged universe devoid of all free will may argue that the selection of activities leading to bad karma may also be predetermined for a certain individual. A Genghis Khan may have been chosen by fate to be an instrument for its own ends. Is it his fault that through his cruelties he acquires enormous amounts of negative karma? I am not a believer in a total predetermination but feel that a degree of free will is open to all of us. It is this very important amount of decision making that creates karma for the next incarnation. Thus, if a Genghis Khan committed himself to the role of conqueror, with all the inherent destruction and cruelties, he did so because of a sense of destiny born from his own desires or frustrations and not based on the inner call that alone determines a person's proper expression in each lifetime.

How do you pay off karma? As we have seen, karma can be either a credit or a debit, depending upon the nature of the event, situation, action, or character of the individual involved. If it is a credit, then it will be paid off automatically through the intervention of the karmic law in due course. If it is a debit, it will have to be wiped out in the next life through positive actions and reactions. Contrary to the popular slogan "opposites attract," *like* attracts *like* in the esoteric world. Good karma brings forth more good, and it seems axiomatic that the payoff for positive karma is an increase over the previously acquired good karma. The extent of this differs from case to case. The status quo is not in keeping with the universal aspect of life: everything moves at all times. Positive karma will not be paid off by negative karma in a subsequent incarnation. But positive results in one lifetime must be based upon corresponding positive factors in the previous one or previous ones. *In other words, everything must be earned.*

Individuals may or may not accept the karmic payoff in good grace, but they cannot prevent the discharge of karma from one incarnation to the next. The idea that someone may refuse to accept the good is not as far-fetched as it may sound: Some individuals, out of extreme modesty or more likely out of a psychological fear that they cannot properly reciprocate, are in the habit of rejecting good things coming to them. With karma, there is no choice. There cannot be any choice, since the law operates naturally, impersonally, directly, without the intermediary of a human element. Even if an individual wanted to reject the blessings stemming from previous positive karma, to whom would the complaint be addressed? Not to the deity, since the deity creates the law but does not administer it. Not the "board of directors," as I like to call them—those advanced souls who have been entrusted with the supervision of an orderly progression from one lifetime to another. They have charge of operating the karmic law, but they do not have the right to suspend it.

Advanced individuals who understand this law can build from one incarnation to the next until they reach the highest levels, at which point they may elect to become members of the elite of beings, sometimes called the masters. To be sure, one does not accumulate good karma deliberately, in a cold-blooded, cunning, or planned fashion. Rather one accumulates it by being in tune with the spirit of the universe, by *training oneself to react* instantly and intuitively in the right way, no matter what the challenge or situation may be.

Thus the matter of acquiring further positive karma is not one of logic but one of feeling. Feeling, in turn, cannot be acquired at will the way one acquires a bank account. It is a delicate expression of soul that results when the trinity of mind, body, and spirit are in harmony, exercising a maximum of interaction and utilizing in full the force inherent in it from the moment of its creation. In popular terms, knowing oneself— understanding one's potentials, strengths, and weaknesses, and accepting oneself with all the faults that may be present; while at the same time placing oneself at the disposal of the forces of fate, realizing that one is but a small particle of a large and unified system, and being alive in the fullest sense of the word— is the sure method by which one increases positive karma.

If one has done something in one lifetime that must be classed as negative karma, it will have to be paid off in some fashion in the next life. Occasionally it may take several lifetimes to be fully paid off, or the neglect, the negative factor stemming from one incarnation, may only be paid off several incarnations later. Every case is individual and different, but one thing is sure: Bad karma must be paid off *eventually*. This is how it works: If an action has been committed in one lifetime that comes under the classification of negative karma, the same situation will not recur in the following lifetime or in one of the next incarnations. Rather, parallel situations will be "thrown into the path" of the individual, to be acted upon by that individual as his or her free will dictates. Since the situations are similar only in terms of merit but not in terms of circumstances, individuals being tested cannot anticipate the situations or connect them with happenings in an earlier lifetime. They are, therefore, solely dependent upon their own resources, their good or bad judgment, as the case may be.

The only exceptions to this rule are the comparatively few cases where reincarnation memories, or rather small traces of them, have been permitted to remain. I have found that this is the case only when a lifetime has been cut short, or when some major situation in one lifetime has not come to fruition. Thus such reincarnation memories seem to be in the nature of bonus arrangements, giving those who have them a small head start in the next incarnation by allowing them some insights as to their previous doings. In this way, they may benefit from the information and apply the knowledge to parallel occurrences—if they are alert to the deeper meaning of the event, of course. Only those conversant with reincarnation theory can properly evaluate such links.

For instance, let us assume that a man has made gains in his business by dealing dishonestly with a friend. In his next lifetime a situation may come his way in which he has the opportunity of dealing again with a friend in some totally different business matter. Sooner or later he will be put to a test: whether or not to take advantage of his friend. If he follows his natural instincts without also listening to the inner voice of harmony, he may simply do the obvious thing and take advantage of his friend. But if he is attuned to the deeper meanings of such challenges, he may reject the opportunity and come to his friend's aid. Instead of taking advantage of a faltering business by buying it out, he might lend his friend support so that the friend could go on with new strength. That would be discharging negative karma. The balance would have been restored.

Everything in the universe must be in balance, and that which is not must swing back and forth until its movement brings it to a point where total harmony reigns again. For when the forces of plus and minus are equal they join each other and create a new whole, which is neither positive nor negative but contains elements of both. Polarity is that which separates, but it also creates the driving force to purify and eventually come together again. When full harmony is reached, polarity serves to keep the balance.

A particularly sensitive point in reincarnation research

concerns illness in individuals when there is no apparent reason for such illness to exist. *Can illness be karmically caused?* Most illnesses are caused by a state of imbalance in the etheric body of the individual. Only accidents or diseases clearly due to neglect should be attributed to physical causes. But some if not all of these illnesses and accidents may be due to a karmic debt. In cases where an individual has physically hurt another, causing that person to be ill or crippled, the individual becomes similarly afflicted in the next incarnation. The perpetrator's suffering wipes out the suffering of the mistreated one. This need not be the identical illness or affliction but may be in a different part of the body; nevertheless, in its impact it would parallel the situation suffered by the other person in the previous incarnation.

Do we then inherit the illnesses and afflictions of our previous sojourns on earth? On the surface it would seem unfair for us to be responsible in this lifetime for something committed by our previous self, living a totally different life and being an entirely different person. Such responsibility and inherited doom smack of the idea of original sin propounded by the Roman Catholic Church and rejected by the majority of progressive thinkers. But it is nothing of the sort. In being given a chance to make up for a wrong done by us in a previous life, even if it means suffering in this one, we are in the end ennobling our own soul, helping it to progress by eliminating the negative aspects from the past. If an illness or affliction has been recognized as karmic, it does not follow that we cannot do something about it. We can deal with it as if it were an illness caused by wrong thinking or an imbalance in our own system. The techniques in dealing with it are exactly the same, and as a result we may eliminate or overcome the karmically caused illness. By doing so we are not setting karma aside. The incidence of the illness or affliction itself is the karmic debt being offered for *payment*: our *efforts* expended on in our own behalf to eliminate the illness or affliction are a proper positive response under the karmic law. By doing the "right" thing about our illness, we would be acquiring positive karma were it not for the fact that we are extinguishing an old negative karma. Thus the slate is clean; there is neither loss nor gain.

Karmic law operates through parallel situations, carefully evaluating conditions in such a way that we are not given any hints that there may be a connection between what is happening to us now and what has happened to us before. Since the majority of people do not have reincarnation memories in the waking condition and only a fraction remember sufficiently in the dream state to be able to draw conclusions from their reincarnation flashes, we can only guess that some event in a past life may be responsible for our present predicament.

But one life must be lived at a time: Decisions and reactions must be based upon our personal feelings, regardless of how many lives we may have lived before. The karmic law would be meaningless if we knew that we were being tested or that some events in our lives were due to a similar event in another lifetime. Likewise the karmic law would be without sense if we did not have free will in deciding, if only intuitively, what to do about every situation we are faced with. A human's free will is the very foundation of our kinship with the Deity: If we were created in his image, as the religionists claim, then it would seem a cruel persiflage if we could not determine our reactions when faced with the forces of destiny.

But bad karma to be worked off and good karma to be increased are by no means the only reference points from incarnation to incarnation. When there are traces of previous memories they are in many cases due to *unfinished business.* Unfinished business may concern itself with a mission in one life that was cut short by tragic circumstances and could not be accomplished. It may have to do with setting things right in some ways, or it may refer to the carrying out of a trust.

Since unfinished business can range almost the entire width of human experiences, it is difficult to pinpoint the telltale marks of such causative factors. But there is present an overriding compulsion, a driving force to do certain things, to be in certain places, to seek out certain individuals or situations, that cannot be explained on the basis of the current incarnation. As a matter of fact, in many instances it goes counter to present inclination. People of one type of background will seek out people of an entirely different background and feel completely comfortable with them, while feeling out of place with their own. This applies to places and occupations as well. Even skills acquired in one incarnation may be remembered, gradually or suddenly, in the next one if they were in some way not fully utilized in the earlier lifetime. This accounts for a number of amazing situations where individuals seemingly possess talents, interests, and inclinations for which there is no rational basis in their present circumstances.

But unfinished business may also pertain to personal matters; it may create difficult problems in one's emotional life. It may even create social and legal difficulties. How does one dispose of unfinished business? First, it is important to recognize it and to put it into the right perspective in relation to the present circumstances. Can one deal with unfinished business under the current circumstances, taking into account one's abilities, powers, environment, and obligations? If there does not seem to be any insurmountable barrier against it, the wisest thing would be to attempt to pick up where a previous lifetime has left off. The more one realizes the nature of the unfinished business, partially through snatches of reincarnation memories, partially perhaps by observing one's peculiar inclinations and unconscious activities, the more one can gradually put oneself into the shoes of the person whose business was left unfinished earlier. Using intuition as much as possible, circumstances will present themselves that demand certain reactions. If the synthesis between present personality and the remnants of the previous one is good, instinctive moves will be made and the unfinished business brought to a conclusion. It may not always be the identical business, to be sure; parallels are also common under such circumstances.

Either way, the matter is taken out of the karmic relationship, and one is able to move forward in the present incarnation. Ignoring unfinished business when one has become aware of it is not advisable. To begin with, it won't go away. One cannot simply suppress it or look the other way, because the more one tries to avoid it, the more it is likely to establish itself in both conscious and unconscious minds. The advice of professional psychics in such matters is also of doubtful value; unless the psychic involved is of superior quality, such readings tend to reflect too much guesswork, generalities, pastoral advice, and otherwise useless material. Far better sources of information lie buried within oneself if one learns to tap such sources through meditation, periods of withdrawal from the world, and a progressive, steady technique of listening to the inner voice, which we all have.

Unfinished business is not due to an accident or neglect of nature. Nature does not err. But there are individual cases where proper application of the universal law demands an interruption of the business at hand, even though on the surface this seems unreasonable. If, as I assume, all data pertaining to an individual are read into a kind of spiritual computer and this spiritual computer comes up with certain negative suggestions based on the sum total of what was fed into it, the smooth continuance of that individual's mission on the earth plane in this particular incarnation must be disturbed in order to satisfy *previously* acquired karma. Even the way in which we are born and in which we die is a karmic matter, determined by and dependent upon previous conditions and reactions. Theoretically at least, only the "young soul," the soul just created by the "system" is relatively free from such burdens, since it comes into the cycle of life without previous testing. But even the new soul brings into its first encounter with life certain environmental factors acquired at the very moment of birth.

The questions still remain: Who decreed the law of karma, and who administers it? If we are to believe that God is contained in all of us and that we are a part of God, then it would appear that the karmic law was also in some way and in some measure created by us, the living universe, in order to have a set of rules to keep this universe in harmony and balance. It appears to administer itself by the very virtue of its infallibility; its omniscience makes it possible for the law to be aware of all that occurs everywhere forever and thus, quasi-automatically, to take the necessary steps to create the conditions that are likely to balance the system for specific individuals.

It may be a little like a Calder mobile, in which the delicate construction can be put into motion by a very slight touch. Eventually it returns to its properly balanced condition. The waves, that is to say, the movements the mobile makes while adjusting itself and returning to its state of perfect balance, may be compared to the encounters between human beings and situations with which they must cope one way or another.

Chapter Twenty-Six

Destiny Encounters and Soul Mates

VERY COMMON OCCURRENCES INVOLVING KARMA, both negative and positive, are the links between millions of people who do not know each other in the present incarnation. Many people have had the experience of meeting someone and having the strong feeling that they have known that person before, yet are unable to determine when and where their relationship began. Sometimes this recognition is sudden and dramatic. Some of these experiences are classed under the déjà vu phenomenon because they give the feeling of "haven't I met you someplace before?" People meet for the first time and are able to describe each other's whims and likes instantly and without previous knowledge. Some people can remember having been together in strange places and under strange circumstances; yet in the cold light of their present lives there is no rational basis for their assumptions. This phenomenon is so widespread, so common, that it appears to me to be one of the prime elements in the reincarnation system. *Links* between people are important, but perhaps even more important is the *recognition* of such links. Undoubtedly the majority of these links are simply overlooked, shrugged off as coincidences, strange occurrences without particular meaning, or are deliberately ignored.

I maintain that two people never meet without some signif-icant purpose being involved. This purpose may come to frui-tion *after* the initial meeting or perhaps at a much later time; but two entities in this universe do not meet each other unless a third purpose is involved and meant to be dealt with. The difficulty lies in recognizing, first, that there is a link between them and, second, what the purpose of their meeting is in terms of universal, or karmic, law. Those who have undergone some esoteric training will perhaps be able to recognize some of the meaning inherent in such meetings. But people who still cling to the materialistic concept of coincidence and accident in na-ture are not likely to see the deeper meanings behind such so-called chance meetings.

Links of this kind are of the utmost importance, not only in accomplishing one's mission in life but also in furthering the other person's purpose. The more we understand the meaning and the meaningfulness of links between people, the more we begin to understand the meaning of the reincarnation system.

Sometimes the pursuit of links can be exaggerated. People who are firm believers in reincarnation may see deep signifi-cance in everyone they meet, everyone in their family and among their friends, to the point where the entire notion be-comes grossly exaggerated. Mistakenly they will attempt to identify everyone they know as having been a close friend or relative in a previous lifetime or perhaps several lifetimes ago. Thus the present mother becomes a daughter in another life, the rejected lover was the successful rival in the last incarnation, the child who reminds one so much of one's grandmother is the grandmother reincarnated, and so forth. Return of a loved one or a friend between one incarnation and the next one is possi-ble, of course, but recognition of such relationships must be based on *evidential factors*: certainly the life readings being dispensed by self-appointed experts for a specific sum of money do not offer such meticulous proof. There is no need to disre-gard scientific standards in this field, where such standards are the only safeguard against delusion whether perpetrated by others or by oneself.

If you meet someone and become convinced that you've lived before in the same place and at the same time, you must search for details of that life together that are capable of being checked out objectively in the files and records of various libraries and research societies. If the life together was in some distant civilization of which there are no research records, such as Atlantis or Lemuria, the matter of proof becomes very difficult, of course. But whenever you are dealing with a known civilization and time in human history, proof of the existence of certain individuals can be found in the majority of cases. Even if the individuals concerned were of minor status and thus not likely to be found in historical records, indirect evidence can be obtained through the knowledge of circumstances, ways of life, and terms used for certain articles or conditions and, in general, by carefully observing knowledge not otherwise explicable in terms of the individual's present circumstances and background.

As yet there is no question that relationships based upon previous lifetimes cannot seriously be considered as bases for close relationship in this life. While the interest in parapsychology and the occult sciences has risen in recent years and reached a kind of plateau of respectability even among the broad masses, this interest still has the aura of curiosity about it. Only a comparatively small segment of the world population truly understands the deeper meaning of living life on the esoteric level.

The theory behind the existence of soul mates goes back to the earliest history of mankind. Even in the Stone Age religion, appropriately called, "the old religion," one of the prime motivations of leading a good and useful life was to be reborn again near the loved one and find the loved one again in the next incarnation. In medieval times the idea of the divinely joined couple runs through many romantic narratives. The German poet Johann Wolfgang von Goethe wrote a novel called *Die Wahlverwandtschaften*, meaning "elective affinities"—relationships by choice. It was his contention that every human being had a perfect mate (of the opposite sex) waiting to be discovered. Goethe expressed in poetic form a philosophy that is probably the deepest and most significant element of all esoteric teachings.

At the beginning, it is thought, the soul was created as an exterior expression of the Godhead, a unit unto itself and therefore neither male nor female but both. Sometime in great antiquity the soul was split into male and female halves and sent forth into the world to prove itself. Through testing and purification, the two halves were forever striving to reunite again. In the process the dynamics of the world were achieved. As a result, a vastly strengthened and purified double soul would emerge to become, perhaps, what the philosopher Nietzsche called Super-man.

Since the soul mates were originally part of a larger unit, they would be possessed of knowledge that need not be explained from one to the other. Consequently one of the earmarks of finding the true soul mate was immediate recognition, instant understanding, and communication beyond logical explanation, even beyond telepathy, accompanied by deep feelings of mutual love. The longing of one soul mate for the other is, in the eyes of the esoteric, the major driving force that makes people search the universe for fulfillment. Only by reaching out to this ideal soul mate can one hope to accomplish one's destiny. It does not follow that every one of us finds the soul mate destined for him or her, but the act of reaching toward it is the important thing. By that very longing, the dynamic force of motivated desire is set into motion, and the multitude of such desires creates the power reservoir whence creative people obtain their inspirations and driving force.

Soul mates are not only physically attuned to each other and consequently perfect for each other in the sexual sense, but they share mutual interests, have identical outlooks on all phases of life, and are in every respect compatible with one another. Soul mates are not necessarily ideal mates in terms of contemporary standards; they may differ greatly in age, social or economic background, or even race. As a matter of fact, some soul mates may be so radically different in outer appearance that the proof of their relationship lies in overcoming their differences rather than in accentuating them.

But soul mates are by no means one of a kind. Every one of us has several potential soul mates, though we may never meet up with any of them. From the material I have investigated and the philosophies I am familiar with, it would appear that each case is different and each personality requires a different set of circumstances and number of soul mates to find his or her whole self again. Some individuals may do so with one perfect soul mate. Some people will find such a soul mate and actually marry that person. The majority rarely do, but those who are esoterically awake will continue to hope that someday they will meet their soul mates, even though they may be married to someone else at the time. This of course creates another set of problems. If they find their perfect soul mates, should they abandon their conventional mates? If they do, they may find happiness, but society may condemn them. If they do not, they will live with a sense of frustration to the end of their physical days.

Those who have the potential for uniting with several soul mates in their lives—usually the leaders of this world, the creative people, those have much to give to the world—find one or several of these potential soul mates as they move through the years. For them to deny themselves the opportunity to unite with them, if only for a limited period of time, would cut off the free flow of the very energies they need to continue their mission on earth.

One has to be sure that the member of the opposite sex one has met is truly a soul mate and that physical desires do not create a mirage. Many are the tests by which a true soul mate can be recognized. Above all, comparison of previously held knowledge about a number of subjects, possibly the question of whether both soul mates felt identical reactions toward each other at the same time, and possible reincarnation memories should all be taken into consideration before a conclusion is reached. On the other hand, conventional social, moral, and religious considerations should be carefully avoided in judging such a relationship. Frequently the very point of such an unusual relationship is that it must be *outside* convention. In overcoming one's fears of conventionality one earns the right to unite with the soul mate. If it is a question of a number of soul mates during a lifetime, both partners should realize that the union may be of a limited duration for a purpose: Once that which was meant to be accomplished by their coming together again has been completed, they must each go their separate ways to unite with other respective soul mates to accomplish still other purposes meant for them as a mean of fulfilling their destiny.

At times a couple becomes involved one with the other without realizing that they are actually soul mates. In the course of time they discover that their relationship is not merely a physical or spiritual or emotional one but develops beyond the usual elements into a deeper relationship, and one day they discover that they are soul mates and stem from a common course. In such cases, of course, it may well be that the couple stays together to the end of their earthly lives, no longer seeking other soul mates. In realizing that each individual may have more than one perfect soul mate to merge with, we should understand this not necessarily as an invitation to a kind of esoteric polygamy but merely one of possibilities. The fact that a number of potentially equal soul mates or combinations of soul mates are in existence may also mean that a particular individual has more than once chance to merge with a perfect partner under different circumstances. This is particularly important in cases where an unhappy love affair creates the false impression in one partner that life's purpose has been aborted and that he or she will never find the same kind of love again. Remember, we are *all* unique, and at the same time, *nothing* in the universe is unique. The uniqueness of self is repeated in myriads of wondrous ways throughout the universe—equal, parallel, similar, and yet not quite the same.

Let us assume that two people meet, both of them not free in the conventional sense and that they discover a deep longing for each other, far beyond physical or emotional desire. If they are esoterically inclined they may discover that they are soul mates. To become one, a perfect union on all levels—physical, mental, and spiritual—is not a question of indulging themselves. The joy of such unions lies not in recognizing their previous relationship but in implementing the opportunity that so patently has come their way for a reason. They cannot afford to overlook the opportunity, to offend fate. They not only have the chance to unite again as they were once united, they have the sacred duty to do so in order to recharge their energies for further accomplishments in tune with the *patterns of destiny*. Avoiding such relationships leads to individual unhappiness and surely will cause the two potential soul mates to slow their progress. Furthermore they will each and individually face a parallel situation again at some time in the future, whether in the same incarnation or in the next one, and will again be tested as to their responsibilities and the maturity of their decisions. It is therefore inescapable that when such conditions are recognized as cases of soul mates, direct and positive action be taken by both partners to fulfill the manifest desire of destiny.

About the Author

Hans Holzer has written 115 books, including *America's Haunted Houses, Great American Ghost Stories, Ghost Hunter,* and many others that deal with the science of parapsychology.

Professor Holzer, who studied at the University of Vienna and Columbia University, holds a Ph.D. from the London College of Applied Science. In addition to having taught parapsychology at the New York Institute of Technology for eight years, he has also written, produced, and hosted a number of television shows, most notably the NBC series "In Search of . . ."

A member of several internationally renowned scientific societies, Dr. Holzer is listed in *Who's Who in America.* He makes his home in New York City.